THE
FBI
STORY

T0056772

THE FBI STORY

LEADERSHIP, INTEGRITY, AGILITY, INTEGRATION

THE U.S. DEPARTMENT OF JUSTICE

Skyhorse Publishing

No claim is made to material contained in this work that is derived from government documents. Nevertheless, Skyhorse Publishing claims copyright in all additional content, including, but not limited to, compilation copyright and the copyright in and to any additional material, elements, design, images, or layout of whatever kind included herein.

All inquiries should be addressed to Skyhorse Publishing, 307 West 36th Street, 11th Floor, New York, NY 10018.

Skyhorse Publishing books may be purchased in bulk at special discounts for sales promotion, corporate gifts, fund-raising, or educational purposes. Special editions can also be created to specifications. For details, contact the Special Sales Department, Skyhorse Publishing, 307 West 36th Street, 11th Floor, New York, NY 10018 or info@skyhorsepublishing.com.

Skyhorse® and Skyhorse Publishing® are registered trademarks of Skyhorse Publishing, Inc.®, a Delaware corporation.

Visit our website at www.skyhorsepublishing.com.

10 9 8 7 6 5 4 3 2 1

Library of Congress Cataloging-in-Publication Data is available on file.

Cover design by Brian Peterson

Print ISBN: 978-1-5107-5052-4
Ebook ISBN: 978-1-5107-5057-9

Printed in China

Table of Contents

Cyberstalking
Woman Sentenced for Harassing Victim on Social Media

The messages were relentless. A California woman couldn't escape the barrage of malicious texts, phone calls, and social media posts originating from a mysterious individual with whom she had no previous connection.

The harassment didn't stop until the FBI intervened and uncovered a trail of threats and extortion that led to a Miami college student—who is now behind bars for cyberstalking.

"An unwanted relationship was being pushed on a victim who ultimately felt terrorized by an obsessed individual she didn't even know," said Assistant U.S. Attorney Jodi Anton, who supported the FBI during the investigation. "The constant intimidation was destroying her life, to the point where she could barely function at work and considered suicide."

The perpetrator, Kassandra Cruz, was completing her criminal justice degree at Florida International University and spent countless hours behind the computer between her studies. In June 2015, she became fixated on a woman she found on a pornography website and tracked down the actress through her social media accounts.

"The victim was an 18-year-old high school student at the time looking for ways to get ahead in life. She made a bad decision trying out pornography," said Special Agent George Nau, who investigated the case out of the FBI's Miami Field Office. "It was something she kept hidden from her family and employers. She didn't realize her past would come back to haunt her 15 years later."

Cruz gained access to two of the victim's social media feeds by creating a fake persona of an attractive male U.S. Marine named Giovanni and sending friend requests. The former adult film actress accepted, and Giovanni began liking and commenting on almost every picture she shared. But the victim's suspicions began to mount in September 2015, when Giovanni started to follow and like the her friends' posts as well.

> *"Even while Cruz was being driven to jail, she still wanted to talk to the victim. She was blinded by her obsession and oblivious to the impact of her crime."*

By the end of the summer, Cruz's fake profiles were blocked, which angered her. She resorted to harassment and often violent threats, which were aimed not only at the victim but also her friends and family. Included in Cruz's messages were a plot to expose the victim's hidden past making adult films as well as demands to be paid $100,000 in return for leaving the victim alone.

Cruz's flurry of e-mails, letters, and social media messages were taking their toll on the victim's personal life and professional career. From the beginning of 2016 until late April, the victim received more than 900 phone calls and text messages on her cell phone alone. Approximately the same amount of unwanted calls were made to the victim's home and work phones before the FBI ended the stalking.

"Cruz had many fake social media accounts, so it was difficult at first to track all of the threats to the source," said Nau. "She would create a new profile as soon as she was blocked. But ultimately, the e-mails, phone calls, and letters led us to her."

A turning point in the investigation took place in May 2016, when the FBI lured Cruz into a video chat with the victim to discuss paying the $100,000 extortion demand. While the conversation further solidified that Cruz was behind the threats, it was the in-person meeting arranged during the chat that allowed agents to finally make an arrest.

In August 2016, Cruz was sentenced to 22 months in prison after having been found guilty of cyberstalking.

"Even while Cruz was being driven to jail, she still wanted to talk to the victim," said Nau. "She was blinded by her obsession and oblivious to the impact of her crime."

Federal Funds Stolen from Non-Profit Health Care Clinics

Investigation Leads to Former CEO

Jonathan Dunning used clinic money to buy this now-shuttered facility, titled the building in his company's name, and charged about $20,000 a month in rent.

The staff of two non-profit health care clinics diligently worked to offer critical medical care and services to the most vulnerable residents—young and old—of the Birmingham, Alabama, region. And to carry out its operations, the clinics received funds from a federal program specifically designed to offer a community safety net for the uninsured, the poor, the homeless, migrant and seasonal farm workers, and public housing residents.

But enter Jonathan Dunning, former CEO of both non-profits who—while working for the clinics and even after he left—orchestrated and carried out a seven-year criminal scheme to defraud the clinics and the federal government out of more than $16 million. The scheme severely affected the quality of care that clinic patients received.

After a joint federal investigation into his activities, Dunning was eventually convicted on nearly 100 counts of fraud and money laundering-related charges and was recently sentenced to a federal prison term of 18 years. He was also ordered to pay $13.5 million in restitution to the entities he defrauded, in addition to an order of forfeiture that divested him of any interest in real property he obtained through his criminal scheme.

The FBI portion of the investigation began in 2011 when the Birmingham FBI Field Office received an allegation that former CEO Dunning was taking money from the two clinics through seemingly illegal contracts with the group of for-profit businesses he had created. Our investigator soon learned that the Department of Health and Human Services Office of the Inspector General (HHS-OIG) had recently opened up its own investigation into Dunning after receiving similar allegations, so both agencies joined forces. An agent from the Internal Revenue Service-Criminal Investigation Division (IRS-CID) rounded out the team.

As a result of the investigation, law enforcement learned that Dunning had begun his scheme to skim some of the federal funds earmarked for the clinics while serving as their CEO, and he was able to continue the scheme even after he left and formed his own businesses, known collectively as Synergy companies. Dunning selected the men who replaced him as CEO for each clinic and was able to steer a variety of contracts to his own companies.

The investigation was extensive—FBI forensic accountants painstakingly examined the clinics' and a related credit union's accounting records. Investigators reviewed Dunning's personal financials and the records of his for-profit businesses, as well as his electronic communications. They also interviewed over a hundred witnesses, including Dunning's former employees from the clinics, persons affiliated with Synergy companies, and bankers associated with real estate transactions.

And investigators also found Dunning living a lavish lifestyle that had been funded by his fraud. Dunning was living large up until the moment of his arrest, which occurred in a luxury hotel room.

What was the impact of Dunning's actions on the clinics he formerly oversaw? It was significant. Less money going to patient care meant that a number of doctors and other staff members had to be let go over time, aging equipment wasn't replaced, and much-needed maintenance on the buildings went undone.

Eventually, as a result of Dunning's actions, one of the health clinics had to close, leaving one less facility in Alabama to care for its most vulnerable residents. But the second clinic remains open for business, although it has changed its name.

Upon Dunning's October 2016 sentencing, FBI Birmingham Special Agent in Charge Roger Stanton said, "Stealing money away from programs that provided health care to poor and homeless people in order to live lavishly is an abominable crime. The FBI and its law enforcement partners are committed to joining forces and putting in the hours, and years if necessary, to stop this kind of crime."

Payback for a Debt Collector

Illegal, Aggressive Tactics Result in Jail Time

John Todd Williams, the owner of a debt collection company based in Georgia, used illegal and aggressive tactics to squeeze millions of dollars from thousands of victims. Now Williams is paying his own debt—to society—in the form of a five-year prison sentence.

The debt collection fraud scheme went on for nearly five years as Williams and those he employed ruthlessly tricked their victims into paying by pretending to be law enforcement officers and lawyers and illegally threatening arrest and other legal action. Some of the victims were so intimidated that they paid debts that had already been paid.

"It was no holds barred in terms of what they told people over the phone," said Special Agent Brian Comisky, who investigated the case from the FBI's New York Division. "They yelled, screamed, harassed. They said, 'We're going to revoke your driver's license. We're going to send you to jail.' It was nasty."

Often working from scripts, Williams and his employees at Williams, Scott & Associates (WSA) gave themselves fake "dunning" names and personas, telling victims they were detectives or investigators. They falsely claimed to be affiliated with law enforcement agencies such as the Department of Justice and the FBI, and regularly used legal jargon to scare and confuse victims.

"They would take legal terms and throw them around," Comisky said, "even though they made no sense." During Williams' July 2016 trial, for example, evidence showed that victims were told that the "statute of limitations" on their "civil legal rights" had expired and that their debt was now a criminal matter

that could only be resolved by voluntary payment or arrest.

> *"What Williams and his collectors were saying—scaring the victims into paying by threatening them with arrest and jail—was fraudulent and illegal."*

Debt collection companies like WSA buy debts—referred to in the industry as "paper"—from businesses whose customers failed to pay. WSA and other third-party collectors buy that debt at a fraction of the debt's value, sometimes for pennies on the dollar. Then whatever they collect is profit. Although the industry has come under scrutiny for predatory collection practices, Comisky noted, "WSA broke all the rules."

"The fact that some of the victims did owe money is not what this case was about," he said. "What Williams and his collectors were saying—scaring the victims into paying by threatening them with arrest and jail—was fraudulent and illegal."

The Federal Trade Commission, mandated to protect consumers, had received multiple complaints about WSA's tactics, and in 2014,

prosecutors at the United States Attorney's Office in the Southern District of New York alerted the FBI about possible criminal activity on the part of the company.

An investigation was opened, and a search warrant executed in May 2014 at WSA's office revealed the bogus scripts employees used to coerce victims. Testimony at trial revealed that approximately 6,000 victims nationwide paid WSA nearly $4 million.

After a jury found Williams guilty of conspiracy to commit wire fraud, a federal judge in November ordered the 50-year-old to serve five years in prison and pay nearly $4 million in restitution to victims.

Comisky, who specializes in white-collar crime and financial fraud investigations, said it was gratifying to put a stop to WSA's illegal practices. "When you heard some of the victims' stories," he said, "you realized that Williams and his employees would go to any lengths to collect."

If you would like to report a crime by a debt collector, contact the Federal Trade Commission: 1-877-FTC-HELP.

For information about dealing with debt collection companies, the FTC offers valuable information on its website, www.ftc.gov.

Seizing Crime Proceeds and Compensating Victims
Forfeiture as an Effective Law Enforcement Tool

Shown is one of the Rutland, Vermont, properties used as a drug house that was seized through the civil forfeiture process and returned to the Rutland community, where it will be rehabilitated for families.

Last fall, the U.S. Attorney's Office in Vermont held a press conference and issued a press release announcing that "the government and its public and private partners have completed an agreement to convert forfeited Rutland drug houses to safe, renovated houses."

So what's the significance of that announcement? The legal forfeiture action it referred to grew out of a multi-agency law enforcement investigation into heroin and crack cocaine dealers who were operating out of various residences on the same street in Rutland, Vermont, spreading their poison throughout the community. Seven subjects were ultimately sentenced to federal prison terms. But beyond that,

through the civil forfeiture process, the government was able to take possession of the very properties that were used in the commission of these crimes and facilitate their return to the Rutland community victimized by the criminals.

The FBI was one of the agencies involved in this investigation, which is just one example of how we use the federal forfeiture provisions. Forfeiture in general as a law enforcement tool allows us to accomplish a number of goals—from disrupting and dismantling criminal and terrorist organizations and punishing criminals to compensating victims and protecting communities.

What exactly is forfeiture? In a nutshell, it's the legal taking of property by the U.S. government because the property was either used in the facilitation of a federal crime or obtained through the illegal proceeds of a federal crime. The FBI, like other federal investigative agencies, began using forfeiture in earnest when Congress passed the Comprehensive Crime Control Act of 1984, which established the Department of Justice's Assets Forfeiture Fund to receive and lawfully manage the proceeds of federal forfeitures.

What sort of items can be seized for forfeiture? Just about anything of value—including cash, financial

THE FBI STORY

accounts, securities, businesses, real estate, jewelry, professional licenses, antiques, artwork, lottery winnings, vehicles of all kinds, high-end electronics, and weapons.

Many—though not all—federal crimes have forfeiture provisions, but just about every law the FBI is charged with enforcing has some forfeiture aspect—from organized crime activities, financial frauds, drug trafficking, and cyber crimes to public corruption, child pornography, human trafficking, and terrorism. In all Bureau cases, the burden of proof to demonstrate that the property in question is forfeitable under the applicable federal law rests with the government.

There are two different kinds of forfeiture—criminal and civil.

In general, criminal forfeiture is an action brought against individuals as part of a criminal prosecution. Their illegal assets can be seized or frozen by the government, and then after a conviction or guilty plea, a forfeiture order is meted out during the sentencing of the defendant(s).

Civil forfeiture, on the other hand, is brought against property rather than the actual wrongdoer—it's not dependent on a criminal prosecution, it's based on the strength of the evidence at hand, it's available whether the owner of the property is living or dead, and it allows us to obtain the assets of fugitives who have escaped the arm of the law or subjects who reside outside our borders.

There are two kinds of civil forfeiture: administrative forfeiture that generally involves property worth less than $500,000, and judicial forfeiture that can be of any value but generally involves property worth more than $500,000. But criminal and civil forfeiture aren't mutually exclusive. In some instances, the FBI—in conjunction with U.S. Attorney's Office—will run parallel criminal and civil forfeiture cases. There are several reasons for this. Parallel proceedings help us get the proceeds of a crime back to the victims more quickly. Also, if the case involves depreciating assets (like cars), we can civilly forfeit those assets faster than in the criminal proceeding, then liquidate the assets and get them back to the victim at a better return than if we had held the assets until the criminal case was completed. We also do parallel cases to ensure we can forfeit the assets civilly in case the defendant flees or dies before the forfeiture order is handed down.

Why use forfeiture at all? First of all, it deprives criminals of the illegal proceeds from their crimes. It helps dismantle criminal organizations and takes away the tools or instruments they use to commit their crimes, and also takes away the funds they use to operate. Forfeiture can also serve as a deterrent to others who might be considering criminal activities—is it worth the risk? And, it can compensate crime victims for the financial losses they suffered.

We've had a lot of success with forfeiture actions in terms of going after criminal enterprises, but our emphasis on compensating victims has paid off as well. In the past two fiscal years, FBI forfeitures—criminal and civil—have allowed the government to return more than $100 million to victims of crime following criminal restitution orders. And since fiscal year 2000, the Department of Justice as a whole has returned more than $4 billion in forfeited funds to crime victims.

Unearthing a Coal Mining Fraud
Investors Bilked out of Millions; 10 Fraudsters Sent to Prison

Left: Salesmen from New Century Coal used sophisticated—but bogus—marketing brochures like the ones shown here to convince investors that the company owned mines that produced high-quality Blue Gem coal. But it was all a fraud, and investors lost millions of dollars.

Brian C. Rose ran a Tennessee company that claimed to be mining and processing a highly profitable type of coal used to manufacture silicon and computer electronics. On the basis of that claim, Rose and his employees raised more than $14 million from more than 160 investors—knowing all along that the only thing they were mining was their victims' cash.

For more than three years beginning in 2011, Rose and his co-conspirators at New Century Coal sold shares in limited partnerships by convincing investors the company owned mines that produced high-quality Blue Gem coal—a scarce commodity that commands premium prices in the marketplace because of its use in computer semiconductors.

"They sold the idea that they had Blue Gem coal," said Special Agent Brian O'Hare, one of the agents who investigated the case from the FBI's Knoxville Division. "But there were never any high-quality mines, and there was never any high-quality coal," he said. "Our investigation led us to the conclusion that this was envisioned as a fraud from the outset."

Thanks to sophisticated marketing brochures and presentations and a persuasive sales force that often traveled to meet with investors, the money started rolling in to

New Century Coal. And Rose and his employees—including Rose's father—were spending it as fast as they could on luxury lifestyles that included buying multiple homes, sports cars, thoroughbred horses, expensive trips to Las Vegas, and other extensive travel.

> *"...there were never any high-quality mines, and there was never any high-quality coal. Our investigation led us to the conclusion that this was envisioned as a fraud from the outset."*

"The salespeople were very talented and very convincing," O'Hare said. "Unfortunately, they knew they were involved in a scam and continued doing it."

New Century Coal fooled some savvy investors, too, many of whom asked to see the mining operation in person before they put up as much as $2 million. Rose went so far as to lease mines and bring in earth-moving equipment, O'Hare explained. "But it was simply for show. The average investor couldn't tell the difference between Blue Gem and regular coal. They assumed the operation was an ongoing, legitimate effort. But it was all a lie."

After several years, the fraud

scheme had grown so large—in excess of $14 million—that one of New Century Coal's employees got cold feet and came to the FBI. "The person didn't want to risk being a party to that kind of a fraud," O'Hare said.

Special Agent Drew Scown opened the investigation into New Century Coal's activity, and, in partnership with the U.S. Secret Service and the Internal Revenue Service, the fraudulent operation was shut down in June 2014. Not long after, Rose and nine others were indicted on a variety of counts of wire fraud, mail fraud, and money laundering.

As of last month, a federal judge in Tennessee had sentenced 10 individuals to a collective 284 months in prison for their roles in the New Century Coal scam. Rose, the ringleader, received a nine-year term.

O'Hare said some of the co-conspirators are currently under indictment in Indiana for a similar investment fraud. "These individuals," he said, "had become highly effective and efficient in their schemes. They would start one, run it until the money ran dry, then start another one. They used aliases to conceal their true identity, and they stayed one step ahead of the law. It seems fraud is in their DNA."

In addition to prison terms for the fraudsters, O'Hare added that investigators have so far been able to recover more than $3 million in assets that will be returned to the victims.

Super Bowl Security

Behind the Scenes Look at Game Day Preparations

When tens of thousands of fans stream into NRG Stadium in Houston for the Super Bowl this Sunday, they will understandably be thinking more about the big game than the behind-the-scenes preparations that have gone into ensuring their safety—and that's just the way law enforcement officials want it to be.

The Super Bowl will put Houston squarely in the international spotlight, and the FBI and its local, state, and federal law enforcement partners have been working hard to make sure the game and the events leading up to it in Houston are without incident.

"We've been working for several years with our partners to make sure appropriate security is in place," said Perrye Turner, special agent in charge of the FBI's Houston Division. "We're going to do everything in our power to make sure it's a safe event."

"On the day of the big game, we will be here, but our presence may not necessarily be seen," said Mark Webster, an FBI assistant special agent in charge in Houston who is coordinating the Bureau's Super Bowl security efforts. "We will have multiple elements in place onsite as well as offsite."

Working with the Houston Police Department—which has the lead role in security planning—and other local, state, and federal agencies, the FBI's primary role is to provide intelligence about possible terror threats. But because the Super Bowl is a major national event, just about every aspect of the Bureau's expertise will be called into play.

"We are using all the elements within our office," Webster said. From SWAT teams and cyber

During the 10 days of festivities leading up to Super Bowl LI on February 5, the FBI will be working closely with the Houston Police Department and other local, state, and federal agencies to keep the city safe. At the Houston Emergency Center, a command post will monitor and coordinate law enforcement and public safety activities.

squads to intelligence analysts and surveillance specialists, FBI personnel will be on the ground at the stadium and will also be staffing command posts set up for the 10-day operational period that includes a variety of festivities leading up to the game on February 5.

At the Houston Emergency Center recently, where the main command post is located, specialists gathered from more than a dozen partner agencies.

"Today is called a rehearsal of concept," said George Buenik, an executive assistant chief with the Houston Police Department responsible for Super Bowl security and police operations. "We invite everybody here to check the equipment, check the hookups, to see where they're going to be sitting, and to also meet some of the other folks that they're going to be working with. We have a great security plan in place," Buenik said.

Matt Slinkard, an assistant chief with the Houston Police Department also involved with Super Bowl security preparations,

noted that this will be the third Super Bowl the city has hosted, along with many other national-level events. "Our city and our counterparts both locally and federally are well prepared and well equipped to deal with these types of events."

He added that even with all the law enforcement coordination, "the community has to be our eyes and ears. We cannot do it by ourselves. If you see something—if something doesn't seem right to you, it's probably not right to us either—say something about it."

The FBI's Turner agreed. "We all have to work together to make this a safe event," he said, expressing confidence that with the extensive planning and resources that have gone into Super Bowl security preparations, "people will be able to come to Houston, be safe, and have a great time cheering on their favorite football team."

Scan this QR code with your smartphone to access related information, or visit www.fbi.gov/superbowl51

NCIC Turns 50

Centralized Database Continues to Prove Its Value in Fighting Crime

Last month, a Tennessee state trooper arrested an Illinois man wanted for questioning in a Kentucky murder. The FBI's National Crime Information Center, or NCIC, had a key assist in the arrest—the state trooper, after spotting a suspicious vehicle at a rest stop, ran the license plate through the NCIC database and received word back quickly that the car had been stolen by a suspect in a Kentucky homicide. A chase ensued, but ultimately the suspect in this case with connections to three different states was taken into custody.

Today, the FBI's NCIC system—created to give our law enforcement partners access to a computerized index of documented criminal justice information whenever and wherever they need it—celebrates its 50th anniversary. Launched on January 27, 1967, the NCIC

database, according to Assistant Director Stephen Morris of the Criminal Justice Information Services (CJIS) Division, is "a cornerstone of the CJIS Division's information-sharing efforts, providing a lifeline to our local, state, federal, and tribal partners 24 hours a day."

> *"[NCIC is] a cornerstone of the CJIS Division's information-sharing efforts, providing a lifeline to our local, state, federal, and tribal partners 24 hours a day."*

The information in the NCIC database can also help law enforcement officers perform their duties more safely—for instance, notifying them if the person in the car they are about to approach might be armed and dangerous.

In the beginning, 15 state and city computers were tied into the Bureau's host computer in Washington, D.C. At the time, NCIC contained just over 350,000 criminal justice records across five different files—wanted persons, stolen articles, stolen vehicles, stolen license plates, and stolen/missing guns. The very first NCIC hit came in May 1967, when a New York City officer radioed in a request for a search of a license plate. Within 90 seconds, he was informed that the car had been stolen the previous month in Boston.

By 1971, all 50 states were connected to NCIC and began making inroads in combating crimes that crossed state lines. And over the next three decades, the database expanded and adapted as new technology and new information needs emerged.

THE FBI STORY

For example, in 1975, a new file was added to record the details of missing persons cases. In 1980, Canadian warrants were added to the database. In 1999, a major technological upgrade—known as NCIC 2000—added new capabilities, including the ability to store digital images and expanded data fields, and also led to near-instant results for queries.

During the last 15 years or so, additional file categories have been added, including identity theft, gangs, known or suspected terrorists, and violent persons.

Currently, the database is organized into a total of 21 files and contains 12 million active records entered by local, state, and federal law enforcement agencies—and it handles an average of 14 million transactions a day. NCIC serves more than 90,000 criminal justice and law enforcement agencies, along with judges, prosecutors, corrections officers, court administrators, and a variety of other criminal justice officials by providing information that can help apprehend fugitives, locate missing persons, identify convicted sexual offenders, uncover weapons used in crimes, locate and return stolen property, and more.

So what does the future hold for NCIC? The CJIS Division is preparing for its next major upgrade, known as NCIC 3rd Generation, or the N3G Project, and is working with its stakeholders to identity new functionalities to modernize and expand the capabilities of the existing NCIC system. CJIS has already conducted the largest user canvass in its history, reaching out to criminal justice users in all 50 states and U.S. territories to help identity additional needs, which is vital input that will be used in the development of the next generation National Crime Information Center.

Here's to the next 50 years of this vital crime-fighting tool!

Shown here are Bureau personnel in the mid-1970s managing the computer storage tapes that contained all NCIC records and transaction logs. This legacy system required operator intervention to ensure that tapes were effectively maintained.

The Origins of NCIC

The FBI first got into the business of collecting, collating, and disseminating criminal identification records and histories in 1924. Over time, Bureau personnel maintained information about crimes with pen and paper, index cards, and typewriters—and they did so effectively—but as the volume of work increased, it was clear that something needed to change.

In 1965, an executive in the then-FBI Identification Division (since renamed the Criminal Justice Information Services Division) proposed that the Bureau lease data-processing equipment to "constructively assist the enforcement efforts of all participating law enforcement agencies" that contributed criminal histories, wanted notices, reports of criminal activity, etc., to the FBI. The original proposal was limited to law enforcement agencies in the Washington, D.C. metropolitan areas, but the value of such a system for all of law enforcement couldn't be ignored.

Director J. Edgar Hoover presided over a meeting during which the decision was made to implement a computer system that would centralize crime information from every state and provide that information to law enforcement agencies around the country. Working with the International Association of Chiefs of Police, the FBI created an advisory board of state and local police to develop nationwide standards and also consulted with the U.S. Department of Commerce to build an effective telecommunications system.

And on January 27, 1967, the National Crime Information Center—soon to be better known by its initials NCIC—was launched.

Office of Private Sector

Enhancing Engagement Efforts to Stay Ahead of the Threat

Brad Brekke, former FBI agent and former chief security officer for an American retailer, serves as the director of the Bureau's Office of Private Sector.

In 1996, the FBI established a private/public partnership program in Cleveland as a way to share information with local information technology experts and others in support of our cyber investigations.

That program, called InfraGard, was a unique effort that was quite ahead of its time—back then, the Bureau did very little with the private sector in terms of engagement. According to Brad Brekke, the head of today's FBI Office of Private Sector (OPS), "We rarely talked to the private sector back in the late 1980s or early 1990s unless we were doing an interview, serving a search warrant, or making an arrest."

However, over the past 20 years—and especially since the events of 9/11—the Bureau has made great strides in engaging

with businesses, sharing information not just on cyber issues but on counterintelligence, counterterrorism, and more traditional criminal matters as well.

But while the number of contacts and information-sharing opportunities between the Bureau and American businesses has grown, the way the process evolved wasn't exactly perfect.

> *"We need to engage with the private sector if we're going to succeed in staying ahead of the threat."*

Explained Brekke, "Interactions were siloed—members of a field office counterintelligence squad might have had a particular point of contact at a company within

their territory, while a criminal investigator might have had a different point of contact at the same company, and someone else at the company might have gotten a phone call from an InfraGard representative or from our Cyber or Counterterrorism Division at Headquarters." He added, "It's just not good business having multiple entities reaching out to the same company."

Brekke also said that much of the FBI's engagement with private industry has traditionally involved Bureau investigators and company employees whose job duties were related to particular cases or particular threats, as well as company representatives—usually security people—that we convey information to through programs like InfraGard. "We haven't worked much with upper-echelon executives, the primary decision makers," explained Brekke.

But things are about to change, and Brekke and OPS will play a vital role in these changes.

The need for OPS was envisioned by Director James Comey and then-Deputy Director Mark Giuliano—both saw that the FBI should have an organized, coordinated, and horizontal approach to interacting with the private sector in today's complex threat environment.

Why interact with the private sector at all? Explained Brekke, "Most of our nation's national security-related and economic infrastructure rests with our private partners—our technology, our innovation, and our intellectual property. So invariably, that's where the threats from—and the victims of—nation states, terrorists, and hacktivists are."

"We need to engage with the private sector if we're going to succeed in staying ahead of the threat," added Brekke. "And staying ahead of the threat—through leadership, agility, and integration—is Director Comey's vision for the Bureau."

Private industry, according to Brekke, has the innovation to mitigate risks. "For instance," he said, "we could never build the systems or the platforms fast enough to mitigate the cyber risk. What we have is the information that gives the private sector a clearer picture of cyber threats so they can more effectively address them. Only by the FBI and private sector working together can the U.S. economy and its national security truly be protected."

Highlights of some of the current efforts by OPS:

- Building partnerships: Among other efforts, OPS is working to determine where the FBI doesn't have relationships with companies where it should, enhance legacy partnership programs like InfraGard and DSAC (Domestic Security Alliance Council) so that they're more effective and vital in today's fast-moving threat environment, and engage with those in the private sector at the "C-suite level"—the chief executive officers, chief information security officers, general counsels, and others who make key decisions for the company pertaining to investment and risk.

- Sharing information: Innovative ways to share information and work more closely together—whether through embedded FBI analysts at private sector companies or with more effective information sharing portals—is where OPS is focused. "Essentially, we are working to take our cooperation to the next level," noted Brekke.

- Providing tools: OPS is working to develop analytical tools and programs to identify gaps in the FBI's private sector relationships regarding both existing threats and over-the-horizon threats, where strategic Bureau engagement is vital.

OPS, which is not involved in investigative work, serves as an entity within the FBI that coordinates—and has a 360-degree understanding of—the Bureau's engagement with the American business community.

And OPS is making sure that companies looking to reach out to the Bureau won't have to try to figure out who to contact for each issue. In addition to the OPS team at FBI Headquarters, there is a private sector coordinator in every field office to provide one FBI voice and connect private industry with the appropriate Bureau contact—no matter what the concern. Said Brekke, "Field offices are centric to our efforts—they are our boots on the ground, the people who actually interact with these companies."

Brekke is perfectly suited to lead OPS. He is a former FBI agent who worked a wide variety of criminal cases in several different field offices, and he also served for more than a decade as a chief security officer for a major American retailer. "Both experiences gave me an insider's view of what the FBI needs and what private sector concerns are," he explained.

His primary message to the private sector? "By engaging with the American business community in a smarter and more effective manner, both the FBI and the private sector will be in a better position to counter today's threats and identify and mitigate tomorrow's."

"And in the end," said Brekke, "it's the American public that will benefit."

New FBI Wanted App
Making It Easier to Find Fugitives and Missing Persons

Scan this QR code with your smartphone to access related information, or visit www.fbi.gov/fbiwantedapp.

You're watching your local news on TV when you see a story on a wanted fugitive in your community. The person looks like someone you've seen living a few blocks away. You grab your cell phone, open the FBI Wanted app, search your city name, and quickly locate the individual's profile with additional pictures and information. The similarity is striking. So you tap the "Call the FBI" button in the app and report what you know.

This situation illustrates exactly the kind of technology-driven crime fighting that is now possible—thanks to a new FBI Wanted mobile application launching today.

The app allows the public to view, search, sort, filter, and bookmark the full range of information issued by the FBI. That includes pictures and descriptions of wanted fugitives, missing persons, crime suspects, deceased victims, and others the Bureau is seeking to locate or identify.

The app is free and works on Apple and Android devices, including smartphones, iPads, and iPods.

Depending on your device, it can be downloaded from the Apple App store or Google Play.

"Since the earliest days of the Bureau—when wanted flyers were tacked to post office walls—the public has played a vital role in helping the FBI and its partners locate criminals on the run and solving cases of all kinds," says Christopher Allen, head of the Investigative Publicity and Public Affairs Unit in the FBI's Office of Public Affairs. "This app is designed to put another digital tool in the hands of concerned citizens so they can help protect their families and communities."

The information in the app is also posted on the FBI website, but the app includes several features and capabilities that make it especially fast and easy to use. For example, with the app you can:

- Access information in one user-friendly interface, with a single tap of the app icon bringing up all Wanted profiles;

- Take advantage of a suite of search and filtering options (see sidebar);

- Easily report information by using buttons that either call the FBI or link directly to the Bureau's online form for providing tips;

- Bookmark individual profiles with one touch, adding them to a favorites page so you can easily access them later; and

- Customize your home screen to display the information that is most relevant or interesting to you.

Along with the TV news scenario described above, the app could be useful in a number of situations. You might see someone who is acting in a suspicious or dangerous manner and wish to determine whether that person is wanted by the FBI. Or you might be interested in which cases the Bureau needs help with in your area.

FBI Wanted is the third mobile app built by the Bureau. The Child ID app, introduced in 2011, allows parents to electronically store their children's pictures and vital information in case their kids go missing; it has been downloaded nearly 350,000 times. The FBI Bank Robbers app was launched in August 2016, publicizing unknown violent and serial robbers sought by the Bureau.

"Thousands of cases have been solved over the years thanks to the watchful eyes of concerned citizens, and that has made the country a safer place for all of us," said Allen. "The FBI Wanted app will help carry on this tradition of partnership. We encourage everyone to download it and report any pertinent tips to the FBI."

A brochure and video on the FBI Wanted app are available online.

Search and Filtering Capabilities

The new FBI Wanted app provides a range of search and filtering options to browse information and locate specific individuals or cases. The app enables you to:

- Quickly scroll through the entire list of Wanted profiles (currently more than 500);
- Use the search feature to locate individuals by name, alias, city, state, country, or any other terms mentioned in the descriptions;
- Sort information alphabetically by the FBI field office working the case;
- List data chronologically according to when it was published or updated;
- Filter profiles by status (deceased, located, etc.);
- View listings by subject or crime categories, including Case of the Week, Ten Most Wanted, Fugitives, Terrorism, Kidnappings/Missing Persons, Seeking Information, Parental Kidnappings, Known Bank Robbers, Endangered Child Alert Program, and Violent Criminal Apprehension Program; and
- Use the search and filtering tools in various combinations—for instance, you can sort all terrorism profiles by field office or list the most recently published kidnappings.

Digital Technologies Help Find Fugitives

Since 1996—when the FBI began posting wanted flyers on its new website—the Bureau has used a number of digital technologies to enlist the public's help in locating and identifying various individuals. These tools include:

- Social Media: The FBI publicizes information about fugitives, missing persons, and other individuals through more than 60 separate social media pages or sites, including a dedicated FBI Most Wanted Twitter page with 50,000 followers.
- Digital Billboards: Since 2007, the FBI has partnered with outdoor advertising companies to place urgent public safety messages—including notifications on wanted fugitives and missing children—on approximately 6,700 digital billboards around the nation. The result has been nearly 60 captures and rescues.
- Audio and Video Podcasts: The Bureau publishes a regular series of podcasts in its Wanted By the FBI series that are available for download on iTunes and FBI.gov. Video podcasts—or vodcasts—can be viewed on YouTube or the FBI website.
- RSS Feeds: On FBI.gov, you can subscribe to 170 different feeds that deliver Bureau news and information. More than 70 of these feeds involve Wanted information.
- Mobile App: Based on the Bank Robbers website, the FBI Bank Robbers App maps the location of robberies locally and nationally and enables people to sign up for new listings.
- Widgets: The FBI has created various widgets or modules that can be incorporated into other websites or blogs, including four related to the Wanted program: Ten Most Wanted, Wanted By the FBI, Predators and Missing Persons, and Most Wanted Bank Robbers.

Wine Ponzi Scheme
Long-Running Fraud Cost Victims Millions of Dollars

In 1980, a California man named John E. Fox opened a wine store near San Francisco called Premier Cru. More than a decade later, when the business was struggling financially, Fox devised a way to make a lot of money—all at his customers' expense.

What transpired on and off during the next two decades was a massive Ponzi scheme: Fox sold millions of dollars of "phantom" wine that only existed on paper and then used some of the proceeds to pay back previous customers who had invested in his fictitious wine futures.

Fox, of course, took millions of dollars for himself, living a lavish lifestyle that included memberships to private golf clubs and buying and leasing expensive vehicles such as Ferraris and a Maserati. He also used his ill-gotten gains to pay for a variety of other personal expenses, not least of which was nearly $1 million on women he met online.

"He had a pretty lucrative scheme going for a time," said Special Agent Scott Medearis, who investigated the case from the FBI's San Francisco Division.

"Like all Ponzi schemes, though, it was destined to fail, but not before his victims lost pretty much everything."

> *"Instead of doing the right thing and closing up shop when the business was no longer viable, he invented inventory he didn't have."*

In the 1990s, Fox began selling "pre-arrival wine" to customers around the country and overseas. He might sell a $100 bottle yet to be produced by a French vineyard that he led people to believe would be worth much more when they took delivery a few years later.

"His customers thought they were getting wine futures," Medearis said, "fancy wine at a good deal." Fox was clever, choosing certain wines because he knew they would sell well. "He put thought into what he would offer," Medearis explained. "Not the rarest wines, because savvy customers would know there wasn't that much available."

Fox conducted legitimate business as well, but if he had 10 cases of a certain wine in his inventory, he might bump that inventory to 30 cases on paper and sell the 20 phantom cases as pre-arrivals.

"He did that off and on when he got into tight spots to generate cash," Medearis said. "Instead of doing the right thing and closing up shop when the business was no longer viable, he invented inventory he didn't have." Just in the years 2010 to 2015, Fox acknowledged that he sold or attempted to sell approximately $20 million worth of phantom wine.

In time, customers complained to law enforcement when they didn't get their wine or their money back. When Fox heard rumors that the FBI had begun an investigation into his business practices, he declared bankruptcy, listing about 9,000 people he owed money to. That didn't protect him from the Bureau's criminal investigation, however, and in June 2016, he was charged with wire fraud.

Two months later, after Fox had already begun cooperating with investigators to provide the details of his long-running scam, he pleaded guilty to the charges against him. "Without the knowledge in his head," Medearis said, "it would have taken us years to unravel the extent of the fraud."

In December 2016, a federal judge sentenced Fox to 78 months in prison. Medearis is satisfied that justice was done, although he understands the frustration and betrayal felt by Fox's many victims. "One victim in Hong Kong lost $1 million," he said. "Another victim invested some of his retirement money and lost it. One father just wanted a great wine to serve at his daughter's wedding, and, of course, that never happened."

Romance Scams

Online Imposters Break Hearts and Bank Accounts

They met online. He said he was a friend of a friend. The woman, in her 50s and struggling in her marriage, was happy to find someone to chat with. "He was saying all the right things," she remembered. "He was interested in me. He was interested in getting to know me better. He was very positive, and I felt like there was a real connection there."

That connection would end up costing the woman $2 million and an untold amount of heartache after the man she fell in love with—whom she never met in person—took her for every cent she had.

It's called a romance scam, and this devastating Internet crime is on the rise. Victims—predominantly older widowed or divorced women targeted by criminal groups usually from Nigeria—are, for the most part, computer literate and educated. But they are also emotionally vulnerable. And con artists know exactly how to exploit that vulnerability because potential victims freely post details about their lives and personalities on dating and social media sites.

> *"The Internet makes this type of crime easy because you can pretend to be anybody you want to be."*

Trolling for victims online "is like throwing a fishing line," said Special Agent Christine Beining, a veteran financial fraud investigator in the FBI's Houston Division who has seen a substantial increase in the number of romance scam cases. "The Internet makes this type of crime easy because you can pretend to be anybody you want to be. You can be anywhere in the world and victimize people," she said. "The perpetrators will reach out to a lot of people on various networking sites to find somebody who may be a good target. Then they use what the victims have on their profile pages and try to work those relationships and see which ones develop."

In the case of the Texas woman who lost everything, it was her strong Christian faith—which she happily publicized on her Facebook profile—that gave "Charlie" an incredible advantage when he began courting her.

"I'm very active on Facebook," said the woman, who agreed to share her story in the hopes that others might avoid becoming victims. "I thought it was safe." After she friended Charlie—without verifying his bogus claim that they had a mutual friend—"he would read my wall, I would read his wall. We would post things, he would like things. Then it got to where we would share e-mails. We started sharing pictures."

Special Agent Christine Beining

According to Beining, this is standard operating procedure for romance scammers, who assume other people's identities to trick their victims. "They make themselves out to be average-looking people," she said. "They are generally not trying to build themselves up too high."

The scammer's intention is to establish a relationship as quickly as possible, endear himself to the victim, gain trust, and propose marriage. He will make plans to meet in person, but that will never happen. Eventually, he will ask for money.

According to the FBI's Internet Crime Complaint Center (IC3), which provides the public with a means of reporting Internet-facilitated crimes, romance scams—also called confidence fraud—result in the highest amount of financial losses to victims when compared to other online crimes.

In 2016, almost 15,000 complaints categorized as romance scams or confidence fraud were reported to IC3 (nearly 2,500 more than

the previous year), and the losses associated with those complaints exceeded $230 million. The states with the highest numbers of victims were California, Texas, Florida, New York, and Pennsylvania. In Texas last year, the IC3 received more than 1,000 complaints from victims reporting more than $16 million in losses related to romance scams.

'I was Looking for Happiness'

When she first encountered Charlie in 2014, the Texas woman recalled, "I was in an emotionally abusive marriage, and things had not been good for probably at least 10 years." Her new online friend seemed to come along at just the right time. "I was looking for happiness," she said. "I thought I could find that with Charlie."

Romance scammers often say they are in the building and construction industry and are engaged in projects outside the U.S. That makes it easier to avoid meeting in person—and more plausible when they ask their victims for help. They will suddenly need money for a medical emergency or unexpected legal fee. "They promise to repay the loan immediately," Beining said, "but the victims never get their money back."

Charlie claimed to be in the construction field. "He was trying to finish up a job in California," the woman said, "and he needed some money to help finish the job. I thought about it long and hard. I prayed about it. I've always been a very giving person, and I figured if I had money … I could send him some [money]. And he promised to have it back within 24 to 48 hours.

I thought, 'I could do that.' It was kind of a statement of faith, too."

She wired him $30,000. A day passed and then another, and she didn't get her money back. "I still thought everything was okay," she said, "just that he was the victim of some bad luck." And then Charlie needed another $30,000.

Empty Promises

For the next two years, the woman believed Charlie's stories after each new request for funds. Everything he said made sense, and, after all, they were in love. Eventually, the woman's financial adviser became alarmed about her steadily dwindling accounts and, suspecting fraud, urged her to contact the FBI.

The subsequent investigation led by Beining resulted in the arrest of two Nigerians posing as South African diplomats who had come to the U.S. to collect money from the woman on behalf of Charlie, who claimed he was paid $42 million for a construction project he completed in South Africa. The woman believed she would be paying to have the money—including the repayment of her $2 million—transferred to the U.S. from South Africa, where Charlie was still supposedly working.

In July 2016, the two Nigerian co-conspirators pleaded guilty in connection with their roles in the scam, and a federal judge sentenced them each to 36 months in prison last December. But Charlie is still at large, presumably in Nigeria, and there may be little hope of bringing him to justice.

"This is a very difficult crime to prove," Beining said. "When someone is using a computer to hide behind, the hardest thing to find out is who they are. We can find out where in the world their computer is being used. It's identifying who they actually are that's the hard part. That is why this individual remains a fugitive."

> *"I don't want this to happen to anybody else. I not only invested money in this man but there is a big, huge piece of my heart that I invested in him."*

It also explains why romance scams are on the rise: It's a lucrative and easy crime to commit, and easier still to remain anonymous and beyond the reach of authorities. "It's not like going in a bank and holding a gun to the teller," Beining explained, "because there are so many leads that you provide law enforcement when you do that. Even if you are able to get out of the bank, we can probably find out who you are and track you down. But with an Internet crime like this, it's much more difficult."

As for the Texas woman, she came forward "because I don't want this to happen to anybody else. I not only invested money in this man but there is a big, huge piece of my heart that I invested in him," she said. "It's not just the finances, it's the emotional part, too—being embarrassed, being ashamed, being humiliated."

Even now, though, she remains conflicted. A part of her still wants to believe that Charlie is real and that their relationship was real— that the e-mail exchanges about church and the phone calls when they sang together and prayed together meant as much to him as they did to her. She even holds out hope that one day Charlie will repay her, as he promised to do so many times.

Otherwise, there is no doubt that he is a heartless criminal who robbed her and broke her heart—and who is almost certainly continuing to victimize other women in the same way.

"I can't even imagine a man, a person, that could be this bad," she said. "I can't think of him that way. ... there can't be a man in this world that could be this horrible to have purposefully done what he's done to me."

 Scan this QR code with your smartphone to access related information, or visit www.fbi.gov/romancescams.

Don't Become a Victim

The criminals who carry out romance scams are experts at what they do. They spend hours honing their skills and sometimes keep journals on their victims to better understand how to manipulate and exploit them.

"Behind the veil of romance, it's a criminal enterprise like any other," said Special Agent Christine Beining. "And once a victim becomes a victim, in that they send money, they will often be placed on what's called a 'sucker list,'" she said. "Their names and identities are shared with other criminals, and they may be targeted in the future."

To stay safe online, be careful what you post, because scammers can use that information against you. Always use reputable websites, but assume that con artists are trolling even the most reputable dating and social media sites. If you develop a romantic relationship with someone you meet online, consider the following:

- Research the person's photo and profile using online searches to see if the material has been used elsewhere.
- Go slow and ask lots of questions.
- Beware if the individual seems too perfect or quickly asks you to leave a dating service or Facebook to go "offline."
- Beware if the individual attempts to isolate you from friends and family or requests inappropriate photos or financial information that could later be used to extort you.
- Beware if the individual promises to meet in person but then always comes up with an excuse why he or she can't. If you haven't met the person after a few months, for whatever reason, you have good reason to be suspicious.
- Never send money to anyone you don't know personally. "If you don't know them, don't send money," Beining said. "You will see what their true intentions are after that."

If you suspect an online relationship is a scam, stop all contact immediately. And if you are the victim of a romance scam, file a complaint with the FBI's Internet Crime Complaint Center at www.ic3.gov.

False Promises

California Man Sentenced for Operating Foreclosure Rescue Scheme

When California homeowners couldn't make their mortgage payments and faced foreclosures during the Great Recession in 2008, some turned to a Long Beach church pastor for help.

For almost six years, Karl Robinson offered mortgage rescue services under his name and through companies such as Stay in Your Home Today, 21st Century Development, and Genesis Ventures Corporation. Now he's serving four years in federal prison for his role in a scheme that brought in nearly $3 million in fees from unknowing clients.

Robinson and a group of co-conspirators attracted distressed homeowners with the promise of delaying foreclosures and evictions. They claimed to offer services that connected clients to experienced consultants who could keep them in their homes for an affordable fee.

It was all too good to be true—until an FBI-led investigation in 2013 determined that the mortgage rescue programs were far from legitimate.

"Robinson joined a growing number of con artists surfacing throughout the country during the subprime mortgage crisis focused on lining their own pockets instead of actually helping clients," said FBI Special Agent Kevin Danford, who investigated the case out of the Bureau's Los Angeles Field Office.

During the housing crisis, opportunistic groups like Robinson's preyed on vulnerable and desperate homeowners through common scams such as offering affordable refinancing with lower monthly payments, low-interest deals, and delinquent mortgage pay-offs.

In 2008, Robinson began offering fraudulent foreclosure delay solutions by taking part in what were known as partial-interest bankruptcy scams (see sidebar). The process went on for months, providing Robinson with a steady flow of income as long as his clients were willing to pay.

> *"Robinson joined a growing number of con artists surfacing throughout the country during the subprime mortgage crisis focused on lining their own pockets instead of actually helping clients."*

Another scam delayed evictions for Robinson's clients whose homes had been sold in foreclosure proceedings. Robinson falsely claimed in state court eviction actions that his clients still had tenants in those homes. Robinson would then file bankruptcies for the fictional tenants, postponing the evictions.

By 2011, clients and lenders were starting to catch on to Robinson's scams. They turned to their local police, who confirmed the suspected fraud and alerted the FBI.

The Bureau opened an investigation on Robinson in August 2013 and subsequently obtained an external hard drive from his home that contained documents such as fake driver's licenses, false identities, and incomplete bankruptcy petition drafts—which revealed the steps he was using to carry out his fraud scheme.

Following his arrest, Robinson confessed to knowingly defrauding his clients and the state and federal courts. Robinson pleaded guilty in August 2016 to the role he played in running the multi-year foreclosure rescue scheme.

"Robinson was able to delay foreclosure sales for more than 100 properties, and he filed at least 200 bankruptcy petitions," said Danford. "His scheme not only impacted more than 60 lenders and clogged both federal bankruptcy court and state and local eviction court systems but also caused undue stress to numerous purchasers."

Partial-Interest Bankruptcy Scams

The scam operator asks you to give a partial interest in your home to one or more persons. You then make mortgage payments to the scam operator in lieu of paying the delinquent mortgage. However, the scam operator does not pay the existing mortgage or seek new financing. Each holder of a partial interest then files bankruptcy, one after another, without your knowledge. The bankruptcy court will issue a "stay" order each time to stop foreclosure temporarily. However, the stay does not excuse you from making payments or from repaying the full amount of your loan. This complicates and delays foreclosure, while allowing the scam operator to maintain a stream of income by collecting payments from you, the victim. (Source: FDIC)

Financial Fraud with a Sci-Fi Twist

Outrageous Scheme Included Impersonating a Canadian Health Official

Howard Leventhal was an imaginative criminal. The scheme he devised to bilk his victims was like a work of fiction—science fiction.

Leventhal claimed to own a company that produced a medical device inspired by the popular television and movie series *Star Trek*. The McCoy Home Health Tablet—supposedly similar to the tricorder used by the show's Dr. Leonard McCoy—was billed as a diagnostic tool that would allow instantaneous delivery of patient data to doctors from the user's tablet or smartphone.

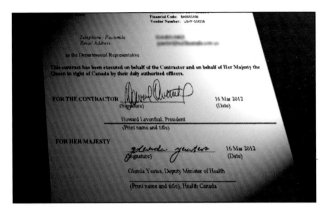

As part of his elaborate fraud scheme, Howard Leventhal claimed that his company was doing millions of dollars of business with Canada. In reality, he invented this contract and forged the signature of Glenda Yeates, then the country's deputy minister of health.

Leventhal raised money by claiming that his company, Neovision, had contracts with the Canadian government. To back up that bogus claim, Leventhal stole the identity of Glenda Yeates, at the time Health Canada's deputy minister of health, and produced fraudulent documents under her signature.

He then targeted factoring companies. Such companies buy or service a business' accounts receivable for a sum less than the receivables are worth and profit by collecting the difference. Factoring companies are a legitimate means for businesses in need of cash to raise funds without taking loans.

In 2012, Leventhal used the bogus Health Canada agreement—which claimed that the organization was doing $13 million worth of business with Neovision—to enter into a factoring agreement with a Florida company. The Florida firm paid Neovision $800,000. Leventhal ultimately used the phony Health Canada agreement to solicit more than $26 million from other potential victims.

"He was going around to different factoring companies and showing that he had contracts with Health Canada," said Special Agent Chris Delzotto, who investigated the case from the FBI's New York Division. "He was actively soliciting investment money for his company and then using that money for his personal benefit."

Leventhal created a sophisticated online presence to give the appearance that Neovision was doing business with Canada. "He also created fake e-mail addresses for other people who are actual Health Canada employees," Delzotto said, "so that if anyone was checking, correspondence would go back to Leventhal and not the Canadian officials."

In fact, no one at Health Canada had ever heard of Leventhal, let alone his futuristic product. An FBI investigation was opened in 2013, and a sting operation was arranged using an undercover agent posing as a wealthy investor. Leventhal was arrested and charged with wire fraud and aggravated identity theft.

While he was out on bail, Leventhal began using an alias—Edward Ben-Alec—and launched a new scheme similar to the one he had just been arrested for.

"He went to great lengths to get a second fraud up and running while he was out on bail," Delzotto said, including forging letters from prominent Illinois politicians to solicit funds for another medical device. "His M.O. was to steal people's identities and use them to fabricate business documents and bank statements."

Leventhal was arrested again and sent back to jail. In December 2013, he pleaded guilty to the wire fraud and aggravated identity theft charges in the Neovision case, and in December 2016, a federal judge in New York sentenced him to five years in prison and ordered him to pay victims approximately $1.3 million in restitution.

"Leventhal was a smart guy who, unfortunately, had no regard for honesty or his victims," said Delzotto, who has been investigating financial fraud case for many years. "He also showed absolutely no remorse for what he did."

African American FBI Special Agents Symposium
Inaugural Event Highlights FBI Diversity

The inaugural African American FBI Special Agents Symposium—organized by former African-American agents and scheduled to coincide with Black History Month—was held in the nation's capital last weekend to recognize the role agents of color have played in the FBI's past and the vital role they will continue to play in the future.

On Friday, February 17, the group visited the National Museum of African American History and Culture. There, participants saw poignant exhibits, including an interactive lunch counter lined with stools from the Woolworth store in Greensboro, North Carolina, the site of many sit-ins and protests against racial segregation.

The next day, they heard remarks from Director James Comey, who thanked the former and active agents on hand for their significant contributions to the FBI. When he became FBI Director, Comey added diversity as a core value of the organization and redoubled the Bureau's efforts to recruit more African-Americans and women to the ranks of special agents.

"The FBI operates in every community of this country," Comey told the group. "To accomplish the

goal of protecting the American people and upholding the Constitution of the United States, we have to be effective." Without diversity in the organization, he explained, "we are less effective."

The group also went to a wreath-laying ceremony at the National

THE FBI STORY

Law Enforcement Officers Memorial, where they had the opportunity to make stone rubbings of the names of those who had died in the line of duty. Later on Saturday, during a visit to the Martin Luther King, Jr. Memorial, the group gathered for a photo to mark the event.

That evening, Lee Woodriffe, daughter of Special Agent Edwin

Woodriffe—the only African-American FBI agent killed in the line of duty—was presented with an American flag that had been flown over the Washington Field Office, the National Museum of African American History and Culture, the Pentagon, the Washington Metropolitan Police Department, and the U.S. Capitol.

Sunday morning, the final day of the symposium, participants took part in a "Blessing of the Badge" ceremony. Active and former agents placed their badges and FBI credentials on a table to be blessed—a symbolic acknowledgement that law enforcement officers must often put themselves in harm's way to serve and protect the American public.

In all, more than 180 active and former agents and their families gathered to celebrate the role African-American special agents have played in the FBI and to pledge continued support for the Bureau's diversity efforts.

Scan this QR code with your smartphone to access related information, or visit www.fbi.gov/aasa2017.

Business E-Mail Compromise

Cyber-Enabled Financial Fraud on the Rise Globally

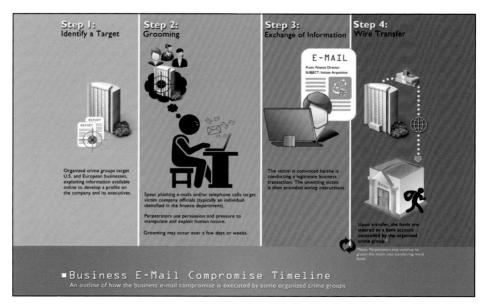

Step 1: Identify a Target

Step 2: Grooming

Step 3: Exchange of Information

Step 4: Wire Transfer

E-MAIL

From: Finance Director
SUBJECT: Initiate Acquisition

Organized crime groups target U.S. and European businesses, exploiting information available online to develop a profile on the company and its executives.

Spear phishing e-mails and/or telephone calls target victim company officials (typically an individual identified in the finance department).

Perpetrators use persuasion and pressure to manipulate and exploit human nature.

Grooming may occur over a few days or weeks.

The victim is convinced he/she is conducting a legitimate business transaction. The unwitting victim is then provided wiring instructions.

Upon transfer, the funds are steered to a bank account controlled by the organized crime group.

*Note: Perpetrators may continue to groom the victim into transferring more funds.

■Business E-Mail Compromise Timeline
An outline of how the business e-mail compromise is executed by some organized crime groups

Since 2013, when the FBI began tracking an emerging financial cyber threat called business e-mail compromise (BEC), organized crime groups have targeted large and small companies and organizations in every U.S. state and more than 100 countries around the world—from non-profits and well-known corporations to churches and school systems. Losses are in the billions of dollars and climbing.

At its heart, BEC relies on the oldest trick in the con artist's handbook: deception. But the level of sophistication in this multifaceted global fraud is unprecedented, according to law enforcement officials, and professional businesspeople continue to fall victim to the scheme.

Carried out by transnational criminal organizations that employ lawyers, linguists, hackers, and social engineers, BEC can take a variety of forms. But in just about every case, the scammers target employees with access to company finances and trick them into making wire transfers to bank accounts thought to belong to trusted partners—except the money ends up in accounts controlled by the criminals.

"BEC is a serious threat on a global scale," said Special Agent Martin Licciardo, a veteran organized crime investigator at the FBI's Washington Field Office. "And the criminal organizations that perpetrate these frauds are continually honing their techniques to exploit unsuspecting victims."

Those techniques include online ploys such as spear-phishing, social engineering, identity theft, e-mail spoofing, and the use of malware. The perpetrators are so practiced at their craft that the deception is often difficult to uncover until it is too late.

"The best way to avoid being exploited is to verify the authenticity of requests to send money by walking into the CEO's office or speaking to him or her directly on the phone. Don't rely on e-mail alone."

According to the FBI's Internet Crime Complaint Center (IC3), "the BEC scam continues to grow, evolve, and target businesses of all sizes. Since January 2015, there has been a 1,300 percent increase in identified exposed losses, now totaling over $3 billion."

Although the perpetrators of BEC—also known as CEO

impersonation—use a variety of tactics to fool their victims, a common scheme involves the criminal group gaining access to a company's network through a spear-phishing attack and the use of malware. Undetected, they may spend weeks or months studying the organization's vendors, billing systems, and the CEO's style of e-mail communication and even his or her travel schedule.

When the time is right, often when the CEO is away from the office, the scammers send a bogus e-mail from the CEO to a targeted employee in the finance office—a bookkeeper, accountant, controller, or chief financial officer. A request is made for an immediate wire transfer, usually to a trusted vendor. The targeted employee believes he is sending money to a familiar account, just as he has done in the past. But the account numbers are slightly different, and the transfer of what might be tens or hundreds of thousands of dollars ends up in a different account controlled by the criminal group.

If the fraud is not discovered in time, the money is hard to recover, thanks to the criminal group's use of laundering techniques and "money mules" worldwide that drain the funds into other accounts that are difficult to trace.

"The ability of these criminal groups to compromise legitimate business e-mail accounts is staggering," Licciardo said. "They are experts at deception. The FBI takes the BEC threat very seriously," he added, "and we are working with our international partners to identify these perpetrators and dismantle their organizations."

The Art of Deception

The organized criminal groups that engage in business e-mail compromise scams are extremely sophisticated. Here are some of the online tools they use to target and exploit their victims:

- Spoofing e-mail accounts and websites: Slight variations on legitimate addresses (john.kelly@abccompany.com vs. john.kelley@abccompany.com) fool victims into thinking fake accounts are authentic. The criminals then use a spoofing tool to direct e-mail responses to a different account that they control. The victim thinks he is corresponding with his CEO, but that is not the case.
- Spear-phishing: Bogus e-mails believed to be from a trusted sender prompt victims to reveal confidential information to the BEC perpetrators.
- Malware: Used to infiltrate company networks and gain access to legitimate e-mail threads about billing and invoices. That information is used to make sure the suspicions of an accountant or financial officer aren't raised when a fraudulent wire transfer is requested. Malware also allows criminals undetected access to a victim's data, including passwords and financial account information.

If you or your company have been victimized by a BEC scam, it's important to act quickly. Contact your financial institution immediately and request that they contact the financial institution where the fraudulent transfer was sent. Next, call the FBI, and also file a complaint—regardless of dollar loss—with the FBI's Internet Crime Complaint Center (IC3) at www.ic3.gov.

Don't Be a Victim

The business e-mail compromise scam has resulted in companies and organizations losing billions of dollars. But as sophisticated as the fraud is, there is an easy solution to thwart it: face-to-face or voice-to-voice communications.

"The best way to avoid being exploited is to verify the authenticity of requests to send money by walking into the CEO's office or speaking to him or her directly on the phone," said Special Agent Martin Licciardo. "Don't rely on e-mail alone."

Here are other methods businesses have employed to safeguard against BEC:

- Create intrusion detection system rules that flag e-mails with extensions that are similar to company e-mail. For example, legitimate e-mail of abc_company.com would flag fraudulent e-mail of abc-company.com.
- Create an e-mail rule to flag e-mail communications where the "reply" e-mail address is different from the "from" e-mail address shown.
- Color code virtual correspondence so e-mails from employee/internal accounts are one color and e-mails from non-employee/external accounts are another.
- Verify changes in vendor payment location by adding additional two-factor authentication such as having secondary sign-off by company personnel.
- Confirm requests for transfers of funds by using phone verification as part of a two-factor authentication; use previously known numbers, not the numbers provided in the e-mail request.
- Carefully scrutinize all e-mail requests for transfer of funds to determine if the requests are out of the ordinary.

19 Indicted in International Fraud and Money Laundering Schemes

Investigators in the U.S. and Abroad Arrest 17

FBI Washington Field Office Assistant Director in Charge Andrew Vale—with U.S. Attorney for the District of Columbia Channing Phillips (right) and other officials—discusses the four indictments announced in Washington, D.C., today involving a transnational organized crime enterprise allegedly responsible for the theft of more than $13 million from victims around the world.

Federal indictments unsealed today in Washington, D.C., charged 19 people in the U.S. and abroad with participating in various international fraud and money laundering conspiracies that resulted in the theft of more than $13 million from more than 170 victims, primarily in the U.S.

Seventeen of those individuals have been taken into custody—some in the U.S. and some overseas—and two remain at large. The Bureau is working with our foreign counterparts to locate and apprehend the two fugitives.

The multi-agency investigation—led by the FBI and the Office of the Inspector General of the U.S. Department of Treasury—involved a number of other federal agencies and international partners abroad joining together to target multi-million-dollar fraud and money laundering schemes committed

by a transnational organized crime network. This particular case resulted in four indictments involving interrelated online vehicle fraud and business e-mail compromise (BEC) schemes along with unlicensed money transmitting and international money laundering.

The investigation began in 2011, when the Bureau's Washington Field Office received information about abandoned property in a hotel room in Washington, D.C. From that, the FBI was able to link the recovered evidence to a transnational organized crime operation involving an online vehicle fraud scheme.

As part of the online vehicle fraud scheme, a network of individuals in Europe allegedly advertised cars for sale on various websites. When car buyers wired the money to the purported sellers' bank accounts in

Washington, D.C., and elsewhere, other co-conspirators who had traveled to the U.S. and opened bank accounts using counterfeit identification documents immediately withdrew the money, laundered it, and then sent it to their associates in Europe. And of course, the buyers never received the vehicles they paid for, but the criminals were able to line their pockets with more than $3 million. Eight defendants were indicted in this scheme.

The investigation into the online vehicle fraud scheme led to the realization that some of the criminals involved in that scheme had branched out to much more lucrative activity—a BEC scheme that resulted in losses of more than $10 million from victim companies. Four additional defendants were charged in this indictment.

According to the indictment related to the BEC scheme, co-conspirators identified and spoofed the e-mail accounts of CEOs or other high-level executives of various international corporations. Using these spoofed accounts, they sent e-mails— ostensibly from a company executive—to mid-level employees working in these corporations' finance departments. The employees were instructed to wire large sums of money to what they thought were bank accounts they normally dealt with, but the account numbers referenced in the e-mails had slightly different numbers and were under the control of the criminal enterprise. Once the funds were transferred, the fraudsters allegedly wired that money out of the bank accounts and into overseas bank accounts before the businesses ever realized they had been duped.

While investigating the above fraud schemes and the efforts to launder the illegal proceeds, investigators uncovered an unlicensed money transmitting network—often referred to as an unlicensed hawala system—operating in the U.S., Europe, and Israel, which allegedly allowed the fraudulent proceeds of the schemes to be distributed from the U.S. to other members of the criminal enterprise in Europe and Israel. Six defendants were indicted for operating an unlicensed money transmitting business after investigators followed FBI undercover funds moving through the unlicensed hawala network in separate transactions in New York and Los Angeles.

And in the fourth indictment, one person was charged with generating hundreds of thousands of dollars in proceeds from various fraud schemes and international money laundering.

The unsealing of the indictments was announced at a press conference today at the U.S. Attorney's Office for the District of Columbia. U.S. Attorney Channing Phillips called the indictments "more than just a simple set of fraud schemes—the investigation uncovered an interconnected web of money launderers and fraudsters and individuals who enabled their criminal activity." He also said that the criminals "could face decades in prison and significant financial penalties" if convicted.

Focusing on the victims, FBI Washington Field Office Assistant Director in Charge Andrew Vale said, "Unfortunately, honest individuals with hard-earned money to spend and enterprising businesses—two essential elements in our global marketplace— were the main targets for these criminals." But according to Vale, because of "the dedication and perseverance by our law enforcement partners in the U.S. and abroad, the FBI's multi-year investigation into these schemes and this international criminal network has yielded the disruption or return of more than $56 million in victim funds."

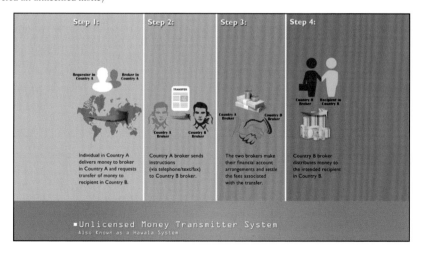

Step 1:

Step 2:

Step 3:

Step 4:

Individual in Country A delivers money to broker in Country A and requests transfer of money to recipient in Country B.

Country A broker sends instructions (via telephone/text/fax) to Country B broker.

The two brokers make their financial account arrangements and settle the fees associated with the transfer.

Country B broker distributes money to the intended recipient in Country B.

■Unlicensed Money Transmitter System
Also Known as a Hawala System

Violent Bank Robber Sentenced to 37 Years

Local/Federal Law Enforcement Partnerships Work

Left: A March 2015 attempted robbery at this bank in Humboldt, Tennessee, resulted in the shooting of a bank manager. A joint law enforcement investigation resulted in a lengthy prison term for the perpetrator. Right: This gun—used by Dominic Williams to abduct and then shoot a bank manager—was recovered by investigators in an alley underneath some leaves.

It was every bank employee's worst nightmare—being threatened at gunpoint by an individual demanding entrance to a bank vault. The employee in this instance, who was one of the bank's managers, told the man she was unable to open it, so he shot her and fled.

The violent and brazen attempted bank robbery took place early in the morning on March 18, 2015 in the small Tennessee town of Humboldt, located approximately 90 miles northeast of Memphis. The perpetrator, Dominic Williams, was apprehended and charged with the crime—and as a result of the joint investigation by the Humboldt Police Department (HPD) and the Memphis FBI Field Office, he was sentenced last month to 37 years in federal prison.

In the early morning hours of that March day, the bank manager left her house and walked to the carport to get to her car. Williams, who had been hiding in front of her vehicle, stood up and, pointing the gun at the manager, asked if "she wanted to die today." He forced her into the driver's seat and demanded that she drive to her bank. Once at the bank, he had her unlock the doors—no one else was in yet—and told her to get money from the cashiers' drawers, but the drawers were empty at the time. He then

demanded that she open the night drop vault, and when she didn't, he simply shot her through the chest and ran off.

The victim, who had played dead after she was shot, was able to call 911 and give a detailed description of her attacker—she also calmly kept pressure on her wounds while awaiting help. And arriving bank employees and other witnesses notified the HPD.

Shortly after arriving on the scene, the HPD police chief saw a suspicious person about a block or so away stripping off some clothing and throwing it into a dumpster. The man was taken into custody, and the FBI was called.

HPD personnel secured the crime scene, and the Memphis FBI's Evidence Response Team processed it. Members of the Violent Crime Task Force from FBI Memphis' Jackson Resident Agency responded as well, interviewing the suspect and witnesses and searching the suspect's home. And fingerprints from Dominic Williams were taken and sent to our Criminal Justice Information Services Division, where analysts linked them to prints taken from an individual by the same name who had committed similar crimes in California as a gang member and had served time in state prison.

All evidence was immediately recovered in or near the bank, except for the gun. The interview team was able to get the suspect to draw a map of where he discarded the gun when he fled the scene—and investigators were able to retrieve it.

Subsequent investigation revealed that Williams, who had recently relocated to Tennessee, used computers to research open source information on bank employees. He also surveilled employees, keeping track of their comings and goings to and from the bank. The bank manager he ultimately focused on lived just a short distance from the bank.

The evidence against Williams was overwhelming—including the court testimony of the woman he nearly killed—and he pleaded guilty in August 2016. According to the FBI case agent from the Jackson Resident Agency, the victim "had learned that the bullet missed her vital organs by the smallest of margins, but she would later recover and continue working hard for the citizens of Humboldt."

The case agent also said that a member of the Humboldt Police Department worked with Bureau personnel throughout the investigative process and was a crucial member of the team. He added, "A strong working relationship was fostered with the Humboldt Police Department that day, and it remains positive to this day."

This case is just one example of the many investigations conducted every day in communities across America where the FBI joins forces with its law enforcement partners to get dangerous criminals off the streets.

FBI Director Addresses Cyber Security Gathering

Varied Group of Cyber Experts Exchange Ideas

This morning, Director James Comey delivered a keynote address at the inaugural Boston Conference on Cyber Security, touching on the current cyber threat landscape, what the FBI is doing to stay ahead of the threat, and the importance of strong private sector partnerships.

The conference, a partnership between the FBI and Boston College's Cybersecurity Policy and Governance master's degree program, also features additional expert speakers and panelists who will be covering such areas as emerging technologies, operations and enforcement, along with real-life cyber and national security experiences focusing on risk, compliance, policy, threat trends, preparedness, and defensive strategies.

Cyber threats, said Comey, are "too fast, too big, and too widespread for any of us to address them alone."

During his remarks, Comey discussed the "stack of bad actors" committing cyber crimes, including nation-states, multinational cyber syndicates, insiders, hacktivists, and—currently to a lesser degree—terrorists ("they have not yet turned to using the Internet as a tool of destruction," he explained, "in a way that logic tells us certainly will come in the future.")

And what are these bad actors after? According to Comey, they're after information, access, and advantage. He further explained, "And we're not only worried about loss of data, but corruption of that data and lack of access to our own information."

The public and private sector can help deter this behavior, said Comey, by reducing vulnerabilities, reducing the threat by holding

On March 8, 2017, Director James Comey delivered the keynote speech at the first Boston Conference on Cyber Security—co-sponsored by Boston College's Cybersecurity Policy and Governance master's degree program—which was attended by cyber security leaders from the academic, analysis, operations, research, corporate, and law enforcement areas.

accountable those who are responsible, and mitigating the damage.

> *"Cyber threats are too fast, too big, and too widespread for any of us to address them alone."*

The FBI Director also laid out the Bureau's five-part strategy to address cyber intrusions:

- Focusing ourselves better inside the FBI in terms of how we operate and who we hire;

- Shrinking the world by clarifying investigative "lanes in the road" here at home and enhancing cooperation abroad;

- Imposing costs on this kind of behavior by locking cyber criminals up and/or calling them out through incidents and sanctions;

- Enhancing the "digital literacy" of state and local partners through training, equipment, and task forces to make them more effective; and

- Working to improve collaboration with private sector entities, the primary targets of cyber intrusions but the majority of whom, according to Comey, don't turn to law enforcement when they're breached.

Comey also spoke about the impact of the advent of "ubiquitous strong encryption" on the work of law enforcement and urged the audience to "continue to engage in what is a very complicated and difficult subject." This so-called Going Dark issue is a growing challenge to public safety and national security that has eroded law enforcement's ability to obtain electronic information and evidence with a court order or warrant.

Binary Options Fraud

A Word of Warning to the Investing Public

Stock options. It's a pretty common investment term meaning, in general, that one party sells or offers to another party the opportunity to invest by buying a particular stock at an agreed upon price within a certain period of time. All perfectly legal and highly regulated—and if the investor takes advantage of the opportunity and the stock performs well, there's money to be made. And if the stock doesn't perform well, the investor knew the risk.

But here's another similar-sounding financial term that the public should be wary of—binary options. While some binary options are listed on registered exchanges or traded on a designated contract market and are subject to oversight by U.S. regulators like the Commodity Futures Trading Commission (CFTC), much of the binary options market operates through websites that don't comply with U.S. regulations. And many of those unregulated websites are being used by criminals outside the U.S. as vehicles to commit fraud.

Binary options fraud is a growing problem and one that the FBI currently has in its crosshairs. In 2011, our Internet Crime Complaint Center (IC3) received four complaints—with reported losses of just more than $20,000—from binary options fraud victims. Fast forward five years, and the IC3 received hundreds of complaints with millions of dollars in reported losses during 2016. And those numbers only reflect victims who reported being fleeced to the IC3—the true extent of the fraud, which has victims around the world, isn't fully known. Some European countries have reported that binary options fraud complaints now constitute 25 percent of all the fraud complaints received.

What exactly is a binary option? It's a type of options contract in which the payout depends entirely on the outcome of a yes/no proposition, typically related to whether the price of a particular asset—like a stock or a commodity—will rise above or fall below a specified amount. Unlike regular stock options, with binary options you're not being given the opportunity to actually buy a stock or a commodity—you're just betting on whether its price will be above or below a certain amount by a certain time of the day.

The perpetrators behind many of the binary options websites, primarily criminals located overseas, are only interested in one thing—taking your money.

For example: You expect the price of an individual stock will be above $80 at 3:30 p.m. today. So you buy a binary option that allows you to place this bet at a cost of $60. If, at 3:30 p.m., the stock price is $80.01, your payout is $100, for a profit of $40. If the price of the stock at 3:30 is $79.99, you lose your $60. Of course, you can buy multiple binary options, which can significantly increase your winnings as well as your losses.

So where does the fraud come into it? The perpetrators behind many of the binary options websites, primarily criminals located overseas, are only interested in one thing—taking your money. Complaints about their activities generally fall into one of three categories:

- **Refusal to credit customer accounts or reimburse funds to customers.** This is usually done by cancelling customers' withdrawal requests, ignoring customer phone calls and e-mails, and sometimes even freezing accounts and accusing the customers themselves of fraud.

- **Identity theft.** Representatives of binary options websites may falsely claim that the government requires photocopies of your credit card, passport, driver's license, utility bills, or other personal data. This information could potentially be used to steal your identity.

- **Manipulation of trading software.** Some of these Internet trading platforms may be reconfiguring the algorithms they use in order to purposely generate losing trades, often by distorting prices and payouts. For example, if a customer has a winning trade, the expiration time is extended until the trade becomes a loss.

Fraudulent binary options website operators go to great lengths to recruit investors. They advertise their platforms—often on social networking sites, various trading websites, message boards, and spam e-mail—with big promises of easy money, low risk, and superior customer service. Potential investors are also cold-called from boiler room operations, where high-pressure salespeople use banks of phones to make as many calls as possible to offer "once-in-a-lifetime" opportunities.

What's being done to combat binary options fraud? The FBI currently has a number of ongoing binary options fraud cases, working with partners like the CFTC and the Securities and Exchange Commission (SEC). And this past January, the Bureau organized the 2017 Binary Options Fraud Summit held at Europol in The Hague, bringing together law enforcement and regulators from throughout North America and Europe to discuss the growing binary options fraud problem.

Special Agent Milan Kosanovich, who works out of our Criminal Investigative Division's Complex Financial Crimes Unit, was one of the FBI's representatives at this gathering. "The summit," he said, "gave all of us the chance to sit down and talk about what we've discovered through our respective binary options fraud investigations, where the challenges are, and how we can all work together."

One of the biggest challenges law enforcement faces, according to Kosanovich, is the fact that the scammers are sophisticated and have operations spanning multiple countries. "So the key to addressing this type of fraud," he continued, "is national and international coordination between regulatory agencies, law enforcement, and the financial industry."

Another important factor, said Kosanovich, is investor awareness and education. "Investors need to be aware of the significant potential for fraud on binary options websites, and they need to make sure they do their due diligence before ever placing that first trade or bet."

What Can You Do to Avoid Being Victimized

- Make sure that the binary options trading platform you're interested in has registered its offer and sale of its products with the SEC. (Registration provides investors with key information about the terms of the products being offered). To do this, you can use the Security Exchange Commission's (SEC) EDGAR Company Filing website.

- Check to see if the trading platform itself is registered as an exchange at the SEC's Exchanges website.

- Ensure that the trading platform is a designated contract market by checking the Commodity Futures Trading Commission's (CTFC) Designated Contract Markets website. Thousands of entities promote binary options trading in the U.S., but only two are currently authorized to do so by the CFTC.

- Check out the registration status and background of any firm or financial professional you are considering dealing with. You can do this through the Financial Industry Regulatory Agency's BrokerCheck website and the National Futures Association Background Affiliation Status Information Center.

- Take a look at the CFTC's RED List, which contains the names of unregistered foreign entities that CFTC has reason to believe are soliciting and accepting funds from U.S. residents at a retail level for, among other things, binary options.

- Finally, don't invest in something you don't understand. If you can't explain the investment opportunity in a few words and in an understandable way, you may need to reconsider the potential investment.

Source: Investor.gov (SEC's Office of Investor Education and Advocacy/ CFTC's Office of Consumer Outreach)

Charges Announced in Massive Cyber Intrusion Case

Two of the Perpetrators Believed to be Russian Intelligence Officers

Russian criminal hacker Alexsey Belan and Russian FBS officers Dmitry Dokuchaev and Igor Sushchin have been indicted on computer hacking, economic espionage, and other criminal charges. Also charged was criminal hacker Karim Baratov.

Four individuals—two Russian Federal Security Service (FSB) officers and two criminal hackers—have been charged by a federal grand jury in the Northern District of California in connection with one of the largest cyber intrusions in U.S. history, which compromised the information of at least 500 million Yahoo accounts.

One of the criminal hackers was arrested yesterday by Canadian authorities. The two FSB officers and the second hacker, last known to have been in Russia, are currently fugitives wanted by the FBI.

The indictments were announced today by U.S. Department of Justice Acting Assistant Attorney General Mary McCord, FBI Executive Assistant Director Paul Abbate, and Northern District of California U.S. Attorney Brian Stretch during a press conference in Washington, D.C.

The FSB is an intelligence and law enforcement agency of the Russian Federation, and it's believed that the two FSB officers work in an FSB unit that serves as the FBI's point of contact in Moscow on cyber crime matters. According to McCord, "The involvement and direction of FSB officers with law enforcement responsibilities make this conduct that much more egregious—there are no free passes for foreign state-sponsored criminal behavior."

According to the indictment, from about April 2014 up to at least December 2016, FSB officers Dmitry Dokuchaev and Igor Sushchin directed this cyber intrusion conspiracy—which involved malicious files and software tools being downloaded onto Yahoo's network—that resulted in the compromise of that network and the theft of subscriber information from at least 500 million accounts. This stolen information was then used to obtain unauthorized access to the contents of accounts at

Yahoo, Google, and other webmail providers.

The indictment says that Dokuchaev and Sushchin paid, directed, and protected two known criminal hackers who took part in the scheme—Alexsey Belan, a Russian national and resident, and Karim Baratov, born in Kazakhstan and a naturalized Canadian citizen and resident. Belan, who has been indicted twice in the U.S. in the past for cyber-related crimes, is currently on the FBI's Cyber's Most Wanted list and is the subject of a Red Notice for Interpol nations, which includes Russia.

The information stolen from the 500 million user accounts came from Yahoo's proprietary user data base, which contained information such as users' names, recovery e-mail addresses, phone numbers, and certain information needed to manually create account authentication web browser cookies.

What were the alleged perpetrators after? In part, they used access to Yahoo's networks to identify and access accounts of possible interest to the FSB, including those of Russian journalists, U.S. and Russian government officials, and employees of U.S., Russian, and other providers whose networks the conspirators sought to exploit. Additional victim accounts belonged to private sector employees of financial, transportation, and other types of companies.

However, the co-conspirators were not above using the information they stole for personal financial gain. For example, Belan allegedly searched Yahoo user communications for credit card and gift card account numbers. He also leveraged the contact lists obtained from at least 30 million Yahoo accounts to perpetrate his own spam scheme.

"This is a highly complicated investigation of a very complex threat. It underscores the value of early, proactive engagement and cooperation between the private sector and the government."

Computer intrusions, by their very nature, are international in scope, so they require an international effort to unmask the worldwide hacking networks responsible for them. And this case was no different. Abbate expressed the Bureau's gratitude to our international partners for their assistance and support leading up to these criminal charges today—specifically mentioning the Royal Canadian Mounted Police, the Toronto Police Service, and the United Kingdom's MI5.

Another important aspect of this case involved the victim companies—including Yahoo and Google—coming forward and working with law enforcement. This collaboration ultimately resulted in countering the malicious activities of state actors and bringing criminals to justice. It also illustrates that the FBI can successfully work these kinds of investigations with victim companies while respecting the various concerns and considerations businesses might have about the impact of going public.

"This is a highly complicated investigation of a very complex threat," said Abbate. "It underscores the value of early, proactive engagement and cooperation between the private sector and the government."

Among the FBI's major investigative priorities are to protect the U.S. against foreign intelligence operations and espionage and to protect the U.S. against cyber-based attacks and high-technology crimes. This case involved both. And it doesn't matter to us whether the perpetrators of such crimes are run-of-the-mill criminals or sophisticated foreign states and their agents. With the help of our partners here and/or abroad, we will identify those responsible and hold them accountable for their actions.

Note: This case may have been resolved since this information was posted on our website. Please check www.fbi.gov/wanted for up-to-date information.

FBI Executive Assistant Director Paul Abbate, with DOJ's Acting Assistant Attorney General Mary McCord looking on, answers questions during a March 15, 2017 press conference announcing the indictments of four individuals on charges relating to the 2014 intrusion into Yahoo's network.

Craigslist Robbers

California-Based Thieves Targeted Big-Money Items and Sellers

For the high-end jewelry sellers on the popular online classifieds site Craigslist, it must have seemed like their ship had come in: A prospective buyer in California offered not only their asking price but would fly them into town and have a limo waiting.

"The individual would think they were going to the jewelry store to meet with the actual buyer," said Special Agent Darin Heideman, who works out of the Oakland Resident Agency of the FBI's San Francisco Division, "when in fact, a co-conspirator would take them to a predetermined location, assault them, and then basically rob them of all their items."

The crew of robbers, based in the San Francisco Bay Area, is estimated to have stolen more than $500,000 in jewelry from victims who traveled from more than six states between November 2012 and December 2013. Five men were charged in 2014 in connection with the violent robberies during which, among other items, a $90,000 Cartier watch, a $14,000 Rolex watch, and a $19,000 engagement ring were stolen. The last member of the crew to be sentenced,

Michael Anthony Martin, 42, of Tracy, California, was handed a term last December of 30 years in prison.

The case illustrates how the FBI and police work together on cases that may at first appear to be local or isolated, but on closer investigation can span multiple jurisdictions. In this case, a Bay Area detective's efforts to solve a "snatch-and-grab" robbery at a Fremont, California coffee shop ultimately led him to more than 20 similar robberies of victims from as far away as Wisconsin and Florida. Fremont Police Department Det. Michael Gebhardt's legwork also uncovered the scheme's mastermind: a prison inmate who personally called Craigslist targets—purporting to be a successful record producer—and assigned his co-conspirators to carry out the plans.

"It's definitely a tale of something that started small and just mushroomed into this massive investigation," said Gebhardt.

It all started in 2012 with the brazen robbery of a Bay Area man who was selling his watch. The

seller and the purported buyer, both local, arranged to meet in Fremont in a public place—a coffee shop. "As they are talking, the potential buyer just grabs the Rolex and takes off running," Gebhardt said.

> *"It's definitely a tale of something that started small and just mushroomed into this massive investigation."*

Video surveillance and the so-called buyer's cell phone number turned up an identity that police were able to link to two more robberies in Bay Area cities. In each case, the victims were selling Rolex watches and the prospective buyers grabbed the goods and ran. "The M.O. [modus operandi] is the same," Gebhardt recalled thinking. "He's targeting people on Craigslist for Rolexes."

Two months later, the detective received word that police in Oakland were investigating five similar robberies, including one they witnessed firsthand during a separate investigation. Oakland police officers arrested three men, who it turned out were associates of the watch thief Gebhardt was investigating for the 2012 coffee shop heist. With some digging, Gebhardt learned his subject was taking directions from his father, an inmate at the California Men's Colony state prison. The father was using a number of relatives, including his son and a cousin in Texas, to lure prospective Craigslist sellers with flights and limos and then have co-conspirators rob them once they were captive.

For the sellers, it might have seemed a safe bet when prospective buyers offered plane tickets and

This ring, shown in an image on a mobile phone belonging to a member of the robbery crew, is believed to be one of the stolen items in the Craigslist robberies.

limos. "That's exactly what they want," said FBI Special Agent Paul Healy, who also worked the case out of Oakland. "They're being told everything's being taken care of."

Heideman said it was a relatively small investment for the robbers. "You have to think—what does a plane ticket cost? Probably $400 to $500. A limo is going to cost a couple hundred bucks," he said. "If you're traveling with a $30,000 diamond, that's just a drop in the bucket to what they are going to steal. They were able to build these personas and build trust where there should not have been trust."

Gebhardt learned of a Wisconsin woman who flew to St. Louis to sell the $19,000 diamond ring she had listed on Craigslist but ended up getting robbed instead. When Gebhardt saw a picture of the suspect, he recognized it was the same guy he'd been trying to run down—the son of the prison inmate. Still other cases—from Florida, Oregon, and Colorado—started to point back to the same prime suspects and associates.

"So we needed one big agency to basically be able to charge

this thing," Gebhardt said. The detective called the FBI, and agents from the Oakland Resident Agency helped set up a sting. They posted an ad on Craigslist hoping to attract the attention of the robbery crew's leader in prison. And it worked.

"He calls me from prison and we set up a deal to sell my Rolex to him," Gebhart said. "I would be flying in from Texas to the Oakland airport. He would have a driver pick me up."

As that plan was coming to fruition, the FBI discovered that another Craigslist seller from Los Angeles was to arrive—with his Rolex—in Oakland on the same day.

"Obviously we couldn't let him get robbed, but we also didn't want to tip him off because we didn't want him to call the guy that was going to rob him," said Heideman. So the investigators posed as Craigslist buyers, contacted the seller in L.A., and outbid the robbery crew. They met him in a bank parking lot in Oakland. "We basically pulled him aside and said, 'Here's what you were about to walk into,'" Gebhardt said. "He was obviously relieved."

"They were able to build these personas and build trust where there should not have been trust."

Meanwhile, on the same day of the sting in Oakland—December 16, 2013—two other simultaneous operations took down the robbery crew's mastermind in prison and arrested his son, who was in hiding in Alabama.

The arrests led to federal indictments in 2014 against five defendants who have since received

sentences ranging from 41 months to 30 years. The father, who cooperated with investigators, was given an addition seven years in prison for his role.

Looking back, the robbery crew was so prolific and violent they had no choice but to expand beyond their local area, agents said. Even limo drivers stopped working with them. "They would literally wear out a jurisdiction," said Healy. "So they would go 40 miles away—or 400 miles away—to another town to do it."

Tips for Staying Safe

The Craigslist website offers tips on personal safety when meeting someone for the first time. The site states, "With billions of human interactions, the incidence of violent crime related to Craigslist is extremely low."

Among the personal safety tips:

- Insist on a public meeting place like a cafe, bank, or shopping center.
- Do not meet in a secluded place or invite strangers into your home.
- Be especially careful buying/selling high-value items.
- Tell a friend or family member where you're going.
- Take your cell phone along if you have one.
- Consider having a friend accompany you.
- Trust your instincts.

Meanwhile, some jurisdictions have moved to create "Safe Lots" for exchanging items from online classifieds. Det. Gebhardt says his department suggests on social media that if people are going to meet, they should meet in their local police department's parking lot.

"If somebody says, 'I don't want to meet there,' then that's probably a red flag about the person you're meeting," he said.

Seeking Special Agents with Diverse Backgrounds
Houston Recruiting Effort Part of National Campaign

When Special Agent Al Tribble joined the FBI 25 years ago, the organization wasn't exactly known for its recruiting efforts—especially when it came to hiring women and people of color.

Much has changed since then. Today, the FBI understands that to effectively protect the American people, its special agents must reflect the diverse communities they serve. That's why Tribble—who specializes in human trafficking and violent crimes against children investigations—participated in a recent recruiting event in Houston aimed at increasing diversity in the ranks of the FBI's special agent corps.

As a veteran investigator and an African-American, Tribble spoke to potential applicants about the satisfaction of being a special agent. "The variety of work that you find in the FBI is unlike corporate America or any other private entity," he said. "There's so much you can do here, and you get to help people. When you take a victim of human trafficking and free her from her captors and reunite her with her family," he explained, "there's no feeling that can beat that."

The FBI's Diversity Agent Recruitment Program began in 2016 with an event in Washington, D.C., that attracted several

hundred potential special agents from diverse backgrounds. The Houston event in January 2017 was attended by more than 200 people who heard from a panel of special agents about the varied paths that led them to the Bureau.

"What we're trying to do is ... let people know that the FBI might be different from what you think."

"I think a lot of people have in their mind what the FBI is and what the FBI does and what an FBI agent looks like," said Special Agent Jenelle Janabajal, a presenter at the event, "and I think what we're trying to do is maybe change some of those ideas and let people know that the FBI might be different from what you think."

Special Agent David Baker, who works with special agent job applicants in the Houston Division, put it another way: "It doesn't matter what walk of life you come from, what color you are, what race you are, what background you have," he said, "there's a place for you in the FBI."

"One of the things that make us very attractive as an organization is that our employees have such different backgrounds," said Perrye K. Turner, special agent in charge of the Houston Division. Turner, who has served as one of the Bureau's national recruiters for nearly two decades, was instrumental in bringing the recent event to Houston. Such employee diversity means that "everybody brings something to the table," he said. "That makes us stronger and more effective as an organization."

Perrye K. Turner, special agent in charge of the FBI's Houston Division, understands the importance of diversity as it relates to the FBI's recruitment efforts—the Houston Division recently sponsored a Diversity Agent Recruitment (DAR) event aimed at potential special agents.

The women, Latinos, Asians, and African-Americans in the audience heard from a variety of FBI agents about what it's like to do good for a living—to take violent criminals off the streets, to hold public officials accountable when they violate the public's trust, to thwart spies who would steal national secrets, and to stop terrorists. And after the official presentation, they were able to talk one-on-one with agents.

> "Our employees have such different backgrounds. That makes us stronger and more effective as an organization."

The event began with a video message from Director James Comey, who told the group that when he joined the Bureau in 2013, he inherited a special agent population that was 83 percent white. Comey made diversity one of the Bureau's core values and began to increase efforts at diversity hiring.

A career in the FBI is like no other, he said. "This in an incredible family where no matter what you look like—black, white, Latino, Asian, Native American, whether you're a man or a woman, whether you're straight or gay—you feel welcome once you join this family."

The statistics bear out that fact. The FBI's turnover rate among agents is less than 1 percent. "That's extraordinarily low," Comey said, "and the reason it's so low is once people become part of this life and see what it's like to have as your mission protecting the American people and upholding the Constitution of the United States, nobody leaves."

Comey cautioned that becoming a special agent is difficult. "We need people of integrity—non-negotiable. We need people of high intelligence—essential to be able to do the complicated work we do. And we need people of a certain physicality. If you're going to be a special agent in the FBI," he said, "we're going to give you a gun on behalf of the United States of America, and you better be able to run, fight, and shoot."

But if you possess those skills, he added, the FBI can be a career like no other. "So here is my challenge to you," he said. "I dare you to take your ability and try to be a part of this organization."

Scan this QR code with your smartphone to access related information, or visit www.fbi.gov/houstondar.

Tam Dao, a special agent in the Houston Division who primarily investigates national security crimes while also serving as a professor at the University of Houston, was born in Vietnam just weeks before the fall of Saigon in 1975.

Alfred Tribble Jr., a special agent in the FBI's Houston Division who supervises investigations into human trafficking, civil rights violations, and violent crimes against children, worked in the banking industry before joining the Bureau 25 years ago.

Hesham Elgamiel, a special agent who supervises a counterterrorism unit in the FBI's Houston Division, was born and raised in Egypt and arrived in the U.S. when he was 15.

Jenelle Janabajal, a special agent in the Corpus Christi office of the FBI's Houston Division, was in the U.S. Marine Corps and attended law school before joining the Bureau.

The FBI in Israel

'Long-Lasting Relationships' Key to Building Cases

An Israel National Police officer stands outside Lahav 433, the investigative arm of the department, in Tel Aviv.

The arrest last week of an individual in Israel suspected of sending threatening messages to Jewish organizations in the U.S. and several other countries provides a glimpse into one of the FBI's key roles overseas.

The FBI and Israel National Police worked jointly to locate and arrest the individual, according to an FBI statement issued March 23. The threatening calls over the last several months fostered fears about a rise in anti-Semitism in the United States. Investigating hate crimes is a top priority for the Bureau, which praised its law enforcement and intelligence partners: "The FBI commends the great work of the Israeli National Police in this investigation," the statement said.

In this and other overseas cases, FBI investigations are greatly helped by having strong relationships already in place with host countries. In Israel, where terrorism is a perpetual threat and American citizens are frequently among those injured or killed in violence between Israelis and Palestinians, the FBI has a long history of working with

the country's national police and intelligence agencies.

"It's immensely important that the FBI and other members of the U.S. intelligence community develop strong, long-lasting relationships with international partners in the intelligence arena and also in law enforcement," said Cary Gleicher, the FBI's legal attaché in Israel. The FBI has more than 63 overseas offices, or legal attachés, and each relies heavily on its local counterpart to support FBI cases.

"Our job is to build and foster long-term relationships."

"The FBI's job overseas is, essentially, to work with the host country to collect evidence and intelligence against interests that may affect us in the homeland or may affect U.S. interests abroad," said Gleicher, who has worked in FBI outposts in Austria, Cambodia, Singapore, and the U.S. Virgin Islands. Gleicher, an agent since 1989 who opened the legal attaché office in Tel Aviv in 1996 and is on his third tour in Israel, said laying a foundation

of cooperation—assisting foreign countries with cases that have a U.S. nexus while seeking their help with FBI cases—is the primary role of FBI agents stationed overseas. "Our job is to build and foster long-term relationships that allow FBI leadership, both at Headquarters and our field offices, to communicate with any host country intelligence and/or law enforcement executives at any time."

In Israel—as elsewhere—the FBI works traditional criminal cases that have connections or subjects within a host country, such as cyber, financial, and organized crime investigations. Earlier this month, for example, an organized crime case that originated in 2011 in the FBI's Washington Field Office led to arrests and charges against 19 suspects in cities in Europe and Israel, as well as in the U.S. Also this month, the FBI added a Jordanian woman to its Most Wanted Terrorists list for her suspected role in a 2001 bombing in Jerusalem that killed 15 people, including two Americans, and injured 122 others, including four Americans.

Rusty Rosenthal, an assistant legal attaché in Israel, said having relationships in place smooths and facilitates these types of complex investigations.

"We're able to hit the ground running, and we're that much further along whenever we need some kind of mutual assistance," said Rosenthal, who has spent more than seven years in Israel on multiple tours, in addition to assignments in Afghanistan, Ethiopia, and Yemen. "We've cultivated and maintained these relationships so that when something does come up—and it may be an emergency and it may be breaking very quickly—we know who to call and get access or the information we need to help advance our interests and also help them."

Indeed, it's a mutually beneficial relationship, said Brig. Gen. Coresh Barnoor, a top investigator in the Israel National Police. "We have to join forces," said Barnoor, who heads a unit at Lahav 433—the investigative arm of the department—that probes

organized crime and financial crimes. "Working together, we can establish cases."

"I say to my police officers, 'Always establish relationships with your colleagues around the world. It's very, very important.'"

Barnoor, a 15-year veteran of the Israel National Police, recalled the cooperation that followed a series of suicide bomb attacks early in his career where Americans were among the casualties. Investigators were able to work together to build a case that ultimately led to indictments in the U.S. against the perpetrators. "I think this was a very, very valuable case besides the investigation," Barnoor said. "We established ties. That's why I say to my police officers, 'Always establish relationships with your colleagues around the world. It's very, very important.'"

In the recent case of the threatening phone messages, the FBI had been working with Israeli

intelligence on the investigation since last September, according to Gleicher, who said the FBI sent more than a dozen agents and technical specialists to Israel in the lead up to last week's arrest.

In addition to a presence at U.S. Embassy Tel Aviv, the FBI has an assistant legal attaché stationed at the U.S. Consulate in Jerusalem. The position was established about five years ago to develop and foster a relationship with the Palestinian Authority.

"Our job is apolitical," Gleicher said. "So, while we're assigned in a nation where the Arab-Israeli conflict is with us every day, it doesn't matter to us whether somebody's wearing a Jewish skullcap—a kippah—or a Palestinian is wearing a keffiyah, we look at everybody as human beings. And our job is to stop them from getting hurt and working closely with our host country intelligence and law enforcement partners to identify and prosecute the bad guys when something tragic happens."

Scan this QR code with your smartphone to access related information, or visit www.fbi.gov/israel.

Israel National Police Brig. Gen. Coresh Barnoor and FBI Legal Attaché Cary Gleicher, seen here at Barnoor's office in Tel Aviv, believe that strong partnerships are key to building cases.

THE FBI STORY

CJIS Division Observes a Milestone

Collecting and Sharing Criminal Justice Information for 25 Years

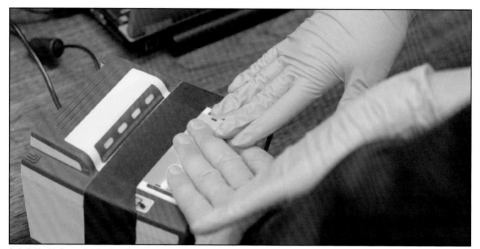

An individual is fingerprinted using a live scan device that enrolls the prints into the Next Generation Identification System at the CJIS Division.

Twenty-five years ago, the FBI's Criminal Justice Information Services (CJIS) Division—the focal point and central repository for all the criminal justice information services within the Bureau—was created.

To understand the significance of the CJIS Division, however, you first have to understand how the FBI's role as the keeper of the nation's criminal justice information evolved.

- Around 1920, there was a push by the International Association of Chiefs of Police (IACP) and others to merge the nation's two major criminal identification records—the federal one at Leavenworth prison and the IACP's own set held in Chicago—and make them available to all of law enforcement. Congress provided the funding, and in 1924, the Bureau of Investigation (as the FBI was called at the time) established its Identification Division, which began accepting

fingerprints and other criminal identification records and also provided crucial identification services for law enforcement across the country and for our own investigations.

- The IACP also saw a need to collect crime statistics nationally that would enable authorities to understand trends and better focus resources. In 1929, the IACP adopted a system to classify, report, and collect crime statistics. But it then recommended that the Bureau—with its experience in centralizing criminal records—take the lead in the effort. Congress agreed, and the Uniform Crime Reporting (UCR) Program was born.

- Fast forward a few years, and in 1967, as computer technology began to make inroads, the FBI launched the National Crime Information Center (NCIC). The NCIC was created to give our law enforcement partners quick access to a computerized

index of documented criminal justice information whenever and wherever they needed it.

"We recognize we can only accomplish our mission by collaborating with and meeting the needs of the agencies we serve."

Over time, various FBI entities continued to develop and implement additional criminal justice information systems, but the problem was that these systems were being developed independently of each other. There had to be a way to coordinate and integrate these systems to ensure that we were providing the criminal justice community with the best products and best service possible.

And there was a way. In February 1992, in a memo proposing the creation of a Criminal Justice Information Services Division, a Bureau executive wrote: "The FBI

THE FBI STORY

has an opportunity to significantly improve the level of information services provided to the criminal justice community. An all-inclusive CJIS will ensure the needs of our users are met and exceeded well into the 21st century, and the technology advancements gained through the creation of CJIS will ensure that the FBI remains in the forefront of criminal justice information systems worldwide."

The establishment of this new office—which was, in effect, a one-stop shop for criminal justice information—was quickly approved by the FBI Director.

The CJIS Division initially included the fingerprint identification services from the Identification Division, the UCR Program from the Information Management Division, and the NCIC program from the Technical Services Division. Over the past 25 years, CJIS has successfully overseen the creation of additional criminal justice services to assist our partners. For example:

• The National Instant Criminal Background Check System, or NICS, launched in 1998, made it possible to determine whether a prospective gun buyer is eligible to buy firearms and explosives.

• In 1999, the Bureau's fingerprint identification process was automated by the Integrated Automated Fingerprint Identification System, or IAFIS. And since then, we've expanded our focus on fingerprint records from local, state, tribal, and federal law enforcement to include those gathered in various counterterrorism operations the U.S. has engaged in worldwide.

• Also in 1999, the National Crime Information Center was upgraded

The main CJIS Division facility is located in Clarksburg, West Virginia.

with more capabilities and additional information files.

• In 2007, the Bureau's Biometric Center of Excellence was established to explore and advance the use of new and enhanced biometric tools, technologies, and capabilities for law enforcement and intelligence personnel.

• In 2010, the National Data Exchange (N-DEx) System—providing criminal justice agencies with an online tool for sharing, searching, linking, and analyzing information across jurisdictional boundaries—was launched nationwide.

• In 2013, Law Enforcement Online (LEO)—a secure network launched in 1995 that gave law enforcement around the country access to sensitive but unclassified information—transitioned into the Law Enforcement Enterprise Portal, or LEEP, a much broader electronic gateway providing law enforcement, intelligence, and criminal justice entities with centralized access to more information, strengthening case

development and enhancing information sharing.

• In 2014, the Bureau announced the full operational capability of the Next Generation Identification (NGI) System, developed to expand the Bureau's biometric identification capabilities and to replace IAFIS.

So what about the next 25 years? There are already plans afoot to enhance services provided by CJIS, including the next iteration of the NCIC, additional capabilities for the NGI system, the development of a national use-of-force data collection, and the expanding and deepening of UCR crime data.

But all of this, according to CJIS Acting Assistant Director Andrew Castor, is being done in consultation with our law enforcement partners. "We continue to be committed to providing the best possible tools to fight crime and terrorism across our nation and around the globe," he explains, "but we recognize we can only accomplish our mission by collaborating with and meeting the needs of the agencies we serve."

Penny Stock Fraud Nets Millions

Scheme Mastermind Among Those Sentenced to Prison

It was a fraud scheme involving penny stocks, but the scheme's mastermind ended up making millions of dollars from unsuspecting investors around the country.

California resident Zirk de Maison, a self-described merchant banker, devised a plan to make himself some easy money off the backs of hard-working folks. From about 2008 to 2013, he created nearly a half-dozen small public shell companies—entities that do no actual business and have no assets. He then offered public shares in the company's penny stocks, which are financial instruments generally worth less than $5 a share.

Why would de Maison deal in penny stocks? Primarily because public information about these stocks and the companies that issue them is hard to find. These very small companies often don't have to file financial reports with the Securities and Exchange Commission (SEC), and their stock usually isn't traded on national or regional stock exchanges.

The companies created by de Maison were purportedly involved in a variety of businesses, including copper and gold mining in South America, high-end diamond trading, and new social media platforms. But in reality, his companies were truly shells—empty inside.

Using fictitious names, de Maison would issue shares in his shell companies to himself and a number of co-conspirators. Then he paid kickbacks to those same co-conspirators—most of them financial brokers—in exchange for using their clients' funds to purchase additional shares of his company stocks.

Besides bribing brokers in several states—including Ohio, California, and New York—to betray the trust of their investor clients by using their money to buy the penny stocks, de Maison found investors through the use of boiler rooms. This technique involved employing high-pressure salespeople to make as many cold calls as possible to potential investors, hounding them to buy shares of stock from de Maison's companies and promising them once-in-a-lifetime opportunities if they acted quickly.

De Maison's scam was a classic pump and dump scheme. The original investors—de Maison and his cohorts—convinced large numbers of investors to purchase stock shares, driving up the price. Those same original investors, including de Maison, would sell their shares when the price of the stock reached its highest level, then the bottom would fall out—the price of the stock plummeted and the rest of the investors were left holding almost worthless shares.

All told, de Maison received and embezzled approximately $39 million in investor money.

The FBI investigation into this particular scheme began in 2013, when our Cleveland Field Office received allegations of illegal activities on the part of an Ohio financial consultant who may have victimized a number of Ohio investors. The investigation into this consultant widened and eventually involved victim and suspect interviews, reviews of e-mails and chat messages, and extensive analysis of financial records. Investigators were ultimately able to unravel the entire scheme, and federal charges were filed against de Maison—who had by that time been living it up in the lap of luxury—and the others.

Zirk de Maison pled guilty in 2015 in connection with his role as the scheme's mastermind. And this past January, he and seven others were sentenced to federal prison for committing securities fraud.

In addition to the criminal case against de Maison and his associates, the SEC—who partnered with the Bureau during our investigation and was of tremendous assistance—also conducted a parallel civil case against the perpetrators.

Don't Be a Victim

According to the SEC, here are some tips that should help members of the investing public avoid being victimized by unscrupulous brokers and others:

- Consider the source. Remember that people touting the stock may well be insiders of the company or paid promoters who stand to profit handsomely if you invest.

- Find out where the stocks trade. Many of the smallest and most thinly traded stocks aren't listed on national or regional exchanges but are often traded in over-the-counter (OTC) markets. Stocks that trade in OTC markets are generally the most risky and the most susceptible to manipulation.

- Research the opportunity carefully. If you can't get a company's current financial statements, check with your state securities regulator to determine if there are issues with the company.

- Watch out for high-pressure pitches. Don't fall for the "once in a lifetime" line until you have a chance to think about and fully investigate the investment opportunity.

Forging Papers to Sell Fake Art

Many Victims May Unknowingly Own Phony Works

Michigan art dealer Eric Ian Hornak Spoutz grew up in a family of artists. His namesake uncle, Ian Hornak, was famous among Hyperrealist and Photorealist painters, and his mother was a gifted painter as well.

Spoutz became an artist in his own right—a con artist peddling fakes. His specialty was forging the paperwork that he used as proof of authenticity to sell bogus works.

His deceit finally caught up to him on February 16, when he was sentenced in New York to 41 months in prison on one count of wire fraud for defrauding art collectors of $1.45 million. The judge also ordered Spoutz, 34, of Mount Clemens, Michigan, to forfeit the $1.45 million and to pay $154,100 in restitution.

Spoutz's scam was straightforward but well executed. He contacted art galleries or auction houses and offered for sale previously unknown works by artists such as American abstract impressionists Willem de Kooning, Franz Kline, and Joan Mitchell. The art did not appear in any catalogs or collections of the artists' known works, said Special Agent Christopher McKeogh from the FBI's Art Crime Team in our New York Field Office.

"He was selling lower-level works by known artists," explained McKeogh, who worked the case for more than three years with fellow agent Meridith Savona and forensic accountant Maria Font. "If it's a direct copy of a real one, the real one is going to be out there and the fraud would be discovered."

Before paying thousands of dollars for works of art, collectors and brokers want assurance the work is real—especially if the work is previously unknown, McKeogh said. Among other things, they look at the provenance—the paper history of an item that traces its ownership back to the original artist—for proof.

Spoutz, who also owned a legitimate art gallery, understood the value of provenance. He forged receipts, bills of sale, letters from dead attorneys, and other documents. Some of the letters dated back decades and looked authentic, referencing real people who worked at real galleries or law firms. Spoutz also used a vintage typewriter and old paper for his documentation.

The old typewriter turned out to be the smoking gun in the case. "We could tell all of these letters had been typed on the same typewriter," McKeogh said. The type of a letter allegedly sent from a business in the 1950s matched the type in a letter allegedly sent by a firm in a different state three decades later. Spoutz also mistakenly added a ZIP Code to the letterhead of a firm on a letter dated four years before ZIP Codes were created.

Another red flag was that many of the people referenced in the letters were dead. And some of the addresses were in the middle of an intersection, or didn't exist at all. "All these dead ends helped prove a fraud was being committed," McKeogh said.

When marketing his fakes, Spoutz stopped just short of saying the works were authentic. "He tried to give himself an out and said they were 'attributed to' an artist," McKeogh said.

Spoutz used sellers all over the country to move his forgeries, some of them fetching more than $30,000. "He looked for people that were not as familiar with a particular artist. Spoutz came across as very scholarly and knowledgeable," McKeogh said.

He also used a number of aliases in the roughly 10 years he ran his scam, and he moved around, from Michigan to Florida to California. He changed the scam over time, selling the works of one artist, then switching to a different artist using a different alias. He was arrested in Los Angeles and charged in February 2016, and pleaded guilty to a single charge of wire fraud in June.

Spoutz produced the fake provenance, but not the fake art. "Spoutz was not known as an artist. He had a source he kept going back to," McKeogh said. The FBI used experts in the field and artist foundations to determine the works Spoutz sold were forgeries.

Many of the fakes passed through auction houses in New York City, McKeogh said, and a suspicious victim eventually contacted the FBI. McKeogh inherited the case about three years ago, when another agent retired.

Although Spoutz has been sentenced, McKeogh and Savona do not believe they have seen the last of the fakes he peddled. The FBI recovered about 40 forgeries; there could be hundreds more that were sold to unsuspecting victims. "This is a case we're going to be dealing with for years. Spoutz was a mill," McKeogh said.

Protecting the integrity of America's art—in all its forms—is a special priority for the FBI and our dedicated Art Crime Team. "It's our heritage; it's who we are. We have to protect it," McKeogh says. "Fake art and fraud schemes like this damage that heritage."

Pharmaceutical Theft
$60 Million Heist Largest in Connecticut History

In the middle of a powerful March nor'easter that was lashing the East Coast with rain and wind, a tractor-trailer backed into a loading dock at a secluded warehouse in Enfield, Connecticut. It was late on a Saturday night. Before dawn the next morning, thieves had made off with $60 million worth of pharmaceuticals—the largest theft in the state's history.

The details of the heist—including a mysterious tip called in to local police a few days later—have all the markings of a Hollywood whodunit, but what's truly remarkable about the 2010 theft from the Eli Lilly warehouse is the investigative work that went into recovering the stolen goods, catching the thieves, and sending them to prison.

The small town of Enfield is about 20 miles north of Hartford. "You would never guess there was a warehouse there with millions of dollars of pharmaceuticals inside," said Special Agent Damian Platosh, who supervised the investigation of the theft from the FBI's New Haven Division. Among a select group of criminals who specialize in cargo theft, however, the facility's location was well known.

These particular cargo thieves—part of a criminal group known as the Cuban Mob—were experts at their trade. They targeted facilities that stored drugs, cigarettes, and consumer electronics such as cell phones. They understood how to conduct surveillance, were proficient at recognizing and disarming alarm systems, and they knew how to load and move freight.

> "They took the cream of the crop, and they loaded the exact number of pallets that would fit into the trailer. They knew exactly what they were doing."

On the night of March 13, 2010, one of the thieves stashed a ladder in the rear parking lot of the warehouse. Later that night, after checking for security guards, the tractor-trailer pulled in and two of the burglars carried the ladder to the building. They climbed atop the warehouse and cut a hole in the roof. Using ropes, they lowered themselves into the facility and disabled the alarm system.

"They knew exactly how that type of alarm system was set up,"

Platosh said. To anyone monitoring the system remotely, it looked as if the storm had knocked out the power. What warehouse employees discovered when they arrived at work was the ladder, the hole in the roof, some discarded tools, and the alarm system beeping as if it needed a battery.

They also discovered the absence of 40 shrink-wrapped pallets of pharmaceuticals, including thousands of boxes of popular medicines such as Cymbalta and Prozac. "They took the cream of the crop," Platosh said, "and they loaded the exact number of pallets that would fit into the trailer. They knew exactly what they were doing."

Because of the magnitude of the crime, the Enfield Police Department called the FBI for assistance. As news of the theft spread in the media, an anonymous caller tipped the police that the people involved in the heist had Cuban names, and one of the thieves was known as El Gato—the cat.

"We started to reach out to our Bureau counterparts who were knowledgeable about cargo theft and the Cuban Mob," Platosh said. Subject matter experts in the FBI's Miami Division, which has a cargo theft task force, suggested that the thieves probably used a "follow car" in addition to the tractor-trailer, and that they would have likely headed south after the burglary and driven about 300 miles before needing to stop and rest.

"Armed with that information," Platosh said, "we started doing a logical investigation. It was classic gumshoe work—finding the right point on the map, checking hotels, car rentals, airline reservations, cell phone tower analysis, that sort of thing."

At the same time, the burglary tools—a particular kind of cutter, work gloves, and other items—were carefully examined. "Our agents were able to determine that that exact combination of gear left at the warehouse was purchased the night before at a big-box hardware store in Flushing Meadows, New York," Platosh explained.

FBI agents and analysts trained in data analysis of electronic transactions also zeroed in on the follow car and where it might have been rented. And then another item left behind at the crime scene—a plastic water bottle—broke the case wide open. DNA on the bottle was matched to a Cuban individual living in Florida with a history of cargo theft.

All of which helped to identify the four suspects involved in the theft: Amaury Villa, Amed Villa, Yosmany Nunez, and Alexander Marquez. The subjects had split up in Connecticut after the robbery and reunited in Florida, where the drugs were transferred into self-storage units in the Miami area.

Agents in Miami put the stolen merchandise under surveillance. "We thought it might be six months or more before the thieves tried to fence the drugs," Platosh said, "so we used that time trying to tie the subjects to other open cargo theft cases."

In October 2011, authorities raided a Florida storage facility and recovered the drugs stolen from the Enfield warehouse. Amed Villa and his co-conspirators were charged with that crime as well as other thefts, including:

Eli Lilly Warehouse

Enfield

190

91

5

Site

Area ☐ of detail

CONNECTICUT

Freshwater Blvd

Map showing location of Enfield, Connecticut, site of an Eli Lilly warehouse where $60 million worth of pharmaceuticals were stolen on March 13, 2010.

- $13.3 million in pharmaceuticals from the GlaxoSmithKline warehouse in Virginia in 2009;

- More than $8 million in cigarettes and a cargo trailer from an Illinois warehouse in 2010;

- Approximately $7.8 million in cell phones and tablets from a Florida warehouse in 2011; and

- More than $1.5 million in cigarettes from a Kentucky warehouse in 2011.

During each of the thefts, Amed Villa and his crew gained entry into the warehouse through the roof, disabled the alarm system, and loaded the stolen goods into tractor-trailers. Villa's DNA was identified on items discarded during the thefts in Connecticut, Illinois, Florida, and Virginia.

Amed Villa pleaded guilty to several counts of theft related to the robberies, and in December 2016, the 51-year-old was sentenced to seven years in federal prison. His three co-conspirators had previously pleaded guilty to charges stemming from the Eli Lilly warehouse theft and are in prison.

"This investigation started in Connecticut and branched out around the country," Platosh said. "The combined effort drew on all of the FBI's investigative strengths and the depth of its resources. It was a great team effort," he said, adding his thanks to the Enfield Police Department, the FBI's Miami Division, and the Major Theft Unit at FBI Headquarters for their efforts.

"These criminals went on a $100 million robbery spree," he said, "but in the end they were brought to justice."

New Top Ten Fugitive

Help Us Catch a Murderer

FBI TEN MOST WANTED FUGITIVE

VIOLENT CRIME IN AID OF RACKETEERING (HOMICIDE)

WALTER YOVANY GOMEZ

A New Jersey gang member wanted in connection with a brutal, premeditated murder has been named to the FBI's Ten Most Wanted Fugitives list, and a reward of up to $100,000 is being offered for information leading to his capture.

Walter Yovany Gomez, in his early 20s at the time of the 2011 murder in Plainfield, New Jersey, was attempting to become a full member of MS-13 by carrying out a gang-ordered killing. It didn't matter that the target was Gomez's friend—the man had allegedly shown disrespect to the gang.

Part of the Plainfield Locos Salvatrucha (PLS) crew, Gomez was assigned the hit when his bosses heard that one of their associates had been seen socializing in a bar with a rival 18th Street Gang member. Ordering a murder for such a sign of disrespect is not uncommon for MS-13, a transnational gang known for its extreme violence.

"To become a full-fledged member of MS-13," said Special Agent Dan Brunner, who is investigating the case from the FBI's Newark Division, "you have to kill someone on behalf of your local clique, or crew. Only then can you get the MS-13 letters tattooed on your body," Brunner explained. "Gomez had not earned his letters yet."

On May 8, 2011, Gomez—known to his friends as Cholo—invited himself and a co-conspirator to the victim's house. Another person was there who was not involved in the plot. The four were drinking, smoking weed, and watching TV. "They were all friends," Brunner said. "The victim had no reason to suspect that he was going to be murdered."

The victim, Julio Matute, partied with his friends all night. Early the next morning, as he was getting dressed to go to work, Gomez grabbed an aluminum baseball bat and struck Matute in the back of his head several times. When he fell to the floor, Gomez cut his throat with a knife, then grabbed a screwdriver and repeatedly stabbed him in the back.

"He was stabbed so many times that when his body was discovered a week later," Brunner said, "police officers thought that he had been shot with a shotgun."

Gomez's fellow attacker was later arrested, but when police went to Gomez's residence, he jumped out a rear window and fled into the woods. Later investigation revealed that he drove to Maryland with assistance from fellow MS-13 gang members.

A Honduran citizen who came to the U.S. illegally, Gomez is not believed to have left the country. He may be residing in Maryland or Northern Virginia, where there are thousands of MS-13 members, Brunner said. Or he may have returned to New Jersey. "He would probably be considered a higher-ranking member of the gang now," Brunner added.

With the exception of Gomez, all of the gang members involved in Matute's murder have been prosecuted. In 2013, Gomez was charged with murder in the aid of racketeering, which carries a mandatory life sentence (Gomez's fellow attacker received a mandatory life sentence).

Brunner believes the $100,000 reward in the case will bring someone forward. "It is unlikely that a fellow MS-13 member would turn Gomez in," he said, "but he works construction doing dry wall, and someone on a construction crew not involved with the gang could recognize him and do the right thing. This is an extremely violent criminal who needs to be captured."

Anyone with information concerning Gomez should contact the nearest FBI office or local law enforcement agency, or submit a tip online.

Note: FBI Ten Most Wanted Fugitive Walter Yovany Gomez was arrested without incident on August 11, 2017, in Woodbridge, Virginia.

New Top Ten Fugitive

Help Us Capture a Murderer

A 26-year-old wanted for the 2015 murder of his wife in Maryland is the newest addition to the FBI's Ten Most Wanted Fugitives list, and a reward of up to $100,000 is being offered for information leading to his capture.

Bhadreshkumar Chetanbhai Patel, a native of India, had been traveling in the U.S. with his 21-year-old wife. At the time of the murder, both were working the night shift at a donut shop in Hanover, Maryland, owned by a relative of Patel's.

Just before midnight on April 12, 2015, while customers were in the front of the shop, Patel stabbed his wife, Palak Patel, multiple times in the back of the shop and left by a rear door.

Investigators theorize that Palak Patel wanted to return to India—their visas had expired the month before—and her husband was against the idea. "The best guess is that he didn't want her to leave," said Special Agent Jonathan Shaffer, who is investigating the case from the FBI's Baltimore Division. "It's possible that he thought he would be disgraced by her leaving and going back to India."

Although the motive remains unclear, and there is no way to know if Patel planned the murder, Shaffer noted that "after the crime, his actions show a very cool and calculated mentality about escaping the scene and fleeing the area."

After the murder, a customer who entered the shop realized something was wrong when no one came to take his order. He alerted a nearby Anne Arundel County Police Department officer, who discovered Palak Patel's body.

FBI TEN MOST WANTED FUGITIVE

UNLAWFUL FLIGHT TO AVOID PROSECUTION - FIRST DEGREE MURDER, SECOND DEGREE MURDER, FIRST DEGREE ASSAULT, SECOND DEGREE ASSAULT, DANGEROUS WEAPON WITH INTENT TO INJURE

BHADRESHKUMAR CHETANBHAI PATEL

"It was horrific what had been done to this young woman," Shaffer said.

Realizing that Patel was an international flight risk, local police requested FBI assistance, and several days after the murder, a federal arrest warrant was issued charging Patel with unlawful flight to avoid prosecution. He has also been charged with his wife's murder.

"Domestic violence homicides tend to be brutal, and this one certainly was," said Anne Arundel County Police Department Det. Kelly Harding, who has handled many domestic violence cases during her nearly 20 years in law enforcement. "We almost always are able to find the suspects in these cases, and they are usually full of remorse, asking 'What have I done?' They are not taking a taxi cab and crossing state lines to escape."

Investigators believe that Patel could be with distant relatives in the U.S. or that he could have fled to Canada. "Or he could have traveled through Canada back to India," Shaffer said. "Those are among the plausible options we are exploring."

Shaffer believes the $100,000 reward will help in the capture of Patel. "Somebody out there who either sees the publicity or knows something already but has been reluctant to come forward will be encouraged by that amount of money," he said. "Whether they do it for the right reasons or just for the money doesn't really matter. Patel needs to be apprehended."

If you have information regarding Patel—who should be considered armed and dangerous—contact your local FBI office or the nearest U.S. Embassy or Consulate, or submit a tip on our website.

Note: This case may have been resolved since this information was posted on our website. Please check www.fbi.gov/wanted for up-to-date information.

Financial Fraud

Stock-Loan Scheme Costs Investors $100 Million

With the substantial proceeds of his long-running fraud scheme, Jeffrey Spanier enjoyed a lavish lifestyle that included buying fancy cars, boats, and this home in Boca Raton, Florida, which he was ordered to forfeit.

An elaborate and long-running financial fraud carried out by a Florida man and co-conspirators cost business executives and shareholders of publicly traded corporations more than $100 million—losses that in some cases forced companies to close their doors.

Jeffrey Spanier, who was recently sentenced to eight years in prison for his role in the scheme, fleeced some very savvy businessmen, including CEOs. "These were sophisticated investors asking the right questions," said Special Agent John Roberts, who investigated the case from the FBI's San Diego Division along with Special Agent Bridgid Cook. "But because of Spanier's deception, misrepresentation, and omission of facts, it was very difficult for these businessmen to see the red flags and to protect themselves."

Beginning in 2004 and continuing on and off for nearly a decade, Spanier's firm, Amerifund Capital Finance, worked in conjunction with San Diego-based Argyll Equities to arrange loans to companies that needed operating capital or an infusion of cash to grow their businesses. In exchange, borrowers pledged company stock as collateral.

"Borrowing against stock is a legitimate concept," Cook explained. "There is nothing illegal or bad business practice about using your stock as collateral against a loan."

In a legitimate transaction, the borrower pays back the loan over time with interest, and the stock certificates are returned. But Spanier and his co-conspirators were anything but legitimate. They never had any money to loan. They financed the deals—and reaped substantial gains—by immediately selling the pledged stock without the borrower knowing. "Spanier would assure clients that their stock would not be sold," Roberts said. "But that is exactly what he did."

A company might have pledged $4 million in stock to get a $3 million cash loan. Sometimes CEOs pledged their personal stock. The business would make interest payments every quarter to service the loan, only to find out years later—after the debt had been repaid—that the stock was gone.

As a result, a number of civil suits were filed against Spanier, but still he kept the fraud going, continuing to insist to new customers that their stock would not be sold. After a lengthy investigation by the FBI, Spanier was indicted in 2012, along with Douglas McClain, Jr. and James Miceli. All were charged with multiple counts of conspiracy, mail fraud, wire fraud, securities fraud, and money laundering.

In 2013, a jury found McClain—president of Argyll Equities—guilty on all counts, and he was sentenced to 15 years in prison and ordered to pay more than $81 million in restitution. Miceli committed suicide shortly before his trial.

In November 2016, Spanier was convicted of conspiring with McClain and Miceli to defraud clients by falsely representing that Argyll Equities was an institutional lender with significant cash to lend to corporate executives and other individuals. The jury rejected defense claims that Spanier was merely a broker who was unaware of the fraud scheme.

"These guys were making tons of money," Roberts said. "They bought fancy houses, cars planes, boats. There was no question that Spanier was on the inside of the conspiracy, not the outside."

At his sentencing in April 2017, a federal judge ordered Spanier to pay more than $20 million in restitution to his victims. Roberts said that while several million dollars in cash and property were forfeited after Spanier's arrest, victims were likely to receive "pennies on the dollar" in restitution. "Unfortunately," he said, "that is usually the case in these types of frauds."

The Scourge of Child Pornography

Working to Stop the Sexual Exploitation of Children

North Hills Man Sentenced to 18 Years in Prison for Producing Sexual Images of Minors. Melrose Man Sentenced to 60 Months for Child Pornography Offenses. Boylston Man Charged with Distributing Child Pornography. Navajo Man from Churchrock Pleads Guilty to Federal Child Sexual Abuse Charge. Vestal Man Pleads Guilty to Distributing and Receiving Child Pornography. Binghamton Man Pleads Guilty to 12 Counts of Distributing Child Pornography.

Rarely a week goes by in the United States that a child pornographer is not charged or sentenced for federal crimes related to the sexual exploitation of children. The press release headlines above from the Department of Justice were issued on a single day last month.

In coordination with local, state, federal, and international partners—both law enforcement and non-governmental organizations—the FBI devotes extensive resources to fighting the sexual exploitation of children. And while the high number of arrests and convictions speaks to law enforcement's successes, there is still much work to be done. According to a 2016 Department of Justice report to Congress, "The expansion of the Internet has led to an explosion in the market for child pornography."

"After you've been doing this awhile, you think you've seen it all, and then you get a new case," said Special Agent Eric Campbell, who investigates violent crimes against children in the FBI's Phoenix Division. "I am surprised by how often I am surprised at what people will do."

Campbell points to one of his recent cases as an example. In

February 2017, a 28-year-old Arizona woman was sentenced to more than five years in prison for mailing child pornography to her imprisoned husband. He was behind bars in Tucson awaiting trial on separate child pornography charges—for which he would eventually receive a 20-year sentence.

Some of the images the woman mailed her husband were of girls as young as 9 years old. "She was trying to sneak them into the prison," Campbell said, "trying to give her husband what he wanted."

The FBI coordinates its efforts to protect children through the Violent Crimes Against Children (VCAC) program. The mission is to lower the vulnerability of children to sexual exploitation, to provide a rapid and effective investigative response to such crimes, and to provide appropriate training and other resources to state and local law enforcement partners.

Investigations are conducted in each of the FBI's 56 field offices by Child Exploitation Task Forces, which combine Bureau resources with those of other federal, state, and local law enforcement agencies. Nearly 400 law enforcement partner organizations participate in these task forces and are assisted by FBI intelligence analysts, victim specialists, and subject matter

experts. The task forces also work closely with the National Center for Missing & Exploited Children (NCMEC).

In addition, because the Internet has blurred traditional notions of borders and jurisdiction, the FBI's legal attaché offices in more than 60 countries around the world coordinate with their foreign counterparts on investigations ranging from child sex trafficking to sex tourism.

Those who engage in the production and distribution of child pornography come from all walks of life and represent varied ages, races, occupations, and education levels. Typically, their crimes are carried out on the so-called dark web—where they can remain anonymous—and their actions are unknown to spouses, families, and associates.

"Most of these guys don't have any criminal history," Campbell said, "and no one has any idea of what they were doing until we catch them." The agent said that the work he and his colleagues do is important, but also emotionally wrenching. "The payoff," he explained, "is that you are able to uncover these perpetrators and shine a light on them, and do everything possible to make sure they are no longer able to victimize innocent children."

2016 Director's Community Leadership Awards

Local Leaders Honored at FBI Headquarters

Scan this QR code with your smartphone to access related information, or visit www.fbi.gov/dcla2016.

FBI Director James Comey today formally recognized 58 individuals and organizations from around the country for their efforts to build stronger, safer, and more cohesive communities.

"This is one of the very best days in the life of this organization," Director Comey said during the April 28 ceremony at FBI Headquarters in Washington, D.C. "We get to recognize and thank people who made the FBI better and the country better."

The annual Director's Community Leadership Awards were launched in 1990 as a way to spotlight individuals and organizations for their work in combating crime, drugs, terrorism, and violence. Today's recipients were also recognized for their work in bridging the relationships between law enforcement agencies and the communities they serve, developing strategies to battle the nation's opioid crisis, and assisting victims of human trafficking, among other efforts.

Honorees are nominated by each of the FBI's 56 field offices, as well as the Bureau's Office of Public Affairs and the Criminal Justice Information Services Division.

In his remarks, Director Comey said this year's recipients embodied the words attributed to the 16th century minister John Wesley, who said, "Do all the good you can. By all the means you can. In all the ways you can. In all the places you can. At all the times you can. To all the people you can. As long as ever you can."

The Director related a story about speaking to young audiences and warning them against losing sight of what really matters in life. He would ask them to close their eyes, imagine they were old, and then ask themselves: Who do I want to have been? "I know some of you want to have been people who made a difference for those who needed you," he would tell the kids, "to have been people who chose lives of moral content, who stood there for the bullied and the picked on and the frightened."

"Why am I telling you this?" Comey asked on Friday. "This auditorium is filled with people who have already answered the question in the most remarkable way. You will have been those people. We're here today to thank you for being that. Because of you, the FBI is better. Because of you, the United States of America is better."

Virtual Ticket to Prison

Investigation of Fraud Scheme Unravels Man's Illegal Bitcoin Exchange

The beginning of the end of an Ohio man's venture into the murky world of cryptocurrencies can be traced back to the moment investigators linked the 29-year-old to a ticket-fraud scheme nearly 2,000 miles away in California.

Daniel Mercede, of Chagrin Falls, was charged last November for using stolen credit card information to buy tickets to concerts and other events from a California-based seller. He would then turn around and sell them through another ticket broker—often for less than he paid—netting himself a tidy profit. He collected more than $400,000 in proceeds, beginning in 2014, through ticket sales and by stealing the personal information of more than 40 victims and using their identities to apply for more than $1.5 million in loans.

The ticket company in California discovered something was amiss when the victims' banks and credit card companies sought their money back. The investigation led straight to Mercede, who had the tickets delivered to his home address or to his parents' house. It appeared to be a straightforward fraud case—until investigators started digging.

"A lot of the material that we got out of his apartment led me to believe there was something greater going on here," said Detective Sergeant Andy Capwill of the Chagrin Falls Police Department. What he found while sifting through thousands of pages of data was evidence of large money transfers, dozens of checking accounts, and what appeared to be a robust business trading in the digital currency and payment network known as bitcoin. "I realized I was going to need some help here," said Capwill, who called the FBI.

In their joint investigation, Capwill and special agents from the FBI's Cleveland Field Office discovered Mercede was buying large quantities of bitcoin from legitimate foreign exchanges and then reselling the bitcoin himself at a premium. The inherent appeal of his business, Cryptocoin Capital Management, was its location in the U.S.—not in Russia or China, where people are leery to send their money—and that it did not require the same lengthy waiting period as the more reputable exchanges.

"A lot of the time, people who want bitcoin want it now, so they will go through more peer-to-peer transactions," said Special Agent Gary Sukowatey, one of the FBI investigators. "He was buying larger quantities and waiting whatever period was necessary to wait, then he would sell it to people that wanted bitcoin right away." The problem, he said, is these transactions are illegal if you don't have a license.

Operating a money transmitting business requires registration through the U.S. Department of the Treasury, which has a bureau—the Financial Crimes Enforcement Network, or FinCEN—dedicated to collecting and analyzing information about financial transactions to combat money laundering, terrorist financing, and other financial crimes.

"You've got to do it the right way," said Special Agent Milan Kosanovich, who specializes in complex financial crimes and investigated the case with Sukowatey and Capwill. "It's perfectly fine to operate as a money exchanger for bitcoin. However, those exchangers, like other financial institutions in the U.S., have specific rules to follow to ensure compliance with anti-money laundering requirements."

In September 2014, Mercede boasted about his profits to a reporter for an online bitcoin publication. He claimed he averaged returns of 8 to 15 percent per day by buying off Chinese exchanges and then selling locally.

Mercede wired funds to make daily purchases of up to $40,000 in bitcoin. Over six months beginning in August 2014, Mercede illegally converted or transmitted $1.4 million. He was sentenced on March 21 to more than six years in prison. The case represents one of the first convictions for what is believed to be an increasingly frequent crime—operating an unlicensed money transmitting business.

The FBI agents stressed that trading in virtual currencies like bitcoin is perfectly legal—with the proper registration, licensing, and record-keeping requirements. "It's easier for people not to do it and hope they don't get charged with it," said Sukowatey. "But as we were able to prove in this case, you can be charged criminally for not being registered."

Capwill, who began the investigation, said he didn't know what bitcoin was at the outset. But he appreciated the learning experience and working the joint investigation with the FBI—as well as the Internal Revenue Service and the U.S. Postal Inspection Service—to its conclusion. "It was a lot of information being shared back and forth between the agencies, which was really helpful," he said. "It's always nice to know there's somebody out there on the other end of the phone that can help you."

'Playpen' Creator Sentenced to 30 Years

Dark Web 'Hidden Service' Case Spawned Hundreds of Child Porn Investigations

The creator and lead administrator of what was believed to be the world's largest child pornography website—with more than 150,000 users around the world—was sentenced this week to 30 years in prison.

Steven W. Chase, 58, of Naples, Florida, created a website called Playpen in August 2014 on the Tor network, an open network on the Internet where users can communicate anonymously through "hidden service" websites—where criminal activity is not uncommon. Chase ran the Playpen website, where members uploaded and viewed tens of thousands of postings of young victims, indexed by age, sex, and the type of sexual activity involved.

The case—and the thousands of follow-up investigations it has launched—is unprecedented in its scope and reach, FBI officials said. It represents the Bureau's most successful effort to date against users of Tor's hidden service sites. And it has opened new avenues for international cooperation in efforts to prosecute child abusers around the world.

"We were only able to pull it off with a lot of support from our international partners and field offices," said Special Agent Dan Alfin, who investigated the case as part of the Bureau's Violent Crimes Against Children section.

The case opened shortly after Steven Chase launched Playpen in the summer of 2014. The FBI, which has numerous investigations involving the dark web, quickly became aware of the site, but "given the nature of how Tor hidden services work, there was not much we could do about it," Alfin recalled.

That is, until December 2014, when Chase slipped up and revealed Playpen's unique IP address—a location in the U.S. The gaffe was noticed by a foreign law enforcement agency, which notified the FBI.

"From that point we took normal investigative steps—seized a copy of the website, served search warrants for e-mail accounts, followed the money—and everything led back to Steven Chase," said Alfin. Chase was sentenced Monday in North Carolina in connection with engaging in a child exploitation enterprise and multiple child pornography charges. His sentencing follows those of two co-defendants who were also administrators on the website— Michael Fluckiger, 46, of Indiana, and David Browning, 47, of Kentucky—who were each given 20-year prison terms earlier this year.

Arresting Playpen's administrators, however, was only the beginning. In January 2015, the FBI, in partnership with the Department of Justice Child Exploitation and Obscenity Section, launched Operation Pacifier—an effort to go after Playpen's thousands of members. Using a court-approved network investigative technique, agents uncovered IP addresses and other information that helped locate and identify users. Investigators sent more than 1,000 leads to FBI field offices around the country and thousands more to overseas partners, Alfin said.

Arrests and other enforcement actions have occurred in countries far and near. Europol, the European Union's agency for law enforcement cooperation, reported arrests, along with Israel, Turkey, Peru, Malaysia, Chile, and the Ukraine. International agencies critical to the investigation included CNCPO Polizia Postale e Comunicazioni of Italian State Police, the United Kingdom's National Crime Agency, and New Zealand's Department of Internal Affairs.

Even some countries where law enforcement cooperation has been historically limited were, in this case, especially helpful in pursuing the FBI's leads on former users and contributors to Chase's Playpen site.

"Members of his enterprise who were raping children, who were producing child pornography all around the world—those cases continue to be indicted and prosecuted," Alfin said.

In addition to taking down the website, the ongoing investigation, as of May 4, 2017, has produced the following results:

- At least 350 U.S.-based individuals arrested
- 25 producers of child pornography prosecuted
- 51 hands-on abusers prosecuted
- 5 American children successfully identified or rescued
- 548 international arrests, with 296 sexually abused children identified or rescued.

The Playpen site has been down for more than two years. But similar sites continue to operate and proliferate on the dark web.

"It's ongoing and we continue to address the threat to the best of our abilities," said Alfin. "As they get smarter, we adapt, we find them. It's a cat-and-mouse game, except it's not a game. Kids are being abused, and it's our job to stop that."

Sovereign Citizens Sentenced
'Stole' Vacant Homes and Filed False Claims to Intimidate Officials

For more than three years, a Pennsylvania group claiming to be sovereign citizens—and therefore not subject to U.S. law—schemed to "steal" dozens of foreclosed homes worth millions of dollars and sell them to unsuspecting victims.

The scheme came to light after local officials in Delaware County, Pennsylvania, received documents declaring sovereign citizen status for three residents. Alarmed, the officials contacted the FBI in May 2010.

Officials had good reason to be concerned: That same month, two so-called sovereign citizens opened fire on police during a traffic stop in Arkansas, killing two officers. The ambush is just one example of how members of the movement often turn to violence.

Sovereign citizens are anti-government extremists who claim the federal government is operating outside its jurisdiction and they are therefore not bound by government authority—including the courts, taxing entities, motor vehicle departments, and even law enforcement.

They also are prone to engage in numerous types of financial frauds and schemes, based on their skewed interpretation of law.

"Most of these sovereign citizens are extremists," said Special Agent Walter Szpak, who investigated the case out of the FBI's Philadelphia Field Office. "When arrested, they don't believe they have committed a crime, and think they have the right to retaliate."

Knowing the potential for criminal and even violent activity by sovereign citizens, FBI agents decided to interview the three people in Pennsylvania who signed the declarations of sovereignty: Steven Hameed, Darnell Young, and Damond Palmer. Hameed and Young were married.

"It's not illegal to file this kind of paperwork," explained Szpak. "This is America; they can say whatever they want. But it's essentially a warning to law enforcement, saying, 'We're about to start committing criminal acts.'"

Which is exactly what Hameed, Young, and Palmer were doing. The trio scoured public records to find foreclosed houses in Delaware County, west of Philadelphia. Then they crafted jargon-laden paperwork claiming ownership on 70 properties worth more than $9 million. Most of the homes belonged to the U.S. Department of Housing and Urban Development (HUD) or Wells Fargo bank.

After staking fraudulent claims to the properties, they listed the houses as rent-to-own opportunities on Craigslist, Szpak said.

FBI agents could not find the three suspects to interview about their claims of sovereign status; they did not live at the addresses listed on their declarations. Agents kept looking, using property records to track them down.

"Every time we went to one of these addresses, someone else was living there," Szpak said. "The tenants had bought or rented the property from the people we were looking for. That's when we realized what they were doing."

As the scope of the fraud became more apparent, the FBI was joined in the investigation by other agencies, including HUD, the Federal Deposit Insurance Corporation, the Federal Housing Finance Agency, and several county and local police departments.

In the midst of the federal investigation, Hameed, Young, and Palmer were charged by local police for offenses such as trespassing. In response, the three played another trick popular within the sovereign movement: "paper terrorism." They filed more than 250 fraudulent IRS forms against numerous state and local law enforcement officials and judges. The fake 1099-DIV and 1099-INT forms falsely claimed that the victims had been paid hundreds of thousands or even millions of dollars in dividends or interest.

Because the forms were fake, the victims did not know they had been filed and obviously did not pay any taxes on the income. In some cases, the IRS placed liens against the victims or seized tax refunds they would have otherwise been owed.

They also added to a growing list of federal charges the trio faced. The three were charged in December 2015 with conspiracy to commit offenses against the United States, bank fraud, and corrupt interference with Internal Revenue laws, among other crimes. All three pleaded guilty in June 2016. Hameed was sentenced to eight years in prison in February; Young and Palmer received shorter sentences in 2016.

The scam left scores of victims in its wake, Szpak said, including people who learned they were not actually home owners. Although HUD and Wells Fargo worked with the unsuspecting victims who bought homes, none were allowed to stay in the homes they thought they owned.

Hogan's Alley Turns 30
The Evolution of the FBI's Mock Training Ground

A squad of agent trainees moves in on the fictitious Dogwood Inn at Hogan's Alley.

It has been called the nation's most crime-ridden town and even the crime capital of the world, but no one has ever been victimized there. This town isn't listed on any official map, but it is visited nearly every day and appears often in the movies and on television.

Hogan's Alley is no ordinary place. It's a mock town where new FBI agents and their law enforcement partners learn the ropes through a series of realistic and often stressful scenarios. Whether investigating criminal and terrorist activities, gathering intelligence, processing evidence, getting into simulated gunfights, or making arrests, agents and other trainees are taught the latest techniques and challenged to make the right decisions—with the help of actors playing criminals, victims, and bystanders.

This year, Hogan's Alley celebrates its 30th anniversary on the grounds of the FBI's Training Academy in Quantico, Virginia. Over the years it has evolved into the cornerstone of the Bureau's practical training program. Every FBI agent hired over the past three decades has gained valuable, real-world experience in this tiny yet always bustling town.

The name—and the training concept—have actually been around quite a bit longer in law enforcement circles. Many decades ago, the use of fake storefronts with mechanical, pop-up bad guys were a staple of police firearms training. The first exercise of this kind appears to have been in 1919 at the U.S. Army's Camp Perry in Ohio on a set built to look like a war-torn French village. It was created for a firearms contest called the National Matches and later used

in police training sponsored by the Army. Contestants were scored on their shooting time and accuracy when hand-controlled cutouts of threatening persons were raised in windows.

By the mid-1920s, these training exercises came to be called "Hogan's Alleys." The name came from a comic strip in the 1890s called the Yellow Kid, which was a romanticized look at the daily life a young boy who lived in a crime-ridden New York tenement called Hogan's Alley.

In its early days, the Bureau used actors and mannequin victims from time to time in its practical exercises. The FBI began including "Alleys" in its training program in the 1940s. In 1945, it started building its first "surprise scenario" training range that incorporated mechanically controlled cutouts.

THE FBI STORY

Surprise target ranges were used at Hogan's Alley in the 1940s and 1950s. Cutouts of targets would mechanically pop up in windows and doors of these ranges and agents would have to quickly react; they were scored on accuracy and response time.

This first FBI Hogan's Alley cost the Bureau $3,000, according former Special Agent Larry Wack. By the early 1950s, Hogan's Alley took on further prominence in FBI training, becoming a centerpiece of Bureau plans to revamp its ranges. When completed, the new Alley included a row of false house fronts, 120 feet long and 10 feet high. Surprise targets appeared in windows along this street front, and agents chose whether or not to shoot.

In 1972, when the FBI opened its Training Academy in Quantico, new facilities were created for agent training. In the mid-1980s, the Bureau began constructing a new home for practical instruction—this time filled with actual buildings, including a bank, a motel, a jewelry shop, and a luncheonette. This new crime town was officially launched in 1987, and it has been a key staple of FBI training ever since.

Over time, the town has grown, adding warehouse facilities, single-family homes, and other typical places where Bureau agents might interact with the public and those who would prey on them. Hogan's Alley may have the highest crime rate in the world, but the Bureau's agent and police trainees have ensured that it also has the highest arrest rate, too.

Con Man

FBI Impersonator Preyed on Women

Anthony Jones was a con man. The 46-year-old Jacksonville, Florida resident impersonated an FBI agent and an investment adviser—and made a habit of preying on women. But like so many scam artists, his lies and deceptions finally caught up with him.

The tawdry tale of Jones and the women he victimized began for Special Agent Steve Burros one January night in 2013, when a Jacksonville Sheriff's Office detective contacted him and said that Jones had impersonated an FBI agent in an attempt to solicit free sex from a prostitute.

Jones had requested a date from an online escort service and promised to pay $200. The prostitute arrived at his apartment, where Jones lived with his wife and three children. "This was all happening in the middle of the day," Burros said. "The wife was at work and the kids were in school."

Shortly after the prostitute arrived, she asked for the money. That's when Jones said he was an FBI agent and that if she didn't have sex with him for free, she would be arrested. When the woman balked, Jones called an accomplice on the phone, who was working from a script.

"He puts the phone on speaker

and says, 'Hey, I got another one for you. I'm just now finishing up the other two warrants,' " Burros said. "And so now, the prostitute believed him." Jones also pointed to a smoke detector in the bedroom and said the woman was being monitored by a hidden camera.

Afterward, though, when the prostitute told her roommate what had happened, the two realized she had been scammed, and they went to Jones' residence to collect the money. The heated argument that ensued led to a police intervention, and Jones ended up being charged with receiving a sex act through force or coercion—and Burros was called in to investigate the FBI impersonation allegation.

Meanwhile, the accomplice on the phone during the prostitution incident was a young woman who knew she was part of a scam but didn't know Jones was trying to get free sex. She had a child with Jones but had no idea he was married and living with his wife and three other children. She, too, was a victim of Jones' many cons.

It turned out that the young woman—the mother of Jones' child—had lost both her parents in a car accident and received a settlement of about $35,000 from the insurance company. Jones lied and told her he was an investment

adviser and that he owned fast food restaurants and would invest the money for her.

"She thought he was investing her money," Burros said, "but instead he was depositing it in his wife's account and spending it on himself." The young woman had no idea what Jones had done until Burros discovered the fraud.

Jones was arrested on January 9, 2013 on the prostitute coercion charge and released on bond subject to electronic monitoring. The following April—aware that Burros was on to his additional financial fraud—Jones cut off his ankle monitoring bracelet and fled. He was on the run for more than two years, until he was captured in August 2015 by the U.S. Marshals Service in Jacksonville.

As for the FBI impersonation, "Jones was not a first timer," Burros noted. He had previously been arrested for passing himself off as an agent to get work done on his house.

In 2016, Jones pleaded guilty to impersonating an FBI agent, wire fraud, and failure to appear. In February 2017, a federal judge sentenced him to five years and six months in prison. Upon release, he has been ordered to pay restitution of nearly $22,000 to the young woman whose insurance settlement he fraudulently gained access to. If he doesn't pay, he could be sent back to jail.

"Anthony Jones was truly a con artist," Burros said. "The money he scammed from this poor young woman was a significant sum for her, and now she is living with her grandparents and raising the child she had with Jones—and so far he has never given her a dime."

National Missing Children's Day 2017

Help Us Find Them

After a teenage girl was reported missing in Virginia earlier this year, the FBI and police worked quickly to reunite her with her family and arrest the man who'd lured her away.

Unfortunately, not all lost children are found quickly, and some never make it home. On National Missing Children's Day, the FBI asks the public for help in locating any of the victims pictured here from our Kidnapping and Missing Persons webpage.

With its partners, the FBI continues its efforts to eradicate predators from communities and to keep children safe. Ready response teams are stationed across the country to quickly respond to abductions. The Bureau offers a full array of forensic tools such as DNA, trace evidence, impression evidence, and digital forensics. And through improved communications, law enforcement also has the ability to quickly share information with partners throughout the world.

The FBI also has several programs in place to educate both parents and children about the dangers posed by predators—in person and online—and to recover missing and endangered children should they be taken. Through the Child Abduction Rapid Deployment Teams, Innocence Lost National Initiative, Innocent Images National Initiative, annual Operation Cross Country, Office for Victim Assistance, Child Exploitation Task Forces, and numerous community outreach initiatives, the FBI and law enforcement partners are working to keep the most vulnerable among us safe and secure.

Note: The children pictured here may have been located since this information was posted on our website. Please check www.fbi.gov/wanted/kidnap for up-to-date information.

Scan this QR code with your smartphone to access related information, or visit www.fbi.gov/missingkids2017.

National Police Week 2017
FBI Remembers Fallen Heroes

In one of many events leading up to National Police Week, attendees gathered for the annual Blue Mass, held at St. Patrick's Catholic Church on May 2, 2017 in Washington, D.C.

The FBI this week honored seven special agents who responded to the 9/11 attacks and later died from illnesses linked to their exposure to toxic air and hazardous materials at the sites. The agents were recognized as part of National Police Week, an annual event that draws thousands of law enforcement officers to Washington, D.C., each May to honor their fallen colleagues.

In the weeks following the 9/11 attacks, Special Agents Steven Carr, William Craig, Jerry Jobe, Robert Roth, Gerard Senatore, Paul Wilson, and Wesley Yoo were among the FBI personnel who recovered the deceased and gathered critical evidence in the largest investigation in FBI history. After scientists confirmed a connection between 9/11 responders and their illnesses, the

agents—who passed away between 2007 and 2015—were added to the FBI's Hall of Honor this week. They ranged in age from 44 to 68 at the time of their deaths.

During a memorial service on May 17 at FBI Headquarters for all agents who have died in the line of duty, FBI Acting Director Andrew McCabe called the fallen 9/11 responders "peacemakers dedicated to protecting the lives of Americans."

"They did their jobs not knowing that responding to the scene of a tragic attack would set into motion another tragedy that they would not realize until many years later," he said.

In 1962, President John F. Kennedy designated May 15 as Peace Officers Memorial Day and the week in which it falls as National

Police Week. Multiple events are held in the nation's capital each year in the days leading up to and during the week, including a candlelight vigil, a Blue Mass at St. Patrick's Catholic Church, a wreath-laying ceremony at the National Law Enforcement Officers Memorial, and several others.

This year's events were underscored by the release of a preliminary FBI report that shows 66 law enforcement officers were feloniously killed last year in the line of duty. An additional 52 officers were killed in line-of-duty accidents, according to preliminary statistics compiled by the Bureau's Uniform Crime Reporting Program, which will release a full report, *Law Enforcement Officers Killed and Assaulted, 2016*, in the fall.

During the 29th annual candlelight vigil, held May 13, 2017 on the National Mall in Washington, D.C., the names of officers added to the National Law Enforcement Officers Memorial wall earlier this year were read aloud and formally dedicated. FBI Acting Director Andrew McCabe was among those who paid tribute to the fallen.

Law enforcement officers participate in a wreath-laying ceremony honoring colleagues who died in the line of duty during an event at the National Law Enforcement Officers Memorial on May 15.

Recognition of the deceased FBI agents made this National Police Week especially poignant. Six of the agents' names were etched into the National Law Enforcement Officers Memorial wall—which displays more than 20,000 names of law enforcement officers killed in the line of duty since 1791—and the seventh will be added next year.

"Each special agent understands and accepts that on any given day, fulfilling your duty as an agent might require you to lay down your life," McCabe said during the FBI service. "We know this because we've heard the names and we've learned the stories of the agents who have gone before us…and now we will all know the names and the stories of Special Agents Carr, Craig, Jobe, Roth, Senatore, Wilson, and Yoo."

Recovering Missing Kids

FBI's Role Part of a Coordinated Response

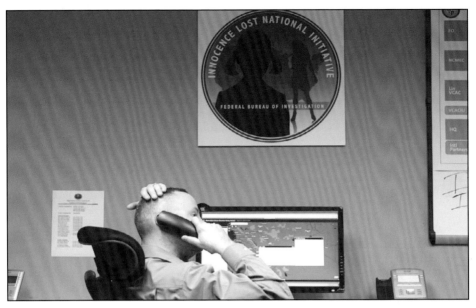

An investigator in the FBI's Violent Crimes Against Children Unit works at a command post in Maryland during a rescue operation last summer.

The disappearance of a Virginia teenager—and her successful rescue, within days, hundreds of miles away—provides a glimpse into the FBI's role when kids go missing and are believed to be in danger.

Police were called when the girl was believed missing, setting in motion an intense process that relies on the resources, expertise, and partnerships of local, state, and federal agencies, including the FBI. Also alerted was the non-profit National Center for Missing & Exploited Children (NCMEC), which last year assisted with more than 20,500 cases of missing children—90 percent of them endangered runaways.

Having determined the girl might be endangered—susceptible to human trafficking, child prostitution, or possibly the victim of abduction—local police referred the case to special agents in the FBI's Washington Field Office (WFO). It was a smooth transition because the agencies work cases together on the region's Child Exploitation and Human Trafficking Task Force.

> "We leverage our 56 field offices across the country—and our 64 legal attachés around the world—to work as a force multiplier."

"We have a robust task force that includes most of the local agencies," said Ray Duncan, assistant special agent in charge of the WFO Criminal Division.

Once reported, the missing girl's description was entered into the FBI's National Crime Information Center (NCIC), an index of criminal justice information available to every law enforcement agency in the country. Last year, there were 465,676 reports of missing kids, according to NCIC, which automatically notifies NCMEC when kids go missing. While not all NCIC reports necessitate federal involvement, the FBI is the lead investigative agency if a missing juvenile is in danger or when children 12 or under disappear.

"Then we will try to step in as soon as possible because we believe those kids are clearly endangered," said Special Agent Rob Bornstein, who supervises WFO's Crimes Against Children squad. "Timing is critical. The earlier we get involved the better."

In the Virginia case, agents and analysts traced the juvenile's

THE FBI STORY

actions from the moment she arrived home from school, dropped off her backpack, and left the house again. Investigators coordinated with local and regional public transit agencies to collect video footage of the girl's movements across the region, and then out of the state. They were able to determine that the girl had been sent a bus ticket, which revealed her destination—more than 1,000 miles away from home. The ticket ultimately led to the identity and location of a subject. Using other sophisticated techniques, the FBI was able to locate the subject that led to the missing child.

WFO investigators, including one of the Bureau's specialized Child Abduction Rapid Deployment Teams, reached out to FBI agents in the field, as well as local authorities, to rescue the girl and make the arrest.

"That's why this worked so well," said Timothy Slater, special agent in charge of the Criminal Division at WFO. "We leverage our 56 field offices across the country—and our 64 legal attachés around the world—to work as a force multiplier. The amount of resources we bring to bear is intrinsic to solving these cases quickly. If we develop information that is outside our area of responsibility, we can contact our agents there to assist."

The number of reports of missing kids last year rose by about 5,000, according to NCIC figures. Investigators said the confluence of kids using cell phones and their easy access to social media has made them more susceptible to predators.

The number of children reported missing has declined significantly since NCMEC was established in

1984 following the 1981 abduction of Adam Walsh, founder John Walsh's 6-year-old son. Robert Lowery, vice president of the Virginia-based agency's Missing Children Division, said reports of brazen abductions have gone down significantly over the years, largely replaced by online predators.

"Offenders are still there and the threat still exists," said Lowery. "Now they're online enticing children."

"There are more and more ways for parents not to know what their children are up to."

"There are bad people out there trying to prey on children," said Bornstein, adding that advances in technology, including encryption, are making it harder to find the bad guys. Parents, meanwhile, just want to keep their kids safe while "there are more and more ways for parents not to know what their children are up to," Bornstein said. This underscores the importance for parents to know who their children are communicating with, what they are posting, and what they are looking at on the Internet.

NCMEC encourages responsible use of social media—rather than fully restricting it, which may have a counter-effect—and honest communication between parents and their kids.

"The key to that is we want parents to not be judgmental with their children if they bring something to their attention," Lowery said. "Sometimes there's a propensity for parents to be judgmental and blame the child for inappropriate conversation when, in fact, these offenders have set the stage for that conversation."

Investigators say resolve and relationships with law enforcement partners play a big role in the Washington Field Office's success rate in recovering missing kids. "We have a lot of priorities in the Criminal Division," said Slater. "But crimes against children are among our highest priorities because these crimes play on the moral fabric of our society."

Many kids, however, remain missing. According to NCMEC, which assists law enforcement and families with missing child cases, about 18,500 of the missing children in 2016 were runaways, who may not want to be found. Posters featuring images and descriptions of missing kids can be found on the FBI website and at missingkids.org, NCMEC's website. If you think you have seen a missing child, contact NCMEC at 1-800-843-5678 or contact your local FBI field office.

National Missing Children's Day

May 25 is National Missing Children's Day, which was established after the May 25, 1979 disappearance of Etan Patz, a 6-year-old New York City boy. His disappearance on the way to school drew national attention to the problem of child abductions. The case remained unsolved for years. His confessed killer, Pedro Hernandez, was found guilty on murder and kidnapping charges earlier this year and sentenced last month to life in prison.

National Missing Children's Day was established by presidential proclamation in 1983 to promote awareness. In 1998, the effort expanded globally when the U.S. and 22 other countries recognized May 25 as International Missing Children's Day.

Report from Chicago

FBI, Chicago Police Department Work to Combat Violent Crime

Tuesday, April 18, 8:15 a.m.: Along the 5100 block of Halsted Street on the South Side of Chicago, a quiet spring morning is interrupted by gunfire. Police respond to a gas station and discover a drive-by double homicide. As they secure the crime scene and work to identify the bodies and recover evidence, distraught family members of the victims begin to arrive, their faces full of anguish and disbelief. They will not be alone in their grief. By the end of the day in a city reeling from violent crime, there will be 13 more shootings and another murder.

Chicago's extreme gun violence—762 homicides last year and more than 4,000 people wounded—has been described as an epidemic. Primarily gang-related, the shootings are often spontaneous and unpredictable, and the toll on victims, families, and entire communities cannot be overstated. That's why the FBI's Chicago Division, working with the Chicago Police Department (CPD) and other agencies, has undertaken significant measures to address the problem.

"The FBI sometimes battles a perception that we are only interested in terrorism or public corruption or large drug-trafficking organizations," said Michael Anderson, special agent in charge of the Chicago Division. "The fact is, we are interested in those things, but in Chicago we are also getting down to the street level to address violent crime, and we are specifically going after the trigger-pullers and shot-callers."

> *"What you are seeing and will continue to see in Chicago is a sustained FBI effort to support and supplement our local partners."*

That street-level focus is in response to a city homicide rate that has "increased exponentially," Anderson said. "The number of shootings is at a level that hasn't been seen here since the early 1990s." As a result, he explained, "what you are seeing and will continue to see in Chicago is a sustained FBI effort to support and supplement our local partners."

That effort involves three major areas:

- The creation in 2016 of a homicide task force—in addition to the FBI's existing violent crimes squad—in which agents work alongside CPD detectives and other law enforcement

officers to assist in solving the city's murder cases;

- Increased intelligence-gathering efforts to identify shooters and "directors of violence," which includes embedding FBI analysts at CPD headquarters; and

- Stepping up community outreach efforts to gain the public's trust and enlist their help in solving crimes and making communities safer.

"Simply put," said CPD Superintendent Eddie Johnson, "the FBI has more resources than we do. We combine the resources we have with the ones they have to fight these crimes."

FBI and CPD personnel working together in the city's most violent neighborhoods "has helped quite a bit," Johnson said. "And we get real-time intelligence from the FBI that we didn't get before. They can look at our crime picture and help us figure out where to best deploy our resources."

Johnson, a Chicago native and 29-year veteran of the police force who spent many years as a patrol officer, believes a key reason for the city's current violence is inadequate gun laws.

"The flow of guns into Chicago is just insane," he said. "You will find that gang members would rather be caught with a gun by law enforcement than caught without one by their rivals. What we have to do through legislation is create a mentality where gang members won't want to pick up a gun," he explained. "You create that by holding them accountable for their actions. We simply don't do a good job of that right now."

Johnson recalled that when he joined CPD in 1988, he and fellow officers responded daily to calls of gang fights in progress. "We rarely hear that call anymore," he said. "What we hear now is a person with a gun or a person shot. They just go straight to a firearm and they resolve their disputes with a weapon."

"Communities are being hijacked by a relatively small percentage of people," Anderson said. "The overwhelming majority of residents are hard-working citizens going to work, going to school, trying to go about their daily lives. These communities are under siege, and they are desperately looking for help."

Of Chicago's 22 police districts, the majority of violent crimes are taking place in a cluster of neighborhoods on the South and West Sides. "A handful of districts—probably five or six—are responsible for the disproportionate number of homicides and shootings," Anderson said.

"We get real-time intelligence from the FBI that we didn't get before. They can look at our crime picture and help us figure out where to best deploy our resources."

FBI and CPD investigators have focused considerable effort on two of the city's most historically violent areas—the 11th District on the West Side and the 7th District on the South Side. "Since we put the task force in place," Johnson said, "we've seen significant drops in gun violence in these two districts. We are making some real positive gains. By no means are we declaring success, but we have seen some really encouraging results."

Driving through the city's most violent neighborhoods—Austin, Englewood, North Lawndale, Auburn Gresham—the streets and parks appear peaceful, and often they are. But when the violence comes, it is sudden and usually without warning. One gang member might have disrespected a rival gang member—increasingly through social media (see sidebar)—and they go looking for each other to settle matters with their guns.

"When I started as a cop," Johnson said, "if you had a gang of 10 guys, maybe two of them at most would be armed. Now if you have a gang of 10 guys, probably nine of them are armed. And we've seen kids as young as 10 and 11 with firearms."

The FBI is working with the Chicago Police Department and others to combat street-level crime while also lending support to communities that are seeking to affect change.

At Chicago Police Department headquarters, personnel in the Crime Prevention and Information Center monitor violent crimes throughout the city using surveillance video and other sophisticated tools. FBI analysts assigned to the center offer additional real-time intelligence that helps police officials deploy resources as efficiently as possible.

In Chicago's most violent neighborhoods, primarily on the South and West Sides, friends and loved ones create street memorials to remember the fallen. Sometimes the victims are gang members killed by rivals, while others are innocent bystanders caught in the crossfire or by a stray bullet.

THE FBI STORY

Special Agent in Charge Michael Anderson describes the FBI's priority in fighting street-level crime: "We're interested in identifying trigger-pullers and shot-callers."

Chicago Police Department Superintendent Eddie Johnson describes how crime and violence has evolved in the city he grew up in: "We've seen kids as young as 10 and 11 with firearms."

Chicago activist Andrew Holmes, who has lost two family members to gun violence, works with the FBI and Chicago Police to strengthen relationships in the communities they serve.

Charles Williams, principal at the Plato Learning Academy, a school on Chicago's West Side, invited the FBI to speak to kids about making good choices.

Investigators agree that gang members are arming themselves at younger ages. "Based on what I've seen over the last year," one FBI agent said, "these guys are carrying around guns as if it's a symbol of their pride or who they are—and the bigger the gun, the better. We are seeing handguns with extended magazines and ammunition drums attached. It's like guns are a part of them, a part of their culture. And they are not afraid to use them."

The FBI is working to reach some of these youngsters before they get involved with gangs—it's one part of the Bureau's larger community outreach effort in the campaign to stop gun violence. At the Plato Learning Academy middle school in the Austin community recently, Special Agent Rob Fortt spoke to sixth-, seventh-, and eighth-graders about the choices they make and the consequences of those choices.

The school's principal, Charles Williams, welcomed the opportunity for the FBI to give students a fresh perspective on law

enforcement and a positive message about making good decisions. Describing the neighborhood's reputation for violence, Williams said he has heard gunshots in the middle of the day from his office, and violent crime is a fact of life. "Our students are surrounded by it, unfortunately. It's just something that permeates the neighborhood."

Gang-related homicides in Chicago are most easily solved when witnesses come forward. But in the city's violent neighborhoods, many who witness shootings or have information don't cooperate with law enforcement, either because they distrust the police or they want to engage in "frontier justice" and seek their own retaliation, the FBI's Anderson said. "So we are putting a lot of resources into community outreach. We are really focusing on going out in the community and building trust. If folks trust law enforcement, they are more likely to report crimes."

"We have to acknowledge that we have a fractured relationship

with the community," the CPD superintendent said. "But we're working hard to rebuild that, and the FBI is helping us do that." Johnson added, "I haven't been to a community meeting yet where people have said they want less police. What they want is the police to be fair, respectful, and to get the bad guys out of their communities. That's what they want. And you start that by having a constant dialogue with them, which we are doing."

Community activist Andrew Holmes represents another important part of law enforcement's outreach efforts. Holmes, who has experienced the tragedy of gun violence firsthand, has been working with the FBI since 2013 on issues involving gun crimes and the human trafficking of children. He is known to law enforcement and residents of violent neighborhoods as a rapid responder when a homicide occurs. He arrives on the streets at all hours of the day

Community activist Andrew Holmes has been working with the FBI since 2013 on issues involving gun violence. He regularly visits high-crime neighborhoods to urge residents to cooperate with law enforcement. In the Auburn Gresham community recently, he spoke to Betty Swanson, block captain of her neighborhood watch group.

and night to counsel and comfort the families of victims. And he encourages witnesses to come forward.

The work is meaningful to Holmes because his daughter was killed in Indiana when she was innocently caught in the crossfire of a gang shooting. And he recently lost an 11-year-old cousin in Chicago who was killed by a stray bullet meant for a gang member. Holmes also visits high-crime neighborhoods, going street to street to hand out pamphlets urging residents to report gun crimes. In the troubled Auburn Gresham community recently, he spoke to Betty Swanson, block captain of her neighborhood watch group.

On the porch of her tree-lined street, Swanson told Holmes that one of her grandsons had been murdered a few months ago. "He was going to visit his mom … after he got off work. Somebody walked up to the car and shot him. He was 28 years old."

Although her street is largely violence-free now because so many

of the residents are senior citizens, Swanson said her block group works hard to keep the area safe, and—like Holmes advocates—that means speaking up when necessary.

"One thing we try to do is to let witnesses know that it's okay to talk," Holmes said. "We ask people to engage with law enforcement. You've got to work with law enforcement. I don't care who it is—FBI, state police, U.S. Marshals, Chicago Police—you have to." Otherwise, the help

needed to save a loved one might come too late. "You've got to reach over and get that phone, call the FBI," he said. "Show these criminals—not this block, it's not happening."

Scan this QR code with your smartphone to access related information, or visit www.fbi.gov/reportfromchicago.

Murder and Social Media

For those unfamiliar with Chicago's rampant gun violence, it would be easy to think that shootings happen because of traditional turf battles—one gang trying to muscle in on a rival's street-corner drug business. But that reality occurred in a time before social media. The new reality is increasingly virtual, and social media is playing a prominent role in the murder rate.

Violence can indeed result from "gang-on-gang and some narcotics territory disputes," said Chicago Police Department Superintendent Eddie Johnson, "but a lot of our gun violence now is precipitated by social media."

One gang member disrespects a rival on social media, and the rival responds in kind. The virtual argument escalates, and the gang members look to settle things with weapons. Using their electronic devices, gang members can often pinpoint their rivals' location.

"Gun in one hand, smartphone in the other," said Special Agent in Charge of the FBI's Chicago Division Michael Anderson. Too often, that makes for a deadly mix. And in many cases, the time between the online dispute and actual shots being fired, Anderson said, "is very short."

Stopping Skimmers
Protect Yourself at the ATM

As Americans hit the road for summer vacation season, many will visit an ATM expecting quick and easy access to their cash. Yet that convenience makes ATMs an easy, year-round target for fraudsters looking to steal your money.

Romanian citizen Ilie Sitariu, 37, and a co-conspirator who has since fled the United States did just that in 2015. From August through October, the Romanians traveled along the I-87 corridor in the Albany, New York, area, going from bank to bank and secretly installing skimming equipment on ATMs—often at night, when their nefarious activities could go unnoticed.

Skimming typically requires two devices to be installed on an ATM or other card reader: one piece skims, or captures, data from a card's magnetic stripe, while an accompanying pinhole camera captures cardholders' PINs as they're entered. While Sitariu's devices were considered relatively primitive—two simple pieces of metal with a skimmer hidden in one and a camera hidden in the other—they were sophisticated enough to do damage. (Some skimming devices incorporate Bluetooth technology, so criminals can access the information remotely without having to return to the ATMs and remove the devices.)

The men left the skimming equipment in place at each machine for about a day before returning to collect it—along with the account numbers and PINs of those who had used the ATMs during that time. They then loaded that information onto another card and used it to pull cash out of the victims' accounts. The money was then loaded onto gift cards to help cover their tracks.

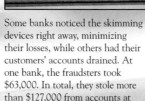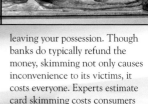

Exterior and interior shots of a strip of metal containing a pinhole camera that was installed on an ATM in the Albany, New York, area.

Some banks noticed the skimming devices right away, minimizing their losses, while others had their customers' accounts drained. At one bank, the fraudsters took $63,000. In total, they stole more than $127,000 from accounts at three banks.

Despite wearing hats and sunglasses while installing the skimmers, security footage from the various ATMs—taken during a relatively short time period at locations in close proximity to each other—helped officials identify the thieves. In these types of cases, data sharing between local law enforcement is critical to catching up to the criminals, as is alerting local banks before they are victimized.

"At the end of the day, greed gets to these people," said Special Agent Paul Scuzzarella, one of the agents who worked the case from the FBI's Albany Division. "They do too much at one time and eventually get caught."

Sitariu, who lived in New York City, is now behind bars thanks to the collaborative work of the FBI, U.S. Secret Service, and law enforcement partners in New York. He pleaded guilty to bank fraud, access device fraud, and aggravated identity theft and was recently sentenced to four years in federal prison.

For skimming victims who find their money mysteriously missing, it's like having your wallet stolen without it ever

leaving your possession. Though banks do typically refund the money, skimming not only causes inconvenience to its victims, it costs everyone. Experts estimate card skimming costs consumers more than $1 billion annually.

Additionally, many ATM skimming cases are linked to Eurasian crime groups, and the stolen funds can wind up overseas as a funding source for international criminal activity, Scuzzarella said.

While law enforcement is constantly working to catch skimmers, the public should take basic precautions to protect against skimming at ATMs, gas stations, and other vulnerable card reader locations.

"You really should be cognizant of where you're using one," Scuzzarella said of ATMs. "If it's in a hidden area in a building, like in a gas station around the corner, who knows who's back there. If it's in the main area, it's less likely someone has tampered with that."

Also, if you notice anything unusual on an ATM, don't use it, Scuzzarella warned. He also noted that covering the ATM keypad could have helped thwart the skimmers in this case.

"I find myself checking more and more," Scuzzarella said of his own ATM use. "When I log in, I notice if something looks different, if it seems as if there's something that's attached. Sometimes it's not very noticeable."

Training Our Partners

National Academy Graduates 50,000th Student

The FBI's National Academy—a 10-week professional course of study designed for law enforcement leaders in the U.S. and around the world—conferred a diploma this week upon its 50,000th graduate.

The academy, located in Quantico, Virginia, where the Bureau also trains its new agents, opened in 1935 and graduated its 268th session on June 7. Among the 228 graduates—which included students from 47 states, 24 countries, seven federal agencies, and every branch of the military— was a University of Alabama at Birmingham Police Department captain accepting the academy's 50,000th diploma.

"Surreal is the best way to describe it," said Capt. Amy Schreiner, who learned only moments before receiving her certificate that she was the milestone graduate. "This just starts the next chapter of my career," she said. "And I want to take the lessons that I've learned here—and the relationships that I've made here—and extend those to further my career."

The 10-week program is grounded in fully accredited academics, with leading-edge practical coursework in a broad array of subjects: intelligence theory, terrorist mindsets, management science, law, behavioral science, forensic science, and the media, to name a few. The students earned more than 3,800 combined credit hours since arriving at Quantico in early April. Students are also tested physically with frequent and taxing workouts, a refreshing change for many of the mid-career officers who have ascended the ranks in their departments and are no longer on a beat. The most valued thing students take from the academy, however, is the

round-the-clock time spent with more than 200 colleagues with varied backgrounds, languages, and personalities but a common goal.

"Building partnerships and networks is what the National Academy does best," said Joshua Skule, executive assistant director of the FBI's Intelligence Branch, during the commencement address. Skule talked candidly about the Bureau's priorities and the difficult work of combating terrorists and spies. The National Academy, he said, is integral to building an international bulwark against common threats.

"If we are to succeed in stopping their networks, we need to strengthen our networks," Skule said.

John Russo, chief of the Rutherford Police Department in New Jersey, spoke on behalf of his class of graduates during the commencement. "This is the highest honor of my career," he said. "And it's been my privilege to work alongside each member of this session."

Like his classmates, Russo plans to take the best practices he learned over the past 10 weeks and apply them in his own department, which benefits not only his community at home but the FBI as well, since the Bureau's biggest asset is local partners.

The inclusion of international students dates back to the academy's beginnings but expanded in earnest in the early 1960s, when President Kennedy signed National Security Action Memorandum No. 177 to enhance the training of overseas officers in the United States. To date, students from 171 countries have gone through the National Academy, and today, at

Capt. Amy C. Schreiner, (right) of the University of Alabama at Birmingham Police Department, is the 50,000th graduate of the FBI National Academy.

Scan this QR code with your smartphone to access related information, or visit www.fbi.gov/na50000.

least 10 percent of each class is made up of international students. Recent graduates hailed from every corner of the globe, including Finland, Japan, Liberia, New Zealand, Thailand, and Albania.

"The men and women graduating here today are the result of the continuous commitment to get better at what we do, working side by side while building friendships," said David Resch, assistant director of the Bureau's Training Division, which oversees the National Academy.

Capt. Schreiner echoed those comments after the ceremony and a succession of high-fives and fist bumps with classmates filing out of the Quantico auditorium to meet family members—some they had not seen in months. The captain posed for pictures alongside the president of the National Academy Associates as they held a large yellow brick commemorating the 50,000 milestone and the academy's culminating physical achievement, a storied and grueling 10-kilometer obstacle course called the Yellow Brick Road.

"The connections I've made here will be lifelong," Schreiner said. "It's a very exciting day but it's also bittersweet because I hate to leave them all. But I know we'll see each other again."

Hate Crime

Historic Sentencing for Gang Member Who Killed Transgender Woman

Investigators at the Mississippi property of Joshua Vallum's father in 2015. Vallum killed Mercedes Williamson, a 17-year-old transgender girl, and was prosecuted under a federal hate crimes law.

A federal prosecution under a 2009 hate crime law resulted in a lengthy prison sentence last month for a Mississippi gang member who killed a 17-year-old transgender woman—and set an important precedent that could benefit other transgender victims.

A judge sentenced Joshua Vallum to 49 years in federal prison under the Matthew Shepard and James Byrd, Jr. Hate Crimes Prevention Act of 2009. The prison term is in addition to the life sentence he received in Mississippi for killing 17-year-old Mercedes Williamson in 2015. Vallum admitted that he killed Williamson because she was transgender.

The Shepard-Byrd Act gives the FBI authority to investigate violent hate crimes, including violence directed at the gay, lesbian, bisexual, and transgender community, and enables the

prosecution of such crimes at the federal level. The act has been successfully applied to other hate crimes, but this is the first time it has been used for a transgender victim.

> "The entire story about why Vallum killed Williamson wasn't public until we charged him at the federal level. And now there is a precedent for future cases."

The FBI's Safe Streets Task Force in Pascagoula, Mississippi (part of the FBI's Jackson Division), investigated the murder because it was initially believed to be gang related: Vallum was a local "enforcer" and a national secretary of the Almighty Latin Kings and Queens Nation gang.

"It was a horrible murder," said FBI Special Agent Jerome Lorrain, who coordinates task force members from local, state, and federal law enforcement agencies. Investigators quickly determined that then-27-year-old Vallum likely killed Williamson because she was transgender. The two met through social media in 2014 and had a sexual relationship for several months. According to the gang, that made Vallum a homosexual, a violation of gang rules that meant he could be killed on sight.

Vallum stopped seeing Williamson, but another gang member confronted him, Lorrain said. At that point, Vallum had two options: he could flee or save face with the gang by killing Williamson.

"Vallum told the other guy he would 'handle the business,'" Lorrain said.

On May 30, 2015, Vallum drove to Alabama to find Williamson and convinced her to get in his car. They drove to his father's house in Lucedale, Mississippi, and he brutally attacked her, stabbing her with a knife and beating her with a hammer. His family called local police after Vallum entered the house covered in blood. Responding officers found Williamson's body in the woods and later contacted the FBI.

Vallum told gang members about the killing the next day. He lied and said he didn't know Williamson was a male until they became intimate, and then he snapped and killed her in a fit of rage.

Vallum later told Task Force Officer Jonathan Carroll the same story in an interview, shortly after he surrendered to law enforcement. Carroll is an officer with the Ocean Springs Police Department in Mississippi and is assigned full time to the FBI Safe Streets Task Force.

In the midst of the investigation, Lorrain's supervisor attended a conference on identifying hate crimes and victims' rights. Two civil rights attorneys from the Department of Justice presented an overview of the Shepard-Byrd Act. Supervisory Senior Resident Agent Rachel Byrd (no relation to James Byrd, Jr.) recognized the possibility for federal prosecution and approached the attorneys.

"The DOJ attorneys were very enthusiastic about prosecuting this horrific murder under the Shepard-Byrd Act," Byrd said.

Vallum found himself facing state murder charges and the federal hate crime charge. In light of overwhelming evidence, he pleaded guilty in state court in 2016, and was sentenced to life in prison. He later pleaded guilty to the hate crime.

Even though he received a life sentence in Mississippi, the federal plea and sentencing are important, Lorrain said. "The entire story about why Vallum killed Williamson wasn't public until we charged him at the federal level. And now there is a precedent for future cases. There have been reports of a number of crimes against transgender people."

Because some states—including Mississippi—do not have hate crime statutes that protect people from bias based on gender identity, the successful federal prosecution of Vallum could help other transgender victims gets justice. The federal sentence also ensures that Vallum will serve at least 49 years in federal prison, regardless of any early release he may be granted on his state sentence.

Joshua Vallum picked up Mercedes Williamson in this car at her home in Alabama, then drove the transgender woman to Mississippi. He attacked her in the car after parking at his father's property, then chased her into the woods and killed her. Investigators found traces of blood in the car.

New Information in Fugitive Case

Donald Eugene Webb Murdered Pennsylvania Police Chief

The FBI has released newly acquired photographs of longtime fugitive Donald Eugene Webb—wanted for the 1980 murder of a Pennsylvania police chief—in the hopes of enlisting the public's assistance in capturing the career criminal who has been on the run for nearly four decades.

Webb, wanted for killing Police Chief Gregory Adams of Saxonburg, Pennsylvania, during a routine traffic stop, would now be 85 years old. A $100,000 reward is being offered for information leading to the fugitive's whereabouts—or the location of his remains.

"These photographs present Donald Webb in a completely new way," said Special Agent Thomas MacDonald, who is investigating the case from the FBI's Boston Division. "The face of this investigation for decades was grainy black and white photos," he said. The new color photographs, taken a year prior to the murder, show Webb from multiple angles in much greater detail. "If he has been living under an alias all these years," MacDonald said, "these photographs might generate the tip that helps us resolve the case."

One of the longest tenured fugitives to appear on the FBI's Ten Most Wanted Fugitives list, Webb was a career criminal who specialized in jewel theft and operated in the Providence, Rhode Island, and Southeastern Massachusetts areas. It is believed he was in Pennsylvania planning a robbery at the time of the murder.

The white Mercury Cougar getaway vehicle Webb was driving at the time of the murder was located several weeks later in Rhode Island, and blood evidence linked to Webb was recovered from the vehicle, leading investigators to believe that he was wounded during the confrontation.

Shown are some of the newly released images of Donald Eugene Webb, taken in the late 1970s.

"There have been few leads on the Webb case for a long time," MacDonald said. But the FBI's Boston Division started an active cold case investigation in 2015. As part of that investigation, the new photos were obtained. "We've been doing a lot of interviews and knocking on a lot of doors," MacDonald explained.

At the time of the murder, Webb lived in New Bedford, Massachusetts, with his wife and stepson. He was known to associate with members of the Patriarca crime family in Rhode Island and with criminals in southern Florida. He was also known to frequent motels in eastern Pennsylvania under the name Stanley Portas. Portas was the deceased husband of Webb's wife.

MacDonald emphasized that the $100,000 reward could be paid

to someone who helps locate Webb's remains if he is deceased. "We want to know one way or the other," he said. "There may be someone out there who had knowledge of his death and is now willing to come forward." It is also possible that Webb is still alive, living under an alias, and that individuals will recognize him from the newly published photographs.

"It might be that someone out there doesn't know that the person they got to know in the 1990s and early 2000s was Donald Webb, and that could help us resolve this case," MacDonald said.

During the investigation, MacDonald has talked to numerous retired agents and police detectives who have worked on the Webb case over the years, and he traveled to Saxonburg and met with police officers there.

"The case still haunts these people," he said, noting that Adams was 31 years old at the time of his death and left behind a wife and two young children. "Resolving this case would be a great victory for law enforcement and for the family."

Note: The remains of long-time fugitive Donald Eugene Webb have been recovered. The Office of the Chief Medical Examiner in Massachusetts positively identified the remains that were recovered by the Massachusetts State Police Crime Scene Services Section, with the assistance of the FBI and Pennsylvania State Police, on July 13, 2017.

Multi-Million-Dollar Financial Fraud

Ponzi Scheme Ends in Prison Time for Former Pro Football Player and Bank Executive

The financial pitch was compelling—help fund short-term loans to professional athletes and get a high interest rate return on your investment, perhaps as high as 18 percent. Equally as compelling were the pitchmen: businessman Will Allen was a former pro football standout who played for the New York Giants and Miami Dolphins; his business partner, Susan Daub, was a former bank executive.

Allen and Daub's Massachusetts company, Capital Financial Partners (CFP), operated out of Florida and took in more than $35 million in approximately three years. But in return for their money, many investors got back headaches, because Allen and Daub were running a Ponzi scheme.

"The company made some legitimate loans," said Special Agent Sheila Magoon, a financial fraud expert who investigated the case out of the FBI's Boston Division, "but relatively early on, they began to defraud investors. Allen and Daub surely knew what they were doing was criminal."

While it might seem surprising that highly paid professional athletes need loans, there are circumstances where that is indeed the case. An athlete just out of college, for example, can sign a lucrative professional contract but might not be paid until he starts playing. A short-term loan would bridge the gap until he gets a regular paycheck.

"Let's say Athlete A wanted a loan of $1 million," Magoon explained. "CFP went looking for specific investors to loan money to Athlete A. That gave investors even more enthusiasm, knowing they were helping a particular player."

Former NFL player Will Allen and former bank executive Susan Daub's company website, parts of which are shown, appeared legitimate and hid from investors the fact that it was being used to run a Ponzi scheme.

Although there was no standard loan amount, Magoon said, investors typically put up at least $100,000. Between 2012 and April 2015, Allen, 38, and Daub, 56, defrauded dozens of investors and diverted some of the funds for their personal use.

> "Relatively early on, they began to defraud investors. Allen and Daub surely knew what they were doing was criminal."

Sometimes the pair collected investor money to fund nonexistent loans and used the money to pay themselves and invest in other unrelated businesses. Other times, they told investors that the athlete loans were larger than they actually were, allowing Allen and Daub to collect more money than they were lending.

To keep investors from discovering the fraud, the pair also used newly invested money to make payments to existing investors.

"We researched what they claimed their business was—what they said they were doing and what they were actually doing," Magoon said.

Working with the Internal Revenue Service Criminal Investigation Division, the investigators conducted interviews and analyzed financial and other records. At the same time, the Securities and Exchange Commission (SEC) was conducting a civil investigation.

In June 2015, Allen and Daub were arrested on criminal charges after being sued by the SEC. In November 2016, each pleaded guilty to wire fraud, conspiracy, and money laundering. Of the more than $35 million Allen and Daub received in investments, less than $22 million has been repaid to date.

This past March, a federal judge in Boston sentenced Allen and Daub to six years in prison and three years of supervised release; they were also ordered to pay restitution of approximately $16.8 million. The judge called Allen and Daub's crimes an "outrageous, extensive fraud."

2016 Internet Crime Report
IC3 Releases Annual Report Highlighting Trends in Internet Crime

Giving someone access to your computer is like giving out a key to your front door. A computer can have your bank account information, family photos, and other private documents and data—information that fraudsters would like to steal. That's why tech support fraud has become a significant trend in online crime, according to the *2016 Internet Crime Report* from the FBI's Internet Crime Complaint Center (IC3).

In tech support fraud cases, criminals convince unsuspecting victims to provide remote access to their computer by calling and posing as tech support personnel from a legitimate company. The criminal can then simply charge your credit card for a fake anti-virus product, or, in more sinister situations, they can steal your personal information or install malware. More than 10,000 incidents of tech support fraud were reported to the IC3 in 2016, with victims losing nearly $8 million. Though anyone can be a victim, older computer users are the most vulnerable targets.

"They'll trick you into letting them into your computer," said IC3 Unit Chief Donna Gregory. "You open the door and allow them in. You may think you're just watching them install a program to get rid of a virus, but they are really doing a lot of damage behind the scenes."

In addition to tech support fraud, the other major fraud categories last year were business e-mail compromise, ransomware, and extortion.

The IC3 receives complaints on a variety of Internet scams and crimes, and it has received more than 3.7 million complaints since it was created in 2000. In 2016, the IC3 received a total of 298,728 complaints with reported losses in excess of $1.3 billion. The IC3 uses the information from public complaints to refer cases to the appropriate law enforcement agencies and identify trends. The IC3's extensive database is also available to law enforcement. Internet users should report any Internet fraud to IC3, no matter the dollar amount. Additional data helps the FBI and law enforcement gain a more accurate picture of Internet crime.

The IC3 publishes the *Internet Crime Report* annually to increase public awareness of current trends in Internet crime. For this report, the IC3 has also created a separate state-by-state breakdown that allows users to select their state from a dropdown menu so they can review local trends in Internet crime. The top states for reported dollar amounts lost to Internet fraud in 2016 were California ($255 million), New York ($106 million), and Florida ($89 million).

Though Internet crime is a serious threat, there are ways to help keep yourself safe online. The IC3 recommends computer users update their anti-virus software and operating system. Additionally, the Internet is an especially important place to remember the old adage: If it sounds too good to be true, it probably is.

"Be aware of what you are clicking on and also what you're posting on social media. Always lock down your social media accounts as much as possible," Gregory said. "Try to use two factor authentication, and use safe passwords or things more difficult to guess. The tougher the password, the harder it is for someone to crack."

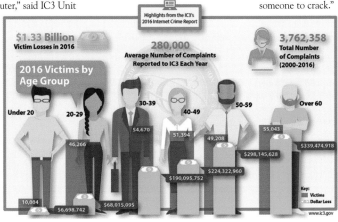

High-Tech Theft
Gang Stole Jeeps to Sell Across the Border

Jeep Theft Locations

Pinpoints represent some of the locations in and around San Diego County where the Tijuana-based Hooligans motorcycle gang allegedly stole Jeeps to sell across the border in Mexico.

- Chula Vista
- Escondido
- Golden Hill
- Grantville
- Hillcrest
- La Mesa
- Lake Murray
- Mira Mesa
- Mission Valley
- North Park
- Ocean Beach
- Ocean View Hills
- Otay Mesa West
- Pacific Beach
- Point Loma
- Scripps Ranch
- SDSU
- Serra Mesa
- Spring Valley
- University Heights
- Vista

Nine members of a Tijuana-based motorcycle gang are facing criminal charges for their roles in a brazen high-tech scheme to steal more than 150 Jeep Wranglers and motorcycles in the San Diego, California, area to sell across the border in Mexico.

According to the charges announced on May 30, members of the Hooligans motorcycle gang canvassed San Diego County looking for specific Jeeps based on the model type and accessories. The gang—a transnational criminal organization with members in the U.S. and Tijuana—was responsible for about $4.5 million in vehicle thefts dating back to 2014.

"The joy ride is over for these Hooligans," Deputy U.S. Attorney Mark Conover said in a statement following the arrests of two of the alleged gang members. Three of the nine suspects are in custody; the rest are fugitives believed to be in Mexico.

Court documents in the case read like a Hollywood script: Gang leaders selected the cars to steal, then "scouts" scoured the streets to find the desired cars and retrieve the vehicle identification numbers. With that information in hand, the leaders would get replacement keys cut. When the thieves returned at night to steal the vehicles, they arrived in groups—often two would work on the car while another stood lookout in a getaway car. One would open the hood to disable the horn and flashing lights while the other opened the driver's door with the new key. He then plugged a handheld device into the car's diagnostic port to program the replacement key's microchip to turn off the alarm and operate the car. With the car now under the thief's control, he quietly drove it away, followed by his accomplices, bound for Tijuana.

It wasn't until September 26, 2014 that the Regional Auto Theft Task Force, which includes 14 law enforcement agencies and the FBI, caught a break when the theft of a Jeep Wrangler was captured on home security video in Rancho Bernardo. The grainy early morning footage shows three men stealing the vehicle by disabling the alarm and using a key and a handheld device to turn on the engine. The driveway theft took less than two minutes. Further investigation revealed a car dealership in Mexico provided the proprietary information for "replacement" keys in nearly 20 of the Jeep thefts.

"The FBI, along with our law enforcement partners, will continue to work day and night to stop these large-scale international crime rings," said Eric Birnbaum, special agent in charge of the FBI's San Diego Field Office.

In addition to laying out details of the case, court records reveal the bravado among the thieves, who coordinated their schemes and bragged on social media. In one exchange in 2015, according to court documents, one subject commented to a co-conspirator on Facebook about his prolific thefts in the U.S.

"You've already cleaned those poor people up," the subject wrote.

"They don't leave me anything outside anymore. Only garage. I have to go around jumping fences and walls," the co-conspirator responded.

"Hahaha, even with that they can't stop us," the first subject wrote back.

Seven of the suspects charged on May 30 are from Tijuana; the other two are from San Diego and Imperial Beach, California. They range in age from 20 to 33. They are all charged with conspiracy to commit transportation of stolen vehicles in foreign commerce and face up to five years in prison if convicted.

The Case of the 'Kung Fu Panda' Fraud

Massachusetts Man Made Bogus Claim Film Was His Idea

Drawing from 1996 Disney Coloring Book   Jayme Gordon's Drawing

A Massachusetts man is behind bars after his scheme to defraud the makers of the animated film *Kung Fu Panda* backfired.

Jayme Gordon claimed that DreamWorks Animation SKG, Inc. stole his idea for the characters and story behind the popular 2008 film, and in 2011, the Boston-area resident filed a civil suit against the studio seeking more than $12 million in damages.

"He said DreamWorks used his ideas, and he claimed to have evidence," said Special Agent Scott McGaunn, who investigated the case from the FBI's Boston Division, "but it was all lies."

Protecting its intellectual property was a serious matter for DreamWorks, and the company spent $3 million defending itself against the charges in a case that dragged on with motions, e-mails, and depositions for more than two years.

Gordon produced drawings that appeared to validate his claims, and his attorneys were convinced he had a strong case. "We later showed that those drawings had been falsified and backdated as part of Gordon's elaborate ruse," McGaunn said.

Investigators learned that months before the release of *Kung Fu Panda*, Gordon saw a trailer for the movie. He had previously created drawings and a story about pandas—which he called "Panda Power"—that bore little resemblance to the movie characters. He proceeded to revise his "Panda Power" drawings and story, and renamed it "Kung Fu Panda Power."

Gordon later filed the copyright infringement suit against DreamWorks, and during the course of that lengthy civil litigation, he perjured himself and provided falsified documents to the court. "He was using the legal system to try and extort over $12 million from DreamWorks," McGaunn said.

Ultimately, in addition to fabricating and backdating sketches that supported his suit, it was discovered that Gordon intentionally deleted relevant evidence on his computer that he was required to produce, and he lied during court-ordered depositions.

The truth came to light when DreamWorks learned that Gordon had traced some of his panda drawings from a Disney *The Lion King* coloring book. Those sketches, which he claimed to have drawn in 1992 and 1993, were copied from the coloring book, which was not published until 1996.

"The coloring book discovery was the smoking gun in the civil case," McGaunn said. Gordon dropped his copyright infringement lawsuit, but he was by no means done with the legal system—he was now the subject of a criminal case for the crimes he had committed. Gordon was ultimately charged with perjury and wire fraud.

At his criminal trial in 2016, Gordon maintained he had not traced his drawings from the coloring book. Instead, he claimed, Disney—like DreamWorks—had copied his drawings and based characters in *The Lion King* on his work. He also claimed that DreamWorks and Disney had copied other characters from his work.

"The jury didn't buy it for a second," McGaunn said.

Gordon was found guilty on numerous counts of perjury and wire fraud. In May 2017, the 51-year-old was sentenced to two years in prison and ordered to pay more than $3 million in restitution.

"It's possible that when Gordon first saw the movie he had believed that DreamWorks stole something from him—that he came up with the original idea for a kung fu fighting panda," McGaunn said. "But even if he did initially believe that, his actions afterward were criminal: He copied and backdated others' drawings, destroyed computer evidence he was ordered to turn over, and lied under oath—all to further his civil suit."

In the end, McGaunn said, "Gordon was using the civil court system to extort DreamWorks in the hopes that they would quickly settle. He was counting on that, but he was sadly mistaken."

Phishing for Photos

Man Tricked Women Into Giving Him Passwords to Access Private Information

Many hackers use the Internet to swindle money or to get revenge on their adversaries. But an Alabama man's online crime was stealing women's personal photos simply for the thrill of invading their privacy.

In e-mails to prospective victims, Kevin Maldonado, 35, purported to be an administrator for their e-mail provider and requested that they change their passwords. He then captured those passwords and accessed their private information—a computer intrusion technique known as phishing.

More than 50 women fell for the scheme. And once Maldonado had their passwords, he could unlock his victims' online lives, including pictures on their cell phones that were backed up to the cloud.

"Getting into these people's personal lives in a deviant manner excited him," said Special Agent Emily Celeste, who investigated the case out of the FBI's Birmingham Division. Maldonado stole and downloaded thousands of photos from unsuspecting women for more than a year, and they never knew it until the FBI notified them.

The case came to the FBI's attention when some of the recipients of Maldonado's e-mail who were suspicious of the message notified their provider, who, in turn, alerted the Bureau. Working collaboratively with the company, the FBI was able to trace the e-mails back to Maldonado's computer in Birmingham, Alabama.

While some of the photos Maldonado stole were explicit, others were simply everyday pictures of children, pets, and family get-togethers. Unlike some similar cases where stolen information is released to

embarrass victims, Maldonado kept the photos on his own computer for his own use.

"You have pictures of your kids all over your phone, family moments, and he harvested them for himself," Celeste said. "It was just disgusting."

> *"Once somebody obtains your password or can answer your security questions, they've opened up your entire world."*

Given Maldonado's random approach to finding his victims, there was minimal connection among them, although many were models or in the fitness industry. Some had been romantically involved with Maldonado, some he had found online, and others lived in his community. After Maldonado accessed one woman's e-mail, he would then use her contacts list to identify future victims.

Maldonado pleaded guilty in federal court in Birmingham, Alabama in February 2017 to computer intrusion, and a judge later sentenced him to six months

in prison and three years of supervised release.

The case is noteworthy because of the perpetrator's motives and the randomness of the targets, but overall, phishing is a common crime. According to the FBI's Internet Crime Complaint Center (IC3) *2016 Internet Crime Report*, there were more than 19,000 victims of phishing and related scams last year.

"Number one is not to ever respond to any type of e-mail request with your username and password," Celeste said. "Also, definitely be careful what you put out online, especially when it ties back to your security questions. Once somebody obtains your password or can answer your security questions, they've opened up your entire world."

Celeste advises using a diverse array of passwords to protect yourself, so if one password is compromised, a thief cannot easily access other accounts.

"Connecting all of those accounts, like most people do, he was able to have control over their lives, and they didn't know it," Celeste said

Dialing for Cash

Pakistani Man Sentenced for Laundering Millions in Telecom Hacking Scheme

A massive international hacking and telecommunications fraud scheme served as a backdrop for an FBI investigation that led to the capture of a Pakistani citizen who played a major role in scamming U.S. companies out of millions of dollars in fees.

From November 2008 to December 2012, Muhammad Sohail Qasmani laundered more than $19.6 million in proceeds from a conspiracy that transformed the telephone networks of American corporations into literal cash cows.

Allegedly led by another Pakistani national, Noor Aziz Uddin—who is currently a fugitive wanted by the FBI—the fraud scheme involved an international group of highly skilled hackers who focused on penetrating telephone networks of businesses and organizations in the United States. Once the hackers gained access to the computer-operated telephone networks, commonly known as PBX systems, they reprogrammed unused extensions to make unlimited long distance calls.

Before a hired group of dialers could freely use the exploited lines, Aziz set up a handful of pay-per-minute premium telephone numbers to generate revenue. While the numbers appeared to be chat, adult entertainment, and psychic hotlines, no actual services were provided. Instead,

the hacked extensions of the U.S. companies dialed into dead air or fake password prompts and voice-mail messages. The longer the lines stayed connected with the fraudulent premium numbers, the higher the bill would be for the unsuspecting businesses. Once paid, the resulting income for Aziz's fake premium lines ended up in the pockets of the criminal enterprise.

Having previous experience running a money laundering and smuggling business in Thailand, Qasmani was a prime candidate for managing the hundreds of transactions necessary to keep the fraud scheme going over the long term.

"Qasmani was a lifelong fraudster with a history of running telephone schemes since the late 1990s. It's how he made his name," said Special Agent Nathan Cocklin, who investigated the case from the FBI's Newark Field Office. "His collective background made him a go-to money mover for Aziz."

In 2008, Aziz recruited Qasmani to oversee the millions of dollars generated from the highly organized operation. Throughout the scam, Qasmani opened numerous bank accounts to avoid detection and shuffled the illicit earnings to more than 650 transferees spanning 10 different countries.

For four years, Qasmani continued to pay the hackers and dialers for their work while retaining portions of the proceeds for Aziz and himself. He kept laundering money even after Aziz was arrested in connection with the scheme and later released by foreign authorities.

A major telecommunications provider discovered the fraudulent activity and reported it to the FBI. The ensuing investigation into the conspiracy hit a major turning point when the Bureau received information that Qasmani would be visiting the United States from Bangkok. Agents arrested him shortly after he arrived at Los Angeles International Airport on December 22, 2014.

Qasmani was sentenced on June 28, 2017 after being found guilty of conspiracy to commit wire fraud. He is now serving a 48-month prison term for his involvement in the scheme.

"Telecommunications fraud not only has a severe impact on victim companies but the industry as a whole," said Cocklin. "While the FBI continues to track down the criminals responsible for this type of crime, businesses can be more proactive by safeguarding their systems and filing complaints with the FBI's Internet Crime Complaint Center at www.ic3.gov."

Health Care Fraud Takedown

Nationwide Sweep Targets Enablers of Opioid Epidemic

Federal officials today announced charges against more than 400 individuals—including doctors, nurses, and licensed medical professionals—for their roles in fraud schemes involving about $1.3 billion in false Medicare billings.

The coordinated nationwide sweep by more than 1,000 law enforcement personnel—operating as part of the Medicare Fraud Strike Force—is the largest action to date. Of the 412 individuals charged, one in four cases involved opioid-related crimes, underscoring the scope of what federal officials are calling a drug-abuse epidemic that is killing approximately 91 Americans every day.

"It's obvious to anyone who picks up a newspaper or turns on the news that the nation is in the midst of a crisis," FBI Acting Director Andrew McCabe said at a July 13 press conference at the U.S. Department of Justice, where he joined Attorney General Jeff Sessions and the heads of the Department of Health and Human Services (HHS) and the Drug Enforcement Agency (DEA) in announcing the charges. "Opioid abuse destroys lives and it devastates families. This week, we arrested once-trusted doctors, pharmacists, and other medical professionals who were corrupted by greed. These people inflicted a special kind of damage."

Additionally, HHS began suspending 295 providers—including doctors, nurses, and pharmacists—so they can no longer participate in federal health programs like Medicare, Medicaid, and TRICARE, a health insurance program for veterans and the military.

The takedown targeted schemes

FBI Acting Director Andrew McCabe speaks at a July 13, 2017 press conference at the Department of Justice announcing results of a Medicare Fraud Strike Force enforcement action as HHS Secretary Tom Price (left) and Attorney General Jeff Sessions look on.

that billed the federal programs for medically unnecessary prescription drugs. It also focused on medical professionals who unlawfully distributed opioids and other prescription narcotics, thereby contributing to the opioid epidemic.

The charges—which span 41 federal districts—are the culmination of deep dives into the submissions and payment data at the federal health insurance programs, which can reveal trends and anomalies that investigators at the HHS Office of Inspector General (OIG) can then probe and send to federal, state, and local law enforcement partners to further investigate. In addition to more than 300 OIG agents, this year's Medicare Fraud Strike Force action included 350 FBI personnel from 28 field offices. The FBI's Health Care Fraud Unit started a Prescription Drug Initiative specifically to go after individuals who overprescribe opioids or seek to profit from illegally selling prescription narcotics.

According to the Government Accountability Office, fraud, waste, and abuse account for more than 10.8 percent of Medicare spending—or $75 billion annually.

"We will use every tool we have to stop criminals from exploiting

the vulnerable people and stealing our hard-earned tax dollars," said Attorney General Sessions. "We are sending a clear message to criminals across this country: We will find you. We will bring you to justice. And you will pay a very high price for what you have done."

Officials laid out case examples to illustrate the scope of the alleged crimes, including:

- In Michigan, six physicians were charged with prescribing medically unnecessary controlled substances—some of which were sold on the street—and then billing Medicare for $164 million.

- In Palm Beach, Florida, the owner of an addiction treatment center was charged in a scheme to submit more than $58 million in fraudulent claims—a case that alleges kickbacks of gift cards, plane tickets, and trips to casinos and strip clubs.

- In Houston, a physician and pain management clinic owner who saw 60 to 70 clients a day allegedly issued medically unnecessary prescriptions for hydrocodone in exchange for $300 cash per visit.

"Their recklessness and their greed puts Americans at significant risk of addiction and death," said Chuck Rosenberg, acting administrator at the DEA, who said four out of five new heroin users started with pain pills and about 600 new users take up heroin every day.

"With great privilege and great authority comes great responsibility to handle and prescribe controlled drugs lawfully, carefully, and thoughtfully," Rosenberg said. "Where and when practitioners fail in that responsibility, we are going to hold them accountable."

It's a hot afternoon in August, and the last of the trainees steps off a coach bus parked outside a dormitory at the FBI Academy. One by one, young men and women from all walks of life make their way toward the entrance with luggage in tow.

A sense of nervous excitement can be felt as supervisors, counselors, and others meet each trainee inside the lobby. They shuffle from station to station and gather paperwork, equipment, class schedules, and dorm assignments. At one of the stops, trainees receive standard-issue polo shirts, khaki pants, and workout gear.

Scan this QR code with your smartphone to access related information, or visit www.fbi.gov/ newagentseries.

The first weeks of training at the FBI Academy can be both exciting and nerve-wracking. For many new trainees, the arrival at Quantico is a significant step in a lifelong journey to becoming a special agent.

This diverse band of trainees is converging on Quantico from across the country with one goal in mind: to complete the Basic Field Training Course and become special agents of the FBI.

The training will be taxing on many levels—academically, physically, and psychologically—and success is far from guaranteed. But through the close bonds inevitably formed by fellow classmates and support from the Academy's training staff, new

agents will endure the challenges that lie ahead.

Over the span of five months, trainees will learn the fundamentals of the special agent tradecraft. They'll root out drug dealers and bank robbers in Hogan's Alley, the FBI's mock town and practical training facility.

The training will be taxing on many levels— academically, physically, and psychologically— and success is far from guaranteed.

They'll expose terrorist cells and learn how to conduct challenging interviews. They'll study legal issues and investigative procedures, gather and analyze evidence, and fire thousands of rounds at the range. Along the way, new agent trainees will work alongside new intelligence analysts to identify threats and develop critical thinking skills.

The intense training regimen is necessary to prepare new agents to carry out the FBI's complex mission

of protecting the nation from a host of major national security and criminal threats—including those posed by terrorists, spies, hackers, gangs, and more—while upholding civil rights and the Constitution of the United States.

Just getting to the Academy was a long and hard-fought journey for the trainees arriving this summer day. They had to compete against tens of thousands of applicants in one of the most grueling selection processes in the country. Navigating the many elements of the application process—including several rounds of interviews and a thorough background check—was its own test. Ultimately, perseverance paid off.

Like their predecessors, this class of new agents comes with a variety of career experiences—some not as traditional as you might expect. The majority of students have military, law enforcement, or criminal justice backgrounds, but there are also former teachers, scientists, IT professionals, entrepreneurs, and more.

In today's global and digitally driven age, diversity on many levels is a necessity for the FBI, and this group was carefully chosen for the wide-ranging set of skills and perspectives they bring to the table.

Many of the trainees are here after deciding to switch careers mid-stream, feeling the need to serve their country or tackle a new challenge. For others, like Liz, being an agent is the culmination of a lifelong dream.

A St. Louis native, Liz worked her way through years of higher education and a career practicing civil law before applying to the FBI. Now she's finally at Quantico,

Special Agent David Lewis recalls arriving at the FBI Academy and feeling uncertain about the months ahead.

Special Agent John Woodill remembers feeling excited the moment he drove through the front gate at Quantico.

suitcase in hand, ready to tackle the journey ahead.

"It felt surreal to finally be here after all this hard work," Liz says. "The best part about the first day was meeting my classmates for the first time and feeling so welcomed. It helped calm my nerves."

It wasn't long after arriving at the Academy that Liz and her fellow trainees received their first of many challenges: the physical fitness test, commonly known as the PFT. It's a demanding circuit that includes sit-ups, a 300-meter sprint, push-ups, and a one-and-a-half-mile run. Passing the test is essential— not only to completing the rest of the Basic Field Training Course but to ensure new agents can effectively carry out their duties.

"Right before the test, everyone was trying to provide words of encouragement and support each other, much like going into a big game," says Liz, who, like all of her fellow trainees, was required to maintain a level of fitness before coming to the Academy. "Our class

rallied and did that for each other. You go out, give it 100 percent, and put it all out on the line. I think we were successful at that."

It's a theme that will be repeated often in the coming weeks.

New agents attend the FBI's Onboarding New Employees (ONE) program before beginning their first week of training. The program introduces employees to the FBI's history, culture, and structure.

New agent trainees must take the physical fitness test, commonly known as the PFT, soon after they arrive at the FBI Academy. It's a demanding circuit that includes sit-ups, a 300-meter sprint, push-ups, and a one-and-a-half-mile run.

THE FBI STORY

Just beside Hogan's Alley, the mock town and training facility at the FBI Academy in Quantico, Virginia, there's a cluster of modern two-story buildings with several classrooms. Inside one of the classrooms, new agent trainees are forming their squads for the morning when they receive word that an "explosion" has occurred in a nearby city.

Over the previous few weeks, the squad has been using the skills they've learned to investigate a simulated hotel bombing and track down the criminals responsible for the attack. With this new report, trainees suspect that the events could be linked to terrorist activity. But before they can identify subjects, the squad needs to gather intelligence, conduct interviews, and dig up more clues.

The agents' partners in this effort are new FBI intelligence analysts who are training right alongside them. Analysts—the men and women who help gather, share, and make sense of information and intelligence from all corners of the globe—have never been more vital to the Bureau's mission in this post-9/11 world. By integrating their training, the FBI is replicating what agents and analysts will experience in their coming cases and ensuring that seamless collaboration is part of their DNA from day one.

"Agent and analyst trainees need to understand each other's respective job roles and how that plays out in the real world," says Carrie Richardson-Zadra, a supervisory special agent with the FBI's Investigative and Intelligence Training Unit. "That's why we have them work together from the moment they arrive at the academy."

Later in the exercise, trainees begin questioning the wife of a suspected extremist (played by a local actor). She's reluctant to talk at first, but by using their newly learned interviewing tactics based on building rapport, the new agents are slowly able to obtain the information they need to stop a potential terrorist attack. If it weren't for the insight provided by the intelligence analysts in their squad, the trainees wouldn't have been so successful.

While trainees are integrated both inside and outside the classroom, specialized courses are provided to students based on what their roles will be in the field. For new agent trainees, the academic side of the training is demanding and includes a broad range of subjects that ground them in the fundamentals of law, ethics (see sidebar), behavioral science, interviewing and report writing, basic and advanced investigative and intelligence techniques, interrogation, and evidence collection.

Agent trainees also receive more than 90 hours of instruction

From day one at the FBI Academy, new agents train alongside intelligence analysts to be more prepared for collaborative work in the field.

and practical exercises focused on tactics, operations planning, cooperating witnesses and informants, physical and electronic surveillance, undercover operations, and intelligence.

> *"Agent and analyst trainees need to understand each other's respective job roles and how that plays out in the real world."*

The rigorous academics are vital to the future success of agent trainees. They will need to learn the basics of federal law, the U.S. Constitution, and the legal process. If agents don't understand all of the details governing searches, questions could be raised during trial about the credibility of recovered evidence.

The intelligence analysts will ultimately graduate before the agents after 12 weeks at Quantico. At that point, new agent trainees begin their tactical training and set their sights on the crooked criminals and gangs waiting for them in Hogan's Alley.

Remembering Why They Serve

FBI agents wield substantial law enforcement powers, including the ability to make arrests and, along with analysts, to build a case that can put a person behind bars. That's why agents and analysts must be grounded in the fundamental principles of ethics and place the utmost value in protecting the innocent and upholding the rule of law.

As part of their ethics training, new agent and analyst trainees make two excursions to the nation's capital that drive home the importance of protecting the public and preventing the abuse of authority.

The first trip, instituted by the Bureau in April 2000, is a specialized tour of the United States Holocaust Memorial Museum. After the tour, agents and analysts talk with museum representatives about how the Nazis took power in Germany in 1933 with the help of civilian police and the horrors that can occur when law enforcement fails to protect and serve with compassion and fairness.

In a second trip, which was incorporated into FBI Academy training in August 2014, students visit the Martin Luther King, Jr. Memorial. The program—put together in partnership with the Memorial Foundation and the National Park Service—reminds trainees of past FBI mistakes, the importance of civil rights for all, and the need for oversight and accountability.

"Visiting the museum and the memorial was a sobering reminder about the misuse of power and the devastating impact of government and law enforcement not being checked," says Jeremy, a new agent trainee. "It reminds us that it's our obligation to routinely calibrate our own moral compasses and always do the right thing for the American people."

It's 8 a.m. on a Monday, and new agent trainees are gearing up to make an arrest at Hogan's Alley. Their subject: a wanted fugitive suspected of extortion and money laundering.

As trainees don tactical vests and holster side arms, team leaders brief their squads on a plan to safely enter the home of a middle-aged man who is considered armed and dangerous.

The trainees break off into their teams and head toward a house just outside of town. Tensions are high as a group of students position themselves just outside the front door with shields in hand. A lead agent knocks loudly and yells, "FBI, we have a search warrant, open the door!"—but the suspect doesn't answer. The agents have no choice but to make a breach.

With flashlights out and weapons drawn, the suspect is safely rooted out, handcuffed, and brought into custody.

This type of exercise is one of many that new agents face while learning tactical and law enforcement skills during the FBI's Basic Field Training Course at the FBI Academy in Quantico, Virginia. Whether it's arresting fugitives or preventing terrorist attacks, Academy instructors have made each scenario as realistic as possible.

"We want to replicate what people are going to see in the field," says M.A. Myers, a section chief at the FBI's Training Division. "The scenarios we've developed are all based on real agent cases. So an exercise in Hogan's Alley is going to closely mirror what our instructors have seen during their own experiences."

Since 1987, the training town has immersed new agents in a variety of intense and lifelike situations that challenge them to make the right call—with the help of actors playing criminals, victims, and bystanders.

"Hogan's Alley is where the rubber meets the road. It's where we get to experience what things could really look like out there," says Sunny, a new agent trainee.

Scan this QR code with your smartphone to access related information, or visit www.fbi.gov/newagentseries.

New agents are tested on a variety of maneuvers behind the wheel at the FBI Academy's precision obstacle course.

Just behind Hogan's Alley, trainees are speeding around a 1.1-mile road track and weaving their cars around orange cones on the precision obstacle course. An instructor is closely watching the maneuvers as new agents push their way to the finish. The driving techniques learned at the Academy's Tactical Emergency Vehicle Operations Center, or TEVOC, prepare agents to handle a variety of dangerous situations like high-speed chases and reversing out of alleyways under fire.

Trainees also spend hundreds of hours across the Academy campus on the range, shooting countless rounds of ammunition. New agents need to protect innocent lives and may be faced with dangerous encounters in the line of duty, so it's necessary to become proficient with a variety of firearms, including the pistol, shotgun, and carbine.

"One of the most important things that we stress at the Academy is firearms training. We spend a lot of time with trainees teaching them how to handle firearms safely and to shoot accurately," said Myers. Trainees must qualify in a series of tests to graduate.

Just a few blocks from the indoor range sits a large field house. Inside the building, a sea of blue exercise mats line the floor, along with fake padded furniture and a partial replica of a commercial airplane—items used by instructors to teach close-quarter defensive tactics like boxing, grappling, disarming, and searching.

In one of the drills, a subject (actually another trainee) refuses to stand up from his desk and

New agents learn to shoot a pistol, shotgun, and carbine at the FBI Academy. Trainees must achieve proficiency with their weapons during their time at Quantico.

be handcuffed, forcing agents to wrestle him to the ground. As they bump up against the padded furniture, it takes two agents to subdue their subject. It's all over in a matter of seconds, but the realistic exercise simulates what could happen when criminals turn violent during an arrest.

For those students without any previous law enforcement or military experience, the tactical training can be one of the most challenging aspects of their time at the Academy. They may have never thrown a punch, shot a weapon, or driven a car at high speeds. But to ensure that agents can safely do

their jobs, instructors must push every trainee to their limits.

"When we first got into the tactical training scenarios, it was a steep learning curve," comments David, a new agent trainee. "You really get to see how difficult it is to learn the special agent tradecraft."

Orders Night

Orders Night—one of the most highly anticipated events of the FBI's Basic Field Training Course—is when new agents and intelligence analysts find out where they're going to start their careers.

Prior to the evening, students are asked to complete a "wish list" of field offices where they'd preferred to be assigned. While some receive their top choices, others are sent to areas that are a complete surprise. There are no appeals.

Throughout the night, each trainee stands up in front of the class, opens their envelope, and shares the result. Before doing so, they discuss their top selections. There is a lot of laughter—and nervous excitement.

"Orders Night is a longstanding tradition at the Academy that has not changed over the decades," says M.A. Myers of the Training Division. "The joke is that we have someone throw darts at a map and that's how we pick where trainees go, but the reality is that we put people where they're needed most. Wherever the agents and analysts end up—whether in sunny Miami or chilly Anchorage—it's their job to convince their families that it's the best place on earth."

On a cold Friday afternoon behind the FBI Academy field house, new agent trainees are shivering in a single-file line waiting to get blasted in the face with oleoresin capsicum—a substance more commonly known as pepper spray.

When it's Liz's turn, she waits with her eyes closed before the instructor asks if she's ready. There's no count to three or warning noise. Before she knows it, her face is burning. To pass this test, Liz has to open at least one eye, attack a punching bag, and defend herself from an assailant who's trying to take her pistol out of its holster.

Amidst the chaos, Liz manages to subdue her subject, and the excruciating exercise is over.

It's one of the final tests at the Academy. Up to this point, more than 800 hours have been spent in and out of classroom learning what it takes to become a special agent. Trainees have worked together,

"The graduation is a moment you'll never forget ... . You've finally reached your dream of becoming a special agent of the FBI."

studied together, and sweated together to complete one of the most challenging experiences of their lives. Now, it comes down to one last event: receiving their FBI badge and credentials on graduation day.

It's a crisp morning in January as hundreds of people file into the auditorium at the Academy. Friends and family members—who have made their own sacrifices over the past five months, with plenty more to come—take their seats and wait in anticipation for their loved ones to officially become special agents.

After being sworn in, Liz makes her way to the wings of the auditorium with the rest of her classmates. Clad in suits, they're all now standing in line, waiting excitedly for their turn to go on stage and complete their journey at the Academy.

"The graduation is a moment you'll never forget—standing up there, raising your right hand, repeating the oath, and then walking across the stage to get your creds and your badge," says Kellie Holland, a special agent unit chief with the FBI's Training Management Unit. "You've finally reached your dream of becoming a special agent of the FBI."

Like the rest of her classmates, Liz couldn't take her eyes off the shimmering gold FBI badge and credentials she now held in her hands. She made it. Now she will head to her first field office in Chicago, where her career as a special agent begins.

In one of their final tests before they graduate from the FBI Academy, new agent trainees are pepper sprayed to learn how to carry out their duties under a variety of challenging scenarios in the field.

The graduation ceremony at the FBI Academy marks the culmination of 20 weeks of hard work and sacrifice, when new agent trainees become special agents of the FBI.

"I'm really excited to get things started. I feel like I'm going into a big family right away," said Liz. "I've already been in contact with my squad mates, and I feel prepared for this next transition. It already feels like an extension of the training I've received at Quantico."

Following the graduation ceremony, before new agents can pack up their belongings and head out to their new field offices, there's just one final item to complete: a stop by the weapons vault to pick up their very own FBI-issued pistol and ammunition. It's a fitting

final lesson on the seriousness and importance of their coming work—protecting lives, putting dangerous criminals and terrorists behind bars, and safeguarding the nation.

The Learning Never Ends

While the graduation ceremony serves as the culminating event for the new agents who have spent countless hours preparing to serve the country, training never stops. As Supervisory Special Agent John Woodill puts it, special agents in the field are constantly striving to improve their tradecraft as they move from assignment to assignment. Individuals assigned to public health cases, for example, must understand the complexities of the industry and the types of violations that may occur.

"There's no success for any individuals who remain locked into certain mindsets as they go about their careers. Lifelong learning is absolutely essential—otherwise, things could get dangerous if you don't stay on your game," said Woodill.

Following graduation, new agents report to their first field office, where they'll be on probation and are assigned a training mentor. Over a three-year period, agents must reach specific checkpoints and objectives before they can operate more independently in investigations.

"After about three years, new agents will begin to get their real sea legs under them," says Kellie Holland, who served in the field for more than eight years as a special agent before eventually becoming a unit chief at the FBI's Training Division. "In my experience, I felt like I got my bearings at that point, and it took me the next few years to fine tune my skillset."

Darknet Takedown

Authorities Shutter Online Criminal Market AlphaBay

FBI Acting Director Andrew McCabe, flanked by Attorney General Jeff Sessions (right) and Deputy Attorney General Rod Rosenstein, announce the takedown of the criminal website AlphaBay, the largest Darknet marketplace in the world, at a July 20 press conference in Washington, D.C.

The largest marketplace on the Darknet—where hundreds of thousands of criminals anonymously bought and sold drugs, weapons, hacking tools, stolen identities, and a host of other illegal goods and services—has been shut down as a result of one of the most sophisticated and coordinated efforts to date on the part of law enforcement across the globe.

In early July, multiple computer servers used by the AlphaBay website were seized worldwide, and the site's creator and administrator—a 25-year-old Canadian citizen living in Thailand—was arrested. AlphaBay operated for more than two years and had transactions exceeding $1 billion in Bitcoin and other digital currencies. The site, which operated on the anonymous Tor network, was a major source of heroin and fentanyl, and sales originating from AlphaBay have been linked to multiple overdose deaths in the United States.

"This was a landmark operation," said FBI Acting Director Andrew McCabe during a press conference at the Department of Justice to announce the results of the case. "We're talking about multiple servers in different countries, hundreds of millions in cryptocurrency, and a Darknet drug trade that spanned the globe."

A dedicated team of FBI agents, intelligence analysts, and support personnel worked alongside domestic and international law enforcement partners to shut down the site and stop the flow of illegal goods. "AlphaBay was truly a global site," said Special Agent Nicholas Phirippidis, one of the FBI investigators who worked on the case from the FBI's Sacramento Division. "Vendors were shipping illegal items from places all over the world to places all over the world."

The website, an outgrowth of earlier dark market sites like Silk Road—but much larger—went online in December 2014. It

took about six months for the underground marketplace to pick up momentum, Phirippidis said, "but after that it grew exponentially."

AlphaBay reported that it serviced more than 200,000 users and 40,000 vendors. Around the time of the takedown, the site had more than 250,000 listings for illegal drugs and toxic chemicals, and more than 100,000 listings for stolen and fraudulent identification documents, counterfeit goods, malware and other computer hacking tools, firearms, and fraudulent services. By comparison, the Silk Road dark market—the largest such enterprise of its kind before it was shut down in 2013—had approximately 14,000 listings.

The operation to seize AlphaBay's servers was led by the FBI and involved the cooperative efforts of law enforcement agencies in Thailand, the Netherlands, Lithuania, Canada, the United Kingdom, and France, along with the European law enforcement agency Europol.

"Conservatively, several hundred investigations across the globe were being conducted at the same time as a result of AlphaBay's illegal activities," Phirippidis said. "It really took an all-hands effort among law enforcement worldwide to deconflict and protect those ongoing investigations."

U.S. law enforcement also worked with numerous foreign partners to freeze and preserve millions of dollars in cryptocurrency representing the proceeds of AlphaBay's illegal activities. Those funds will be the subject of forfeiture actions.

AlphaBay's creator and administrator, Alexandre Cazes—who went by the names Alpha02 and Admin online—was arrested by Thai authorities on behalf of the U.S. on July 5, 2017. A week later, Cazes apparently took his own life while in custody in Thailand.

Because AlphaBay operated on the anonymous Tor network, administrators were confident they could hide the locations of

AlphaBay by the Numbers
Until law enforcement shut it down, AlphaBay was the largest online dark market in the world, where criminals could anonymously buy and sell drugs, weapons, and a range of other illegal goods and services.

- 200,000 Users
- 40,000 Vendors

- 122 vendors advertising Fentanyl and 238 vendors advertising heroin
- More than 250,000 listings for illegal drugs and toxic chemicals
- More than 100,000 listings for items including fraudulent identification documents, malware and other hacking tools, firearms, and counterfeit goods
  As of early 2017

More than $1 billion in illegal transactions in Bitcoin and other cryptocurrencies
Between 2015 and 2017

As of December 2015

The Takedown
Multiple servers were seized worldwide, and the site administrator was arrested in Thailand. The combined efforts of global law enforcement agencies represents one of the most sophisticated and coordinated takedowns ever in the fight against online criminal activity.

THIS HIDDEN SITE HAS BEEN SEIZED
Since July 4, 2017

the site's servers and the identities of users. "They understood that law enforcement was monitoring their activity," said FBI Special Agent Chris Thomas, "but they felt so protected by the dark web technology that they thought they could get away with their crimes."

The FBI and its partners used a combination of traditional

investigative techniques along with sophisticated new tools to break the case and dismantle AlphaBay. "The message to criminals is: Don't think that you are safe because you're on the dark web. There are no corners of the dark web where you can hide," Thomas said.

The operation to seize AlphaBay coincided with efforts by Dutch law enforcement to shut down the Hansa Market, another prominent Darknet marketplace that was used to facilitate the sale of illegal drugs, malware, and other illegal services. After AlphaBay's shutdown, criminal users and vendors flocked to Hansa Market, where they believed their identities would be masked.

"Taking down two major dark sites at once is considerable, and it took a lot of effort, a lot of expertise and teamwork," said FBI Acting Director McCabe. "As this level of teamwork and coordination shows, we will go to the ends of the earth to find these people and to stop them."

Global Threat Requires Global Partnerships

The takedown of AlphaBay—and another prominent site on the Darknet known as Hansa Market—required months of planning among law enforcement agencies around the world and was one of the most sophisticated coordinated takedowns to date in the fight against online criminal activity.

The operation to shut down AlphaBay was led by the FBI and involved law enforcement authorities in Thailand, the Netherlands, Lithuania, Canada, the United Kingdom, and France, along with Europol. It is expected that hundreds of new investigations will be generated worldwide as a result of the takedowns.

Europol played a central coordinating role in both cases. In early July, days before AlphaBay servers were seized, Europol hosted a command post staffed with representatives from the FBI, the Drug Enforcement Administration, and the Department of Justice, along with its own members. The command post was the central hub for information exchange during the AlphaBay operation.

In parallel to these operations, Europol hosted an international Cyberpatrol Action Week in June, where more than 40 investigators from 22 European Union member states and representatives from the FBI and other U.S. law enforcement agencies joined in an intelligence-gathering exercise to map out criminality on the Darknet. The focus was on vendors and buyers who were actively involved in the online trade of illegal commodities including drugs, weapons and explosives, forged documents, and cyber crime tools. Analysis of the results and dissemination of the resultant intelligence is ongoing.

Seizing the Moment

Vermont Civil Forfeiture Leads to Renewal of Homes, Community

A unique public-private agreement returned three seized homes used by drug traffickers back to the community of Rutland, Vermont, where a non-profit organization will renovate and sell them at an affordable price with the stipulation that the owner reside there.

There was no mystery about what was occurring at the three multi-family rental houses on Park Avenue in Rutland, Vermont: strangers dropping in around the clock, police responding to neighbors' complaints, discarded syringes turning up in nearby yards.

"My grandson that lives here got to where he wouldn't even go outside for two years," said Michael Moran, who has lived with his family in a home on Park Avenue for more than 25 years. He raised his own kids in the modest house and watched helplessly, beginning around 2011, as his tree-lined street turned from a respectable working-class enclave to a notorious destination for drug sellers and buyers at the height of the state's opioid epidemic. Living across the street from one drug house and next door to another, Moran said, the routine for his grandson had become "come home from school and go in the house."

The Park Avenue homes were well known to local police, who made occasional arrests but were unable to appreciably stem the flow of drugs and money. It wasn't until they partnered with civic leaders, researchers, and federal law enforcement agencies that a more holistic solution took hold. Rather than the piecemeal arrests, investigators worked with local police to build a long-term investigation that included surveillance, informants, and undercover work, including at least six controlled drug buys. The case ultimately led to arrests and convictions in 2014 of seven drug dealers who had lived in the houses. Federal officials also moved to seize the houses in 2015 after it became clear the absentee owner knew of the illegal activity and did nothing to stop it.

"Property used to facilitate drug trafficking is subject to forfeiture," said Joseph Perello, an assistant U.S. attorney for the District of Vermont, which filed for the civil forfeiture. "You look at the facts to see whether or not the landlord took reasonable but safe steps to rid the residences or the rental properties of drug dealings. Here, we concluded that he did not."

Unlike criminal forfeiture, which is a legal action brought against individuals as part of a criminal conviction, civil forfeiture is brought against property and is not dependent on a prosecution. The legal measure is based on the strength of available evidence—in this case, the overwhelming testimony of witnesses to the landlord's complicity.

"It's a very worthwhile tool," said FBI Special Agent Chris Destito, who helped investigate the case out of the Burlington, Vermont, office of the Bureau's Albany Division. "It's an effective tool for us to get the landlords to be a little more aware of what's happening in their units and not allow it."

In many cases, proceeds from forfeitures go back to victims. And in some cases, a portion of funds help support law enforcement programs. In Rutland, where the effort to eliminate the drug houses was part of an expansive strategic goal to rehabilitate the greater neighborhood, an idea took hold to try something new.

With the three houses vacated and boarded up and the city still owed back taxes and fines, the U.S. Attorney's Office and the city of Rutland struck an agreement last year to renovate the derelict properties into affordable homes. Under the arrangement and pursuant to the civil forfeiture of the properties, the U.S. Marshals Service transferred the houses to the city, which, in turn, cancelled its taxes and fines and then transferred the properties to a local non-profit, NeighborWorks of Western Vermont, which paid $82,500 to settle with the banks holding the properties' mortgages.

"The properties were seized and they were transferred to a housing partner of the community—within

Rutland earned a dubious reputation in recent years as a destination for both traffickers and users of opioids. A recent civil forfeiture measure took aim at absentee landlords who turn a blind eye to renters they know are using their rental properties to traffic illegal drugs.

One of three homes seized on Park Avenue in Rutland. A non-profit organization is restoring the properties, much to the delight of neighbors. "The transformation is palpable," the former mayor of Rutland said.

a thriving railroad town and later a manufacturing hub—efforts are underway to eliminate blighted properties and return some multi-family homes back to their original, smaller size.

"It wouldn't have happened without the federal partners being invested in seeing our community succeed."

"They all have a history of being kind of family-oriented. Our hope is to bring them back to exactly that," said Ludy Biddle, executive director of NeighborWorks. "We will repair these homes and sell them to families to live, I hope, happy lives in this neighborhood again."

While the renovations have not yet started, the tenor of the neighborhood has already changed for the better. A block party on Park Avenue last month drew hundreds of people from around the city, showing a renewal is already underway. "The transformation is palpable," the former mayor said.

The party was held on the lawn of one of the seized homes, directly across from Michael Moran's house. "For the longest time, nobody would walk up and down these streets at night," Moran said. "We fought and fought and fought, and this is where we're at today. I see things getting better. And this is a nice neighborhood. It really is."

the community—to provide home-ownership opportunities and—I can't say it enough—to transform the community," said Chris Louras, who was mayor of Rutland during the period when the drug dealers were arrested and the homes were seized and turned over to the city. "It wouldn't have happened without the federal partners being invested in seeing our community succeed."

Once renovated, the homes will be either owner-occupied single-family residences or duplexes or condos in which the landlord must live on-site, according to the agreement. The city's aim is to bring stability to the street, the neighborhood, and the city, where just one in three homes is owner-occupied. With an excess of housing stock in Rutland—once

Scan this QR code with your smartphone to access related information, or visit www.fbi.gov/vermontforfeiture.

THE FBI STORY

Adopt-a-School Program
Reducing Crime, Empowering a Community

All the evidence led to the University of Hawaii's West Oahu campus, to a field that appeared to contain a shallow grave. Taking direction from their FBI mentor, two teams of young investigators began to excavate the site, using trowels and soft brushes, working methodically until the freshly exposed earth revealed the outlines of a skull.

In 2009, Special Agent Arnold Laanui helped establish the FBI Honolulu Division's Adopt-a-School program at Waipahu High School. Since then, one of the state's most troubled schools has undergone a renaissance.

For the students from two different high schools, the hands-on dig was part of a mock kidnapping case they were investigating, and the culmination of a yearlong introduction to the FBI and the workings of the criminal justice system. For Special Agent Arnold Laanui, the exercise capped another successful year for the FBI Honolulu Division's Adopt-a-School program—and it reaffirmed his passionate belief that one of the best ways to reduce crime in at-risk communities is to provide the right educational opportunities for young people.

Nearly a decade ago, Laanui, one of fewer than 20 Pacific Islanders in the FBI agent ranks, wanted to bring an Adopt-a-School program to his home state. The Bureau began the national outreach initiative in 1994 to help young people stay away from crime and drugs while learning core values that would make them

good citizens. Since then, agents and other FBI employees around the country have volunteered thousands of hours to make a positive impact on the lives of youngsters in predominantly disadvantaged neighborhoods.

To determine which Hawaiian school would be best served, in 2009 Laanui researched Oahu communities with the highest crime rates. The neighborhood of Waipahu, encompassing approximately a four-square-mile area not far from the high-rise resorts and tourist beaches of Waikiki, showed surprising statistics.

"The data revealed that nearly half of the juvenile criminals in the state of Hawaii were coming out of that one area," Laanui said. "That one little plot of land represented the most crime-ridden neighborhood in the state."

Another fact was also of interest: From 2008 to 2010, nearly half the students at Waipahu High School had failed to graduate on time. Only 52 percent of the students who had entered the school as freshmen during those years had graduated four years later. Did the other 48 percent, having dropped out, resort to criminal activity because there were few other options? If you could design a program to keep those youngsters in school, engaged, and graduating on time, wouldn't that result in lowering the community's crime rate?

Laanui had his school—"in the toughest neighborhood in Hawaii"—and a clear vision: "From the start," he said, "the Adopt-a-School program was a very deliberate attempt to re-engineer an entire neighborhood really at its core."

The FBI's Honolulu Division implemented its Adopt-a-School program nearly a decade ago at what was then an at-risk high school in a troubled neighborhood. Today, the program is showing tangible, measurable results that show lower rates of drug use and truancy at the school.

Waipahu High School was full of energy on a recent spring morning as young people made their way to and from class. Motivational words—*Ambition, Courage, Perseverance*—appear on stairwells, and students' murals grace many of the walls. Today, the school is a safe place for young people to learn and explore, but that was not always the case.

"When I first became a police officer in 2000," said Anson "Kaipo" Paiva, a member of the Honolulu Police Department, "Waipahu was a completely different neighborhood. There was high crime, a lot of truancy. In certain areas, officers could not go in alone. Two officers would service a 9-1-1 call, and one would stay outside and watch the cars to make sure they weren't vandalized."

Officer Kaipo, as he is now fondly known to the many Waipahu students he teaches and counsels, was a patrol officer back then. When police showed up in the neighborhood, kids would run. Officers regularly responded to the high school for brawls and drug busts. "Pretty much every time you got called there," he said, "somebody would get arrested."

After eight years, Officer Kaipo left patrol and joined the community policing team. Now, instead of arresting kids, he gets to mentor them through a number of initiatives, including the Adopt-a-School program.

"Showing these kids what they're capable of is an eye-opening experience for them," he said. "When they start accepting that what they can do is great, and they can actually create the community they want, it changes everything."

The Adopt-a-School program brings together students from two different high schools to solve a mock kidnapping case, culminating in a dig at a fictional crime scene. The mock-investigation is part of a two-day field training exercise called PROVE (Practical Observation and Vocational Experience).

Standing at the front of the classroom, Laanui addresses his students as he always does, with the same initial greeting, spoken in native Hawaiian: "Kings and queens of Waipahu, let's begin."

"All learners, all students want to be treated with a certain degree of respect," he said, and that simple greeting confers not only respect but expectation. Today's lesson—leading up to the following week's mock investigation and dig—is about how to sketch a crime scene. After classroom instruction, the junior and senior boys and girls head outdoors where shell casings, items of clothing, and other pieces of "evidence" have been planted. They learn to work together to preserve the scene, to take notes and measurements, and to sketch what they have found, just as FBI investigators would.

After Laanui chose Waipahu High School for the Adopt-a-School

program in 2009—with the enthusiastic support of the school's principal—he spent a year writing curriculum for the program that aligned with Hawaii Department of Education standards. (That process made him realize he needed more than the law degree he had earned on his way to becoming an FBI agent, and he went on to earn a doctorate in education.)

"We put together a curriculum based on sound educational philosophy," Laanui said. Lessons were designed around five general principals, what Laanui calls "the Five Ps"—purpose, passion, persistence, practice, and positivism.

Waipahu's Adopt-a-School program has two main components. Eligible ninth-graders—averaging more than 100 students per year—can participate in a Leader Lab where they receive blocks of instruction on ethics, relationships, strategies for success, and leadership. They also work in teams to design projects for the benefit of the school and the neighborhood. The Leader Lab concludes with a "Shark Tank"-like presentation where student teams "sell" their projects to community leaders who help fund the best ideas.

If those freshmen express a career interest in the criminal justice system, as juniors and seniors they can enroll in the school's Academy of Law and Justice Administration, which Laanui helped to establish. There, rather than take a physics class, students might take forensic science. Instead of classic history, they might study social justice or criminology and law. "The academy is geared toward inspiring the future detectives, special agents, attorneys, and judges of Hawaii," Laanui said.

In addition, the Honolulu Police Department sponsors a program for sixth-graders called Real and Powerful, better known as RAP. Administered by Officer Kaipo, RAP provides guidance on dealing with bullying, cyberbullying, drugs, peer pressure, and other topics.

Taken together, starting in sixth-grade students are exposed to core messages about how to make good choices, how to set goals and achieve them, and how to plan for a successful future that involves giving something back to the community. "We keep injecting positive messages and building positive relationships with people," Officer Kaipo said. "Eventually, the only thing that can happen is positive."

Changing the culture of a school—especially one that had historically underperformed—does not happen overnight. Laanui understood that a long-term commitment was required. So did Waipahu High School's new principal in 2009. Keith Hayashi immediately saw the potential of the Adopt-a-School program and encouraged Laanui to include 120 students in the inaugural cohort, far more than Laanui had planned for—and a majority of those students were at high risk for dropping out.

In those early years, the program included a trust-building ropes course held off campus where students and teachers needed to work together to complete a physically demanding set of obstacles. Part of the course involved scaling a 10-foot wall.

"Students were helping each other, hoisting each other up, jumping up. They got over," Hayashi remembered. "Some of the teachers struggled, as I would have, and

Anson "Kaipo" Paiva, a member of the Honolulu Police Department's community policing team, helps a Waipahu High School freshman in the Adopt-a-School program as he prepares to make a presentation in a *Shark Tank*-like competition. Student teams "sell" projects to benefit the school and the neighborhood to community leaders, who act as judges and help fund the best ideas.

the kids helped them, not only physically, but they encouraged them to try."

Eventually, everyone made it over the wall, and the students and teachers began to see each other in a different way, Hayashi said. "I think that was the beginning of a really great journey for us at Waipahu."

Although he credits the students, teachers, parents, school administrators, and community advocates for their hard work over many years in transforming the school, Hayashi has special praise for Laanui. "He has helped to build a culture at our school where students take care of each other," the principal said. "Teachers and students look at each other with mutual respect. They work together. Adopt-a-School has made a difference."

Statistically speaking, only about 40 of the initial 120 Adopt-A-School freshmen were on track to remain in school by the start of their junior year. But a combination of factors—the ropes course, the message of empowerment, Laanui's engaging curriculum and his commitment—made something special happen.

"Our cohort had the largest matriculation rate and persistence rate into the sophomore year," Laanui said. "When they continued

to persist into their junior year, we didn't realize we were influencing the culture on the entire campus, because the students who were least likely to succeed were persisting, and not only persisting but persisting at a very high and successful rate. That seed," he said, "was a contagion that started to spread throughout the entire campus."

The Adopt-a-School program at Waipahu High School has been so successful because a core group of individuals—including (from left) Special Agent Arnold Laanui, community advocate Lorrie Kanno, and Honolulu Police Department officer Anson "Kaipo" Paiva—are among those who made a long-term commitment to the program.

Today, the incidence of violence and drug use on campus is down by more than 50 percent. Truancy and suspension rates have dropped by more than 50 percent as well. "As a result," Laanui explained, "I see an almost one-to-one match in the reduction of juvenile delinquency rates in the neighborhood—a more than 50 percent reduction, which I anticipate will result in a dramatic

reduction in adult criminality well into the future."

Simply put, "the neighborhood has changed because the school has changed," he said. "What we are seeing now that we are entering our eighth year in the program is a renaissance in the neighborhood, and it's our former students that are leading a lot of that change. And many of those students," he pointed out, "were on a track to drop out of school."

The dig site at the University of Hawaii's West Oahu Campus has revealed a second skeleton, along with telling evidence. The excavation is part of the Adopt-a-School program's two-day field exercise called PROVE—Practical Observation and Vocational Experience.

"It is basically an attempt to mimic a multi-jurisdictional criminal investigation," Laanui said. Months earlier, Laanui—with the help of a University of Hawaii forensic anthropology professor—buried two authentic lab skeletons, along with evidence including a murder weapon, at the site. Then Laanui crafted a crime scenario revolving around the sale of fake marijuana online and a double kidnapping involving students from Waipahu High School and Sacred Hearts Academy, a private girls' school on Oahu.

Waipahu students in the Academy of Law and Justice Administration take part in the PROVE project to apply what they have learned throughout the year—interviewing witnesses, creating a timeline of events, conducting a search, crime-scene sketching and photography, gathering evidence, and taking comprehensive notes.

Prior to beginning the two-day **PROVE** field exercise, Special Agent Arnold Laanui "deputizes" students from Sacred Hearts Academy in Hawaii. The students will need to apply the forensic skills they have learned throughout the year to solve a mock kidnapping case that has all the earmarks of a real law enforcement investigation. Among the skills required are collecting and processing evidence and crime-scene sketching. The FBI Honolulu Citizen's Academy Alumni Association (HNCAAA) has been a strong supporter of the Adopt-a-School program.

There is also an added wrinkle. Laanui has been teaching the same blocks of instruction at Sacred Hearts Academy, and both schools' students must work together to solve the crime.

"The project has been deliberately designed so that their investigations intersect," he said, "and only by collaborating and cooperating with each other—which is often the way it works in the real world—are they able to solve the case."

At the dig site, Waipahu students work alongside their counterparts from Sacred Hearts, whom they have just met in person that morning. Although they come from significantly different cultural, social, and economic backgrounds, the students quickly form a partnership.

"You've got to work together as a team," said Kendrik Dang, a junior at Waipahu High School. "It's always a team effort." Dang, who had never met an FBI agent before joining the Adopt-a-School program, said the experience—including the PROVE Project—makes him want to pursue a career in criminal justice.

After her experience working with Laanui, Sacred Hearts senior Angelina Gomes said she, too,

"might seriously consider a career in law enforcement or maybe the FBI." Gomes likened the investigative process to a puzzle where all the clues fit together to solve the crime. "What's important," she said, "is not to have a closed mind and always think of a lot of possibilities."

For Waipahu High School, the possibilities seem endless.

Principal Hayashi pointed to the school's successes: the significant reduction in truancy, suspensions, and behavioral issues, the increase in academic achievement, on-time graduation, and the overall positive culture at the school. He noted that Waipahu teachers are making a "huge" statement by sending their own children to the school, which did not always happen. "My daughter is a junior here," he said, "and I wouldn't have it any other way."

As for Laanui, he is proud of what the Adopt-a-School program has accomplished. "You can't deny the numbers," he said. "You have this intervention and you reduce crime by more than 50 percent."

"The research in the area of truancy is clear," he added. "If you have absenteeism and behavioral and conduct issues, these are the

conditions in middle school that contribute to dropouts. Unless you come up with a better program that will engage students—so that they build better relationships with each other and with their teachers—then learning is not going to continue." If learning does not continue, he said, "students become disengaged, turn to truancy, truancy leads to delinquency, delinquency leads to adult criminality, and that can be multi-generational."

That unfortunate chain of events occurs in countless schools around the country, turning them into dropout factories. Could Hawaii's Adopt-a-School model work at other schools as well as it has at Waipahu High School?

Laanui believes it can, as long as there is a strong partnership between law enforcement, the school, the community, and dedicated individuals who are willing to make a long-term commitment. "By strategically targeting truancy," he said, "you can short-circuit what will eventually become adult criminality. The return on investment we get out of a program like this is incredibly high."

Scan this QR code with your smartphone to access related information, or visit www.fbi.gov/ hawaiiadoptaschool.

New FBI Director
Christopher Wray Takes Oath of Office

FBI Director Christopher Wray takes the oath of office during his swearing-in ceremony at the Department of Justice on August 2, 2017.

Christopher Wray was sworn in today as the eighth Director of the FBI in a ceremony at the Department of Justice in Washington, D.C. Attorney General Jeff Sessions administered the oath of office.

"It is the honor of a lifetime to serve as Director," Wray said in a statement Wednesday. "I long ago grew to know and admire the FBI from my earliest days as a line prosecutor to my years as assistant attorney general. I am excited, humbled, and grateful, therefore, to have this chance to work side-by-side again with these fine professionals for the good of the country and the cause of justice."

President Donald Trump nominated Wray for the position in June to replace former Director James Comey. The U.S. Senate confirmed the nomination yesterday.

"Chris has the experience and the strength of character that the American people want in an FBI Director," said Attorney General Sessions, adding that he looked forward to working with Wray every day to keep the country safe.

Stopping a Violent Burglary Ring
Jewelry Store Heist Began with Kidnapping

Watches and jewelry stolen during a 2013 Fairfield, Connecticut, robbery and kidnapping were recovered from the residence of one of the thieves in the robbery crew.

Timothy Forbes was a career criminal who specialized in robbing jewelry stores. He and his crew had progressed from smash-and-grab thefts to what they considered a more reliable method: kidnap store employees and force them to provide after-hours access to the jewels.

In the spring of 2013, members of the burglary ring conducted surveillance on employees at a Fairfield, Connecticut, jewelry store, going so far as to attach a GPS tracking device under one of their cars to learn where they lived.

Around 9 p.m. on April 11, 2013, three of Forbes' crew, wearing masks and gloves, forced their way into an apartment in Meriden, Connecticut, brandishing handguns. The terrified victims—two of whom worked at the Fairfield jewelry store—were bound with duct tape, and their heads were covered with pillowcases, towels, and jackets. The kidnappers then forced the jewelry store

employees into a vehicle and drove them to the store while a remaining kidnapper stayed behind to guard the other victims.

Forbes arrived at the store in a separate vehicle, and the thieves proceeded to steal jewels, watches, and loose diamonds estimated to be worth more than $3 million. After the robbery, Forbes notified his associate at the apartment, and the victims there and at the store were left bound as the criminals made their getaway and fled the state.

The kidnapping and robbery had gone off without a hitch, and Forbes thought he had considered all the angles. What he failed to anticipate, though, was how an alert neighbor and strong law enforcement partnerships would undo his careful plan.

When the victims were able to free themselves, they called the police. Meriden Police Department officers conducted interviews and did an initial neighborhood canvass the

night of the robbery. A resident came forward with information he wasn't sure was relevant but that "broke the case open," said Special Agent Jennifer Berry, who worked the investigation from the FBI's New Haven Division.

The neighbor told police that one night nearly two weeks before the kidnapping, he noticed a suspicious silver car on the block with out-of-state license plates. One man was sitting in the driver's seat, and another man was on the ground next to what turned out to be the vehicle of one of the victims. The neighbor dialed 911 but hung up when the suspicious car drove away.

When the car returned 30 minutes later, the neighbor used a pair of binoculars to write down the New Jersey license plate number. He thought maybe the men in the car were buying or selling drugs. It was later learned that Forbes and one of his crew had been trying to remove the GPS tracking device from the victim's car.

A frame from a security video shows one of the suspects exiting a jewelry store robbed by the crew in Connecticut.

had been previously sentenced to prison terms ranging from seven to nearly 15 years for their roles in the kidnapping and robbery.

"This was a really good case," Berry said, "because we were able to get a lot of bad guys off the streets. We couldn't have done it without this great partnership and the help of a concerned citizen."

Investigators quickly identified the silver car as a rental vehicle, and with that information identified the woman who rented the car. Through the phone number she used on the rental application, investigators were able to tie Forbes and his crew to the robbery and kidnapping.

"Through detailed analysis of cellular phone records," Berry said, "we knew exactly when Forbes was in the parking lot where the neighbor spotted him and dialed 911. Eventually we were able to show where all the thieves were before, during, and after the robbery based on calls that were made. That evidence was compelling."

Forbes had been on something of a robbery spree. He had been involved in at least three other similar jewelry store robberies, including a 2012 theft in York, Pennsylvania, in which a jewelry store owner was shot and permanently disabled. (Forbes was sentenced in 2016 to 14 years in prison for his role in that robbery.)

Within six weeks of the Connecticut kidnapping and robbery, Forbes and his four associates were arrested.

"This case is a great example of partnership," Berry explained. "The local police departments in Fairfield and Meriden conducted victim interviews, the Connecticut State Police helped process crime scenes, and the U.S. Marshals Service assisted us with the extensive cell phone analysis. Everybody worked well together."

"The concerned neighbor who wrote down the license plate saved us months of work," Berry said, "and who knows how many more robberies the ring would have done during that time?"

Of the more than $3 million in stolen jewels, Berry said, "very little was recovered." Forbes and his crew—who had all grown up together in Allentown, Pennsylvania—were fond of gambling and high living.

In January 2017, Forbes pleaded guilty to kidnapping, robbery, and the use of a firearm during the Connecticut robbery. Last month, a federal judge sentenced the 35-year-old to 19 years in prison. His crew

Financial Fraud

Lengthy Prison Term for Estate Planner Who Betrayed Clients

Julie Kronhaus was a well-regarded estate planner with impressive training and credentials. She was a licensed attorney, a certified public accountant, and had earned a master's degree in taxation. Unfortunately, she was also home-schooled in fraud.

Between 2009 and 2015, according to court records, Kronhaus defrauded clients and banks out of approximately $2.7 million. The Florida resident often acted as a trustee for her clients and held their money in bank accounts she controlled. With that access, she diverted money into her law firm's bank accounts and used it to afford a lavish lifestyle that included clothes-buying sprees and regular trips to New York and Europe.

"She loved to spend money and live extravagantly," said Special Agent Samantha Medico, who investigated the case from the FBI's Tampa Division. "At one point she had racked up a $1.5 million balance on her American Express card."

The scam worked for so long in part because of the faith placed in Kronhaus by her clients. "When people in the Orlando area and even out of state asked about the best people to handle estates," Medico said, "her name would often come up. She had a good reputation and a good client base."

Medico, a veteran white-collar crime investigator, explained that clients would typically seek out Kronhaus "at a low point in their lives, often involving a death in the family. They would trust her to handle all the estate matters. She would prepare wills and was supposed to distribute money according to those wills," Medico said. "She had a fiduciary responsibility to protect her clients' assets, and she didn't do that."

"She had so much to begin with. Why would she do something like this? It was just greed. She did it because she could."

One of her victims was a child who had been awarded a settlement as the result of a medical malpractice suit. The judge in the case ordered a third party—Kronhaus—to act as the child's financial trustee. "She had complete access and control of the account," Medico said, "and either failed to pay the child's mother for mounting medical expenses or stalled making payments."

One out-of-state victim, himself a lawyer, became suspicious of Kronhaus' actions regarding his accounts and contacted

law enforcement. Investigators eventually subpoenaed bank records in that case, which revealed an extensive fraud that ultimately led to more than a dozen victims. "We kept finding victim after victim," Medico said. "If Kronhaus was short in one account she took money from another account to cover payments. And she was preparing false statements to cover her tracks."

In 2016, Kronhaus was arrested and charged federally with wire and bank fraud. In January 2017, the 52-year-old pleaded guilty to the charges, and last month a judge sentenced her to 10 years in prison and ordered her to pay nearly $3 million in restitution to her victims.

"In many ways, this was a typical fraud case," Medico said. "Except that I have never seen someone so educated and with so much opportunity who committed this type of fraud. Kronhaus already had money," Medico said. "That was the toughest part to comprehend. She had so much to begin with. Why would she do something like this? It was just greed. She did it because she could."

On the Front Line

Public Access Line Marks Five Years

Scan this QR code with your smartphone to access related information, or visit www.fbi.gov/pal5years.

The FBI's Public Access Line plays a key role in investigations by serving as the central intake for all the calls and public leads made to the FBI's 56 field offices across the country.

On April 16, 2013, the FBI's Public Access Line call center was on high alert. Just 24 hours earlier, two homemade bombs detonated near the finish line of the annual Boston Marathon, killing three people and injuring hundreds of runners and spectators. Customer service representatives fielded scores of calls from eyewitnesses with information that could help the FBI and local law enforcement track down the bombers.

Less than a year after opening its doors, the Bureau's central contact center for all the calls and public leads made to the FBI's 56 field offices was playing a key role in a major investigation.

Since 2012, the Public Access Line has received more than two million calls that have resulted in thousands of actionable tips and leads for special agents and intelligence analysts. The unit, which is part of the Bureau's Criminal Justice Information Services (CJIS) Division in Clarksburg, West Virginia, was established five years ago this month.

Whether it's a tip on a missing child, a bomb threat, or financial fraud, the access line is responsible for receiving and vetting information from the public, then disseminating it to the field. In addition to the Boston Marathon bombing in 2013, the unit has been essential in other major events—like the mass shootings in San Bernardino, California, in 2015 and at the Pulse Nightclub in Orlando, Florida, in 2016. For major cases such as these, the FBI uses a dedicated tip line—1-800-CALL-FBI—as a primary means to collect nationwide leads and tips.

"Over the past five years, we've assisted in numerous cases that have led to arrests and the capturing of fugitives," said a supervisory special agent with the Public Access Line unit. "The work we do saves time for agents so they can continue to conduct their investigative work."

Prior to 2012, field offices handled their own calls, which placed a heavy burden on Bureau resources. The access line was born out of the necessity to streamline investigations by centralizing how public information is gathered. Today, the unit vets every tip and complaint that is made to FBI field offices. And it doesn't stop at a phone call. Customer service representatives also assist with online leads that are captured through the FBI's web portal, tips.fbi.gov.

"We're the voice of the FBI," said a lead customer service representative with the Public Access Line unit. "The access line is on the front line serving a very important role for the Bureau. We're building those initial relationships with the public so information can get out into the field in a timely manner."

So far this fiscal year, Public Access Line personnel have answered more than 617,000 calls and processed in excess of 611,000 online tips. Their efforts have saved countless hours of investigative work for FBI field offices.

Currently, the unit has more than 150 members on its staff fielding public leads and tips 24 hours a day, seven days a week. Representatives are not only trained to gather integral information to aid in potential investigations, they're also taught essential listening and communication skills. This level of training is especially important during times when public assistance is needed the most.

"When something devastating happens, we're here," said a customer service representative with the access center. "We impact the public more so than a lot of people would imagine."

Cold Case Homicide

Law Enforcement Hopes Advances in Technology Can Help Solve Tammy Zywicki's Murder

This week marks the 25th anniversary of the kidnapping and murder of Tammy Zywicki, but the FBI and the Illinois State Police have never stopped searching for the young woman's killer—and they are actively pursuing new investigative strategies that could help solve the case.

On August 23, 1992, Zywicki was a 21-year-old college senior who played sports and was passionate about photography. She had driven her brother to college in Evanston, Illinois, and was on her way to Iowa, where she was in her final year at Grinnell College. Her mother called the Illinois State Police that night to report that her daughter had never arrived.

That afternoon, Zywicki's car—a 1985 Pontiac T1000—was found abandoned by a state trooper on Interstate 80 near Utica, Illinois. At the time, it was reported that a tractor/trailer was seen near Zywicki's vehicle, and the trucker was described as a white male about 40 years old, over six feet tall, with dark, bushy hair.

Nine days later, Zywicki's body, stabbed and possibly strangled, was found wrapped in a sheet and blanket and bound in duct tape—nearly 500 miles away in Missouri.

"A lot of people are still passionate about this case," said Special Agent Amanda Becker, who has been working on it for the past two years from the FBI's Chicago Division. "No one has forgotten Tammy—not her family, her high school and college friends, and certainly not law enforcement. I am very motivated to find her killer."

"These cold case homicides are always difficult cases," said Lt. Jeff Padilla, an Illinois State Police detective who has been working on

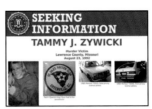

SEEKING INFORMATION
TAMMY J. ZYWICKI
Murder Victim
Lawrence County, Missouri
August 23, 1992

the investigation for the past six years, "but this case has so much evidence that still exists, it should help us be able to bring justice to Tammy and her family."

The FBI and the state police have been working closely together to review and catalogue the extensive amount of physical evidence in the case. The goal is to determine which evidence will best lend itself to the newest forensic techniques for DNA extraction.

Padilla estimated that more than 200 pieces of physical evidence exist in the case file. To date, a definitive DNA profile has only been extracted from one item—a beer can found near where Zywicki's car was abandoned that may or may not have anything to do with the crime.

"That profile has never returned a match with any known offender," Padilla said, "and beyond that, we don't currently have any other profiles because the technology used then was inadequate."

Advances in DNA testing mean that the same evidence—the blanket, sheet, and duct tape Zywicki was wrapped in, shoelaces found at the scene, and other significant items—could reveal the killer's DNA.

"I'm hopeful this new technology will help us," Padilla said. "I am convinced the DNA and the suspect are in the case file. It's just a question of finding them."

Some of Tammy's personal property is known to be missing, including a Cannon 35mm camera, a musical wristwatch with an umbrella on the face, and a distinctive patch issued by Zywicki's soccer team for only one year. The patch was missing from the shorts she was wearing.

If the killer kept the soccer patch, camera, or watch, Becker explained, a tip from someone who recognized the items could help lead to his capture. "There continues to be a $50,000 reward offered in this case," she added. "Even after 25 years, a concerned citizen doing the right thing can help us solve this case."

JoAnn Zywicki, Tammy's mother, is happy that the investigation continues and that the latest DNA techniques will be used. "I'm glad to see they are pursuing that," she said. "It's good to see the FBI and the Illinois State Police working together." She added that her daughter's tragedy "has brought a lot of attention to cold cases, and that's important."

Milestone years such as the 25th anniversary of her daughter's death can be particularly hard, JoAnn Zywicki said, but she also sees the positives. "It always amazes me how many people remember Tammy in different ways," she said. "She did make her mark." As to whether Tammy's killer will ever be captured, JoAnn Zywicki said, "I never give up hope."

Note: This case may have been resolved since this information was posted on our website. Please check www.fbi.gov/wanted/seeking-info for up-to-date information.

Wanted: Your Campus ID

Credit Card Scheme Targets University Bookstores

The June announcement says schools began reporting the fraud last April and sustained losses of several thousands of dollars in each occurrence.

Students at colleges and universities across the country are being warned of a credit card scheme that enlists them to help purported classmates buy high-end electronics at their campus bookstores.

A number of universities last spring reported their bookstores lost thousands of dollars in purchases that were made with stolen credit card information. Investigators found similar patterns in each of the cases: perpetrators claiming to have lost their student ID cards enlisted unwitting students to essentially vouch for them at the counter with their valid IDs. The perpetrators then made their purchases—in many cases, high-end electronic products—with a bogus credit card that matched their bogus identification.

Investigators believe campus bookstores may be targets for this scheme because they generally offer specific discounts for students, who may not see anything wrong with helping out an unlucky stranger claiming to be classmate.

"Students are being used to facilitate this activity," said FBI Special Agent Jennifer Gant, who manages the Bureau's Campus Liaison Program, which started in 2008 to help improve communications between the FBI and U.S. colleges and universities. The program originated in the FBI's Counterterrorism Division as a way to build relationships and increase two-way information sharing before a crisis. Each of the Bureau's 56 field offices has a special agent or task force officer whose duties include building and maintaining connections with school leaders and campus police in their regions.

"If we have information, we share it with them—because our ultimate goal is to keep campuses safe," Gant said.

In June, the FBI released a public service announcement through its campus liaison agents warning of the credit card scheme. The announcement offers the following tips on how to protect against the scam:

- For students, don't agree to facilitate a purchase for someone who does not have a valid student ID.

- For school administrators, establish a procedure at your campus bookstore that includes a provision against allowing a purchaser to use a credit card in someone else's name.

- For victims, notify campus police or campus public safety.

This was not the first announcement warning students they may be targeted in fraud schemes. In May, the FBI warned students about a fake "education tax" scam, where perpetrators call students, claim to be from the IRS or the FBI, and demand immediate payment with the threat of arrest. Another scam involves criminals contacting students' parents, claiming their kids have been kidnapped, and demanding ransom money be sent to a third party for the safe release of the students. The students are often in class at the time and cannot answer phone calls from the parents, furthering the plausibility of the scam. Other scams are variations on common fraud schemes, where scammers pose as someone they are not in order to elicit sensitive information (names, dates of birth, Social Security numbers, bank accounts) to advance a crime.

If you believe you are a victim of a scam, contact your local authorities or, in the case of online crimes, the FBI's Internet Crime Complaint Center (IC3) at www.ic3.gov. Crime tips can also be submitted at tips.fbi.gov.

Sex Traffickers Sentenced
Father and Twin Sons Preyed on Underage Girls

A Chicago man who enlisted his twin sons to recruit underage girls for a family-run sex trafficking operation will spend nearly 17 years in prison—and his sons will serve even longer terms.

Nathan Nicholson, 45, and his 24-year-old sons Myrelle and Tyrelle Lockett victimized multiple girls and women—even kidnapping one of them.

"I've seen cases of families being involved in prostitution and other crimes, but I've never seen anything quite like this, with twins being used to recruit victims," said Special Agent Michael A. Barker, who investigated the case with Special Agent Carrie J. Landau out of the FBI's Chicago Division.

The twins had spent several months in juvenile detention for sex trafficking in 2010, putting them on the radar of the FBI and sheriff's deputies in Cook County, Illinois. They started working for their father shortly after their release.

As young adults, the Locketts looked for minor girls at Chicago-area malls. They flirted with girls, introduced themselves as "talent scouts," and asked if they wanted to make money by "dating" men. They introduced interested girls to their father, who photographed them partially nude. Nicholson made them have sex with either or both twins as a test before putting them to work.

The twins lured victims into prostitution in other ways, too. One of them had an underage girlfriend who posted pictures of herself flashing money and expensive items on her Facebook page. "All of her girlfriends would see that and hit her up on Facebook," Barker said. The girlfriend introduced her

interested friends to the Locketts.

The twins also targeted girls through Facebook on their own, focusing on teens who lived in the Muncie, Indiana, area. They fed girls compliments, Barker said, hoping to get a response.

"Sometimes, the Locketts were very blunt. They would say, 'I want good-looking girls to prostitute. You'll get rich, I'll get rich,'" Barker said. "Some girls were just sick of being poor. And these guys took advantage of that.

The victims rarely saw much or any of the money they collected as prostitutes. Nicholson and the Locketts also controlled the girls through terrible violence—including rape—and drugs. "These girls were essentially slave labor," Barker said.

The Lockett twins eventually started recruiting for themselves instead of their father, Barker said. All three men advertised on the Internet to find customers; Nicholson had his own website that showed pictures of the girls and his phone number.

As the FBI and Cook County deputies were building a case against the three, the Locketts kidnapped an 18-year-old woman in Minnesota and took her to Chicago in 2013. She managed to escape and contact the police. The abduction created new pressure on investigators, Barker said.

"We knew what they were doing, and we were building up our case. Then this happened, and we moved fast," Barker said. Authorities arrested Myrelle the day after the young woman escaped, Tyrelle was arrested in May 2014, and Nicholson was arrested in July 2015.

"Many of these girls had parents who loved them. … As parents, you have to be involved with everything your kids do, with all their electronic devices and their personal lives."

A search of Nicholson's home uncovered a bank of cell phones, a client list, a list of girls with their street names, and his ratings of the girls working for him. His computer contained photos of the victims as well as of his sons. Authorities also used a search warrant to capture incriminating material from the twins' Facebook profiles.

Law enforcement also recovered two minors actively working for Tyrelle at the time. Victim specialists from the FBI's Chicago Field Office helped the victims, including some adult females.

Nicholson pleaded guilty last year to one count of sex trafficking of a minor. A federal judge sentenced him in March to 16 years and eight months in prison. The twins each pleaded guilty to one count of transportation of a minor with intent to engage in prostitution and were sentenced by the same judge to 17 years and eight months. All three were also ordered to pay restitution to some of their victims.

For Barker and Landau, the case serves as a potent reminder for parents: "Many of these girls had parents who loved them. The problem is, some of them worked odd and long hours, and they were just tired and overwhelmed," Barker said. "As parents, you have to be involved with everything your kids do, with all their electronic devices and their personal lives."

Hurricane Harvey
Avoid Fraudulent Charitable Contribution Schemes

Texas National Guard soldiers arrive in Houston on August 27, 2017 to aid residents affected by Hurricane Harvey. (Texas Army National Guard photo)

Federal authorities are issuing warnings to potential donors wishing to aid victims of Hurricane Harvey that unscrupulous scammers may set up shop in the storm's wake.

"Criminals can exploit disasters, such as Hurricane Harvey, for their own gain by sending fraudulent communications through e-mail or social media."

The Federal Trade Commission (FTC) and the U.S. Computer Emergency Readiness Team (US-CERT) this week warned that phishing scams and bogus e-mail solicitations may target potential givers. US-CERT warned users to be cautious when handling unsolicited e-mails with subject lines, hyperlinks, and attachments related to Hurricane Harvey. And the Department of Justice (DOJ) on Wednesday issued a reminder to be vigilant about potentially fraudulent activity on the heels of a disaster.

"E-mails requesting donations from duplicitous charitable organizations commonly appear after major natural disasters," said US-CERT, an organization within the Department of Homeland Security that analyzes and responds to emerging cyber threats.

"Be alert for charities that seem to have sprung up overnight in connection with current events," the FTC warned.

The National Center for Disaster Fraud, which was established by the Justice Department to investigate fraud in the wake of Hurricane Katrina, said in a press release this week that tips regarding suspected fraud should be reported by phone to (866) 720-5721 or online at disaster@leo.gov. Suspected Internet-based fraud can also be reported to the FBI's Internet Crime Complaint Center, or IC3, at www.ic3.gov.

To assist those seeking guidance, the Federal Emergency Management Agency (FEMA) tweeted a link to "trusted sources for helping out with #Harvey," which takes users to the website for National Voluntary Organizations Active in Disaster. The Virginia-based non-profit group describes itself as an "association of organizations that mitigate and alleviate the impact of disasters" and counts many well-known national aid organizations among its members. FEMA also posted a link to a list of the organization's members in Texas.

The agencies offered these tips (among others) to individuals who are considering making donations:

- Donate to charities you know and trust.

- Designate the disaster to ensure your funds go toward disaster relief.

- Never click on links or open attachments in unsolicited e-mail.

- Don't assume that charity messages posted on social media are legitimate. Research the organization.

- Verify the legitimacy of any e-mail solicitation by contacting the organization directly through a trusted contact number.

- Beware of organizations with copycat names similar to but not exactly the same as those of reputable charities.

- Avoid cash donations if possible. Pay by credit card or write a check directly to the charity. Do not make checks payable to individuals.

- Legitimate charities do not normally solicit donations via money transfer services. Most legitimate charity websites end in .org rather than .com.

- Make contributions directly, rather than relying on others to make a contribution on your behalf.

After Hurricane Katrina hit New Orleans and the Gulf Coast region in 2005, the immediate devastation was followed by years of complaints of fraud. In the four years after Katrina, the fraud task force—consisting of more than two dozen local, state, and federal agencies, including the FBI—received more than 36,000 complaints. By 2009, more than 1,300 individuals had been indicted for Katrina-related crimes.

If charitable giving after past disasters is any indication, millions of aid dollars will flow in the coming weeks and months to areas affected by Harvey's damaging storms and flooding. Federal agencies want to make sure those

contributions end up where donors intend, and not in the hands of criminals.

"Unfortunately, criminals can exploit disasters, such as Hurricane Harvey, for their own gain by sending fraudulent communications through e-mail or social media and by creating phony websites designed to solicit contributions," the National Center for Disaster Fraud warned.

"The FBI is dedicated to investigating and preventing this type of fraud, especially when it involves preying on individuals during times of great need."

Perrye Turner, the special agent in charge of the FBI's Houston Division, echoed these warnings: "As we all work to rebuild the Houston/Gulf Coast region and look for ways to help, it's important to perform due diligence before giving contributions to anyone soliciting donations or individuals offering to provide assistance to those affected by Harvey, whether the solicitations are in person, via e-mail, or by telephone," Turner said in a statement. "The FBI is dedicated to investigating and preventing this type of fraud, especially when it involves preying on individuals during times of great need."

National Center for Disaster Fraud
Phone: (866) 720-5721
E-mail: disaster@leo.gov

Cold Case Solved

Decades Later, Murderer Brought to Justice

James Ricks was sitting in his car late on a summer night in 1967 in North Little Rock, Arkansas when he was startled by tapping on his car window. Two criminals were fleeing a store they had robbed when their getaway car broke down. They stole Ricks' car—and his life—but decades would go by before his killer was brought to justice.

The pair of criminals shot Ricks, a 27-year-old African-American father of a young daughter, and locked him in the trunk of his own 1964 Oldsmobile. After driving around with a wounded Ricks in the trunk, they shot him again in the back of the head and left him in a wooded area in rural Arkansas.

James Leon Clay, 20, and his brother Leon Junior Clay, 25, were convicted of interstate vehicle theft for stealing Ricks' car and for the robberies they'd committed earlier that night. But the men were never charged with Ricks' murder, despite having stolen his car and leaving fingerprints inside the vehicle. Ricks' body was found by hikers two months later on August 27, 1967.

Cold Case Heats Up

Nearly 50 years later and 1,100 miles away in Delaware, Special Agent Justin Downen—working out of the FBI Baltimore Division's Dover Resident Agency—received a call from a man who said his brother-in-law's prison cellmate had confessed to the murder. Though Downen was not familiar with the killing, the story piqued his interest. So Downen and Officer Derrick Calloway of the Laurel (Delaware) Police Department interviewed the cellmate of James Leon Clay, by then in his 60s, at Sussex Correctional Institution in Georgetown, Delaware. (Calloway was familiar with Clay because he had investigated the bank robbery—unrelated to the Ricks murder—that landed Clay in prison.)

Clay's cellmate, who was imprisoned on drug charges, gave the investigators a detailed account of the killing—the circumstances, type of gun used, Clay facing Ricks' family in the courtroom when he was charged with stealing the car. The cellmate, who slept in the top bunk, took detailed notes on their discussions while Clay talked from the bottom bunk.

Clay told the cellmate he regretted killing Ricks, and that his brother, who had since died, had told him to do it.

"I think some of it was bragging a little bit," Downen said of Clay's willingness to confide in his cellmate. "He's an old man in prison, and you wonder how much he wanted people to be a little bit scared of him. I don't know how much of it was ego and wanting people to think he was a tough guy, or how much of it was just boredom."

After additional investigation, it became clear that the story checked out.

"There's just no way this story isn't true," Downen said after listening to the story and seeing how it corroborated with known details of Ricks' murder. "Then it was just a matter of how we would prove it. The case is 50 years old, so the only way we get a conviction is to get the guy on tape admitting to it."

Waiting Game

There were a number of challenges with getting that proof, one being that the cellmate had since moved to a minimum security prison out of state.

So the investigators decided to simply wait for Clay's release and try to get a second confession—this time on tape.

"It wasn't like we were working it every day or even every week, we just had to have the willingness to wait him out and take the long approach," Downen said.

Two years went by. Downen was assigned to other cases. Calloway transferred to another police department. Given their workloads, they could've easily moved on from the case or not acted on the tip, but investigators were committed to seeing it through to the end.

"No one was tracking this case. No one would've criticized us if we didn't follow through on this case from 50 years ago with nothing more than a tip from someone in prison," Downen said. "We knew it was the right thing to do, and we would want someone do it for us. That's what justice is about."

'Chance' Encounter

Downen called the Delaware prison system occasionally to check on Clay during those two years. In August 2014, he got the answer he'd been waiting for: Clay was released that morning. It was time to get their taped confession.

Given where Clay and his old cellmate had met and bonded, the probation office seemed the most likely place for their "chance" meeting, so Downen, Calloway, and officials from the Delaware Department of Probation and Parole came up with a plan to have the two former cellmates in the lobby at the same time as they were arriving for meetings with their probation officers.

James Ricks (holding guitar) in an undated family photo. Ricks was murdered in 1967, and his killer, James Leon Clay, was brought to justice nearly 50 years later. (Photo Courtesy of Julius Ricks)

Right on schedule, the cellmate arrived at the probation office when Clay did, wearing a hidden recording device. Clay recounted everything, both in the office and as the two men continued to chat in Clay's truck.

Clay was quickly arrested and returned to Little Rock, where he was charged with Ricks' murder. After the judge declared his taped confession admissible, Clay pleaded guilty to the murder charges and was sentenced to 20 years. He was 67 at the time of his arrest in 2015 and will likely spend the rest of his life behind bars.

Justice Achieved

For Ricks' family, the years without justice and closure for their loved one were difficult, especially knowing that the Clay brothers had been convicted of other crimes but would be released.

Ricks' brother described James Ricks as a friendly and fun-loving young man.

"It was hard on me," said Julius Ricks, who is now 74 and still lives in the North Little Rock area. "I would often think about him. Me and my brother and my sister, we'd always talk about it. We wondered what happened to the guys. It was rough; I won't lie. I really missed him."

He was surprised to receive a phone call from the FBI that his brother's killer had confessed.

"That was a miracle, what they did," Julius Ricks said. "It was just a miracle when they called and said that the guy had talked in jail."

Putting a killer behind bars—even nearly a half-century after the crime—was also worth the patient effort for Downen and the other investigators involved.

"It's really easy to put yourself in the shoes of that family and think about what it would be like to lose a loved one under those circumstances and not have justice," Downen said.

Staying Ahead of the Threat

National Security Summit Focuses on the State of U.S. Intelligence

Director Christopher Wray speaks at the Intelligence & National Security Alliance Summit on September 7, 2017, in Washington, D.C.

The FBI is working tirelessly to stay ahead of the evolving terrorist threats facing the United States—including small-scale attacks that are often difficult to disrupt, FBI Director Christopher Wray said today during a meeting of intelligence and national security leaders.

Speaking at the Intelligence and National Security Alliance Summit in Washington, D.C., Wray said that while large-scale terrorist strikes like the September 11 attacks remain a threat, violent radicals are increasingly engaging in smaller plots on vulnerable soft targets that are planned quickly, decreasing the amount of time the FBI and other law enforcement agencies have to intervene.

"If the lifespan is much shorter, which it is with a lot of the homegrown, violent extremist types of situations, the need for us as a community to be more agile ... is much greater," Wray said.

The summit is an annual conference for government,

military, and private-sector personnel, sponsored by national security industry groups AFCEA International and the Intelligence and National Security Alliance. This year's theme was "The State of U.S. Intelligence: A Time of Transition, Challenge, and Innovation."

Wray was joined in a panel discussion by top leaders in the intelligence and national security communities, including National Security Agency Director Admiral Michael Rogers, National Geospatial Intelligence Agency Director Robert Cardillo, Defense Intelligence Agency Deputy Director Melissa Drisko, and National Reconnaissance Office Principal Deputy Director Frank Calvelli. FBI executives Paul Abbate, Joshua Skule, and Scott Smith also participated in breakout sessions during the two-day conference.

The leaders on Wray's directors' panel discussed a variety of intelligence topics, touched on national security investigations,

and took questions from the audience.

When asked about his thoughts on assuming leadership of the FBI, Wray said the organization has grown since he initially worked with the Bureau during his earlier career as a Department of Justice prosecutor and administrator. He cited the organization's efforts to keep up with technology advancements, the growth in partnerships, and expansion of the intelligence program as positive changes he has noted since his term began last month.

"The things that were great about the Bureau still are great about the Bureau," Wray said. "People are mission-focused. No matter what job they have, they're very passionate about it. They are determined to be the best at what they do." He added that employees "bring the kind of integrity that I always found so attractive when I was working with them as a line prosecutor and later in main Justice after 9/11."

Partnerships and intelligence are two key factors in staying ahead of the threats posed by terrorists, hackers, and criminals, Wray said. The FBI is "very focused on building ties with all of the communities it protects," he explained, noting how much the organization's partnerships with state and local police and the private sector have expanded in recent years.

He also praised the evolution of the FBI's intelligence program, including the integration of intelligence into everything the organization does. "You can see how intelligence is driving everything," he said.

Safe Online Surfing Internet Challenge
Free Cyber Safety Program Redesigned for New School Year

In the Safe Online Surfing (SOS) Internet Challenge, students navigate through various games and activities on their grade-appropriate island. The SOS website is accessible year-round at https://sos.fbi.gov, but the testing and competition is only open to registered teachers and schools from September through May.

The FBI's Safe Online Surfing (SOS) Internet Challenge—a free, educational program for children that teaches cyber safety—has been redesigned for the 2017-2018 school year, with new graphics and updated content.

The new SOS program, created for students in third through eighth grades, covers age-appropriate topics, such as cyberbullying, passwords, malware, social media, and more. The program also provides teachers with a curriculum that meets state and federal Internet safety mandates.

While taking the course, participating students "surf" their way through a variety of Internet safety challenges at each grade level, with characters guiding them through the games. The latest version of SOS allows the program to work on more devices, including tablets. The content has also been refreshed to address current cyber safety challenges, and the island-theme graphics have been updated.

"Just as we teach our children to lock the front door for their physical safety, we have to teach them the online equivalents of those things in the digital age, like creating a strong password," said Unit Chief Jonathan Cox of the FBI's Office of Public Affairs. "SOS helps to make students better digital citizens in a fun and educational way."

Last school year, more than 700,000 students across the country completed the program and took the test, a 41 percent increase from the previous school year. More than 1.5 million students have participated and taken the exam since the original program was launched in 2012.

The SOS activities are open to anyone, though to participate in the testing and challenge, teachers must register their classes. Teachers manage their students' participation in the program; the FBI does not collect or store any student information. Each month from September through May, the classes with the top exam scores nationwide receive an FBI-SOS certificate and, when possible, they are visited by local FBI personnel to congratulate them.

SOS Internet Challenge Program

Select Teacher Feedback from the 2016-2017 School Year:

- *"Thank you so much for this wonderful opportunity. My classes have really enjoyed this activity."* - Huntsville, Alabama, teacher

- *"I truly feel like our students gained so much from your Safe Online Surfing lessons! Thanks for helping to educate our precious children and keep them safe!"* - Vega, Texas, teacher

- *"This is a great program. I thank you for making it available to students. My classes will be participating again next year!"* - Phoenix, Arizona, teacher

- *"The SOS program has been a very effective tool which has provided the students … the knowledge they need to be safer online and when using technology."* - West Long Branch, New Jersey, teacher

Usage Statistics:

- During the 2016-2017 school year, 12,560 schools in 49 states, Washington, D.C., and the Virgin Islands completed the program.

- Since October 2012, the FBI SOS website has been visited more than 2.5 million times.

Bankruptcy Fraud

Wife Stole Husband's Identity, Retirement Account

Veteran financial fraud investigators had never seen anything like it before: A bankruptcy scam in which an Indiana woman stole her husband's identity—while they were still married—and began to loot his 401(k) retirement fund and other assets.

"This was certainly a unique case," said Special Agent Doug Kasper, who supervised the investigation from the FBI's Indianapolis Division. Even after 58-year-old Patricia Bippus-Allen was sentenced to five years in federal prison in July after pleading guilty to conspiracy to commit bankruptcy fraud, subornation of perjury, wire fraud, and aggravated identity theft, investigators remain uncertain about her motive or what she did with the money.

What is certain, however, is that Bippus-Allen devised an elaborate bankruptcy fraud to gain access to her husband's wages, and she made multiple unauthorized withdrawals from his 401(k) retirement account—all with the help of her brother, who impersonated her husband.

In September 2010, Bippus-Allen filed a joint Chapter 13 bankruptcy petition in both her and her husband's name in the U.S. Bankruptcy Court for the Southern District of Indiana. Her husband of more than 25 years had no idea she had done so.

"He trusted his wife to handle all the family finances," said Special Agent Paul Medernach, who investigated the case. "He never used a computer, and never saw his pay stub because his check went into his bank account through direct deposit."

"For husbands or wives who might have similar ideas about defrauding their spouses, they should know there are serious penalties for such actions."

During the course of the bankruptcy proceedings, Bippus-Allen created documents bearing the forged signature of her husband, and she made excuses about why he could not attend meetings. In one instance, she provided her bankruptcy attorney with a letter from a doctor stating that her husband was under his care and would be hospitalized for at least 30 days, during which he could not see visitors or take phone calls.

"That was all a lie," Medernach said. "She faked the letter and the doctor's signature. Her husband had never been under the doctor's care."

In March 2011, Bippus-Allen attended a meeting of creditors that her husband was also required to attend. That's when she persuaded her brother, David Bippus, to impersonate her husband. Both stated under oath that he was her husband, and a bankruptcy plan was confirmed requiring monthly payments to Bippus-Allen's trustee for 60 months. Approximately $74,000 was deducted from the husband's direct deposit

paychecks, without his consent or knowledge—and Bippus-Allen gained access to those funds.

During the same time period, Bippus-Allen transferred money on multiple occasions from her husband's 401(k) account into her own personal bank accounts by purporting to be her husband and by providing false documentation. In all, those unauthorized withdrawals totaled more than $24,000, not including more than $16,000 in loans she took out on her husband's 401(k) account—again, without his knowledge or consent.

The idea that a disgruntled wife or husband would want to steal a spouse's money is perhaps not that surprising, Medernach noted. "But not many spouses would go to these lengths—to find someone to impersonate a spouse and to forge documents like doctor's notes and a driver's license."

The scam might have continued to work if not for an unbelievable coincidence: A relative of the victim happened to work as a paralegal for an Indiana bankruptcy attorney and saw his name on the bankruptcy court's docket. She asked the husband if he was aware of it, and he was not. The relative contacted law enforcement.

FBI investigators worked closely with the U.S. Attorney's Office to unravel the fraud and to bring charges against Bippus-Allen and her brother. "The U.S. Attorney's Office was eager to prosecute this case because it sends a clear message," said Kasper. "For husbands or wives who might have similar ideas about defrauding their spouses, they should know there are serious penalties for such actions."

A Psychological Twist

Mother and Son's Companies Bilked Medicare out of Millions

A Louisiana man and his mother were sentenced in July to lengthy prison terms for fraud schemes spanning six years that bilked Medicare for more than $13 million in bogus claims. The two were among 243 doctors, nurses, and medical professionals who were charged in 2015 in what, at the time, was the nation's largest Medicare fraud takedown.

Rodney Hesson, 47, and his mother, Gertrude Parker, 63, together owned eight psychological services companies that operated in Louisiana, Mississippi, Florida, and Alabama. Hesson's companies operated as Nursing Home Psychological Services, and Parker's companies operated as Psychological Care Services. The pair was convicted in January for billing the federal health insurance program more than $25 million for services at nursing homes that were either unnecessary or not provided.

Medicare Fraud Strike Force investigators discovered patterns of billing irregularities originating from Hesson and Parker's companies beginning in 2009 and referred the matter to the FBI's New Orleans Field Office, which investigated the case with the Office of Inspector General for the Department of Health and Human Services.

"The case was difficult because there were multiple schemes in play," said Special Agent Jennifer Terry, one of several agents who worked the case. She amassed spreadsheets of data illustrating how inconceivable it was for the subjects' companies to bill what they did. "One of the things they were doing was billing impossible hours. If Mr. Hesson worked 365 days a year without taking a day off, he would have had to work in

excess of 30 hours a day to be able to equate to some of his billings."

Meanwhile, at the facilities where Hesson's companies claimed to provide services, there was compelling evidence that some treatments, like psychological testing, could not have been delivered as claimed. "There were patients who were in a state where they just couldn't be tested," Terry said. "Some had severe dementia. Some of them couldn't speak at all. We found files showing some patients were completely unresponsive and yet their billings were for psychological tests."

Two psychologists who worked for Hesson admitted to repeatedly testing nursing home residents even though they were incapacitated. In their plea agreements last September, John Teal, 46, of Jackson, Mississippi, and Beverly Stubblefield, 62, of Slidell, Louisiana, admitted that some of their clients could not have meaningfully participated in testing.

The fraud case against Hesson was not without precedent. In 2011, he was indicted on state charges in Mississippi for fraudulently billing Medicaid, the joint federal and state health insurance program for low-income and needy people. In that case, he was sentenced to

five years suspended jail time and three years of house arrest. The sentence in 2012 also excluded his companies from billing all federal health care programs, cutting a primary source of income. Just before his sentencing, however, he resigned from his companies, changed their names, and sold them to his mother, Gertrude Parker, who investigators say paid him for the purchase during his house arrest. The companies that emerged from that arrangement are the same companies involved in the schemes that led to charges against Hesson, Parker, Teal, and Stubblefield.

Hesson was sentenced on July 13 to the statutory maximum of 15 years in prison and ordered to pay $13.8 million in restitution. Parker was sentenced on the same day to seven years in prison and ordered to pay $7.3 million. They were scheduled to begin their prison terms this month.

Coincidentally, the pair's sentencings were on the same day federal officials announced the results of this year's nationwide sweep targeting Medicare fraud. The announcement of charges against more than 400 doctors, nurses, and medical professionals for $1.3 billion in false Medicare billings was said to be the largest action to date.

Idaho Drug Ring Dismantled

11 Sent to Prison for Dealing Methamphetamine

The opioid epidemic is battering American communities and rightfully commanding national attention. In certain areas of the country, however, the illicit drug of choice is methamphetamine, and that powerful stimulant is every bit as addictive—and devastating—as heroin, fentanyl, and prescription opiates.

In the southwestern corner of Idaho, in an area surrounding the city of Boise, "we're on the front end of the opioid epidemic," said Special Agent Doug Hart. "We've seen increases in heroin use—it's coming our way—but meth is still king."

In its wake, meth leaves a trail of crime and addiction that ultimately leads back to the dealers who supply the drug and reap substantial profits.

Early in 2015, Elizabeth Gaytan, a street-level dealer, sold meth on numerous occasions to undercover police officers working with the FBI-led Treasure Valley Metro Violent Crime Task Force. The task force, composed of local, state, and federal law enforcement agencies, is part of the FBI's nationwide Safe Streets Violent Crime Initiative.

Investigators later learned the identity of Gaytan's supplier—Stacy Duane Wilfong—a gang member who led a larger group that distributed drugs throughout the Treasure Valley. "That took us one more step up the ladder," said Hart, who worked on the investigation from the FBI's office in Boise, part of the Bureau's Salt Lake City Division.

Gaytan and others involved in the meth trade in the Treasure Valley were associated with gang activity and "a lot of violence," Hart said. "There had been shootings and stabbings and home invasions involving her residence, all related to the drug trade."

A court-ordered wiretap of Wilfong's phone during the course of less than one month revealed hundreds of calls to co-conspirators related to the distribution of meth and other drugs, Hart said. "We were also able to determine who was supplying Wilfong. The investigation enabled us to go up three levels and take off the main suppliers."

Members of the Treasure Valley Metro Violent Crime Task Force were aided in the investigation by the Organized

Crime and Drug Enforcement Task Force (OCDETF), a federal entity that supplies funding for law enforcement efforts to dismantle major drug trafficking organizations.

In December 2015, Wilfong, Gaytan, and nine others were indicted by a federal grand jury in Boise for conspiring to distribute controlled substances. "This group was responsible for dealing multiple pounds of meth," Hart said.

In July 2017, Idaho resident John Matthew Caviness, Jr. was sentenced to four years in federal prison for his role in the meth ring. He was the last of 11 subjects to be sentenced in the case. Wilfong, the 40-year-old ringleader, was sentenced in October 2016 to more than 18 years behind bars. Gaytan received a prison sentence of more than eight years for her role in the conspiracy.

"We dismantled a violent group of individuals who distributed meth throughout the Treasure Valley," Hart said. "But they were one group of many." The veteran investigator, who has been working gang and drug investigation cases for more than two decades, noted that so-called "super labs" in Mexico can produce 50 pounds of meth a day, and the drug usually hits American streets uncut.

"When I started doing drug buys in 2008, we bought ounces and tested them at 9 percent and 11 percent purity," he explained. "The purity is now essentially 100 percent, and availability has increased substantially. If we dismantle these groups and reduce supply, the price of meth should go up, but that's not happening," he said. "That's the type of drug problem we are facing."

2016 Crime Statistics Released

Violent Crime Increases, Property Crime Decreases

Violent crime increased for the second consecutive year, while property crime decreased for the 14th straight year, according to the FBI's annual report on national crime statistics released today. There were an estimated 17,250 murders in the U.S. last year, an 8.6 percent increase from 2015.

Overall violent crime rose 4.1 percent last year, while property crime fell 1.3 percent compared to 2015 figures.

Crime in the United States, 2016 is a compilation of information reported to the FBI's Uniform Crime Reporting (UCR) Program by more than 16,000 law enforcement agencies nationwide.

The report showed there were an estimated 1.2 million violent crimes in the U.S. last year. Though the violent crime numbers rose from 2015 to 2016, the five-year and 10-year trends show an increase from 2012 (up 2.6 percent) and a decrease from 2007 (down 12.3 percent).

Additional statistics from *Crime in the United States, 2016* include:

- Last year's data shows there were 95,730 rapes reported to law enforcement, based on the UCR's legacy definition.
- Of the violent crimes reported to

police in 2016, aggravated assault made up 64.3 percent, while robbery was 26.6 percent. Rape (legacy definition) accounted for 7.7 percent of the violent crimes reported last year, and murder made up 1.4 percent.

- About 7.9 million property crimes were reported to the UCR, with losses (excluding arson) of about $15.6 billion.

- The report estimates that law enforcement agencies made about 10.7 million arrests in 2016 (excluding arrests for traffic violations).

The 2016 report has been streamlined from 81 information tables to 29, but it still includes key

data on major categories—such as known offenses and number of arrests—that researchers, law enforcement, and the public expect. *Crime in the United States, 2016* also includes the additional publications *Federal Crime Data, Human Trafficking,* and *Cargo Theft.*

In his message accompanying the report, FBI Director Christopher Wray called on law enforcement agencies to continue transitioning to the more informative National Incident-Based Reporting System (NIBRS). Use of NIBRS data, which will be the national standard for crime reporting by 2021, will provide additional transparency. Wray called for the country to "get beyond anecdotal evidence and collect more comprehensive data so that we have a clearer and more complete picture of crime in the United States." He also noted the creation of the FBI's database to collect law enforcement use-of-force statistics to facilitate an informed dialogue within communities.

"The more complete the data, the better we can inform, educate, and strengthen all of our communities," Wray said.

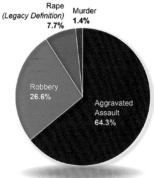

Violent Crime in 2016

Rape (Legacy Definition) 7.7%
Murder 1.4%
Robbery 26.6%
Aggravated Assault 64.3%

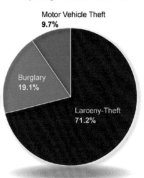

Property Crime in 2016

Motor Vehicle Theft 9.7%
Burglary 19.1%
Larceny-Theft 71.2%

From *Crime in the United States, 2016.*

New Top Ten Fugitive

Help Us Catch a Murderer

FBI TEN MOST WANTED FUGITIVE

UNLAWFUL FLIGHT TO AVOID PROSECUTION - MURDER IN THE FIRST DEGREE, ATTEMPTED MURDER IN THE FIRST DEGREE, CONSPIRACY TO COMMIT MURDER IN THE FIRST DEGREE, UNLAWFUL POSSESSION OF A FIREARM IN THE SECOND DEGREE; MURDER IN THE SECOND DEGREE

SANTIAGO VILLALBA MEDEROS

Photograph taken in 2009   Photograph taken in 2005

A Washington state gang member charged with two murders in 2010 has been named to the FBI's Ten Most Wanted Fugitives list, and a reward of up to $100,000 is being offered for information leading to his capture.

Santiago Villalba Mederos, a member of the violent Eastside Lokotes Sureño gang, is wanted in connection with two separate shootings in Tacoma, Washington, that resulted in the death of a young woman and the serious wounding of her brother, and a month later, the murder of a young man. Mederos was a teenager at the time of the killings.

"To have committed two homicides at such a young age shows how violent he was and how violent the gang was," said Special Agent Terry Postma from the FBI's Seattle Division. "The younger gang members tried to earn respect from the older guys by these extreme acts of violence."

In February 2010, Mederos—who goes by the nickname "Pucho"—allegedly fired multiple shots into a random car, killing a 20-year-old woman and wounding her brother. The following month, during a robbery that turned into a fight

when bystanders became involved, Mederos allegedly fired a single gunshot toward the group, striking and killing a 21-year-old innocent bystander.

> "We believe he is still extremely dangerous and a threat to the community, wherever he is."

"In both the cases he's wanted for, none of the victims had anything to do with gangs," said Steve Reopelle, a homicide detective with the Tacoma Police Department who has investigated both murders.

Based on witness reports, it is believed that Mederos—19 years old at the time—fled to Mexico after the murders. He may have returned to the U.S. since 2010, which is why investigators are looking for the public's assistance in both countries. In addition to Washington state charges including first- and second-degree murder, Mederos has been charged federally with unlawful flight to avoid prosecution. Naming Mederos to the Ten Most Wanted Fugitives list means that the case will get much wider exposure and public attention, and the reward for his

capture increases to as much as $100,000.

"We believe there are a lot of people that have information on his whereabouts," Reopelle said. "The reward will be a great incentive for someone to come forward. Mederos has been on the run for a long time. We need the public's help to apprehend him."

The FBI and the Tacoma Police Department have been working closely together to bring Mederos to justice. "We believe he is still extremely dangerous and a threat to the community, wherever he is," Postma said.

Mederos, now 26 years old, speaks English and Spanish. He is known to have ties to the states of Guerrero and Morelos in Mexico. He also has ties to Washington state. He is approximately 5 feet 10 inches tall and weighs 140 pounds. He has black hair, brown eyes, and distinguishing tattoos: the letter "S" on his left shoulder and the letter "E" on his right shoulder.

Anyone with information concerning Mederos should take no action themselves, but instead immediately contact the nearest FBI office or local law enforcement agency. For possible sightings outside the United States, contact the nearest U.S. Embassy or Consulate. The FBI's Seattle Field Office can be reached at 206-622-0460. The U.S. Embassy in Mexico City can be reached at 011-52-55-5080-2000. Tips can also be submitted at 1-800-CALL FBI or online at tips.fbi.gov.

Note: This case may have been resolved since this information was posted on our website. Please check www.fbi.gov/wanted for up-to-date information.

Director Wray Formally Installed

Ceremony Held to Recognize Appointment of Eighth FBI Director

During Christopher Wray's formal installation ceremony at FBI Headquarters in Washington, D.C., today, Attorney General Jeff Sessions called the new Director a "great leader" and "one that is right for the time."

"Leading such a critical organization as the FBI where violent crime, national security, public corruption are key responsibilities, and when technology presents even more new challenges every day, it requires qualities of intelligence, integrity, objectivity, and most of all, I think, good judgment," Sessions said. "Director Wray meets that test in full. His judgment and integrity will always lead him."

Wray, a former U.S. attorney and assistant attorney general in the Justice Department's Criminal Division, was formally sworn in August 2, 2017 in a private ceremony. Today's event publicly marked the beginning of Wray's tenure, with hundreds of FBI employees, current and former federal officials, and other dignitaries in the audience.

In his remarks, Wray pledged to uphold the "simple, yet profound" mission of the FBI: to protect the American people and uphold the Constitution of the United States.

"That mission hasn't changed, and it won't change, not as long as I have anything to say about it. We're going to abide by the rule of law and our core values," Wray said. "We're going to follow the facts independently, no matter where they lead and no matter who likes it. And we're going to always, always pursue justice."

Wray thanked the FBI's workforce and commended their "drive and passion for service." He recalled

Director Christopher Wray addresses the audience during his formal installation ceremony at FBI Headquarters on September 28, 2017.

From left: FBI Deputy Director Andrew McCabe and Attorney General Jeff Sessions joined Director Christopher Wray and his wife, Helen Wray, on stage during the ceremony.

his previous interactions with the FBI in his prosecutorial career and said he was excited to lead the organization. He also noted how much the threats to the country have evolved in recent years and vowed that the FBI will continue to adapt to be one step ahead of them.

"The threats we face are significant, and the premium on vigilance doesn't stop," Wray said "I am determined to do the very

best I can to put the FBI in the best position to meet those threats and to make this extraordinary institution even better and even stronger."

National Cyber Security Awareness Month 2017

Protecting Yourself Online in an Interconnected World

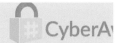

As hacks, data breaches, and other cyber-enabled crime become increasingly commonplace, this year's National Cyber Security Awareness Month is an important reminder of the need to take steps to protect yourself and your family when using the Internet. Launched in 2004 by the Department of Homeland Security and the National Cyber Security Alliance, the annual campaign held every October is designed to help the public stay safe online and to increase national resiliency in the event of a cyber incident.

"Cyber risks can seem overwhelming in today's hyper-connected world, but there are steps you can take to protect yourself and reduce your risk," said Assistant Director Scott Smith of the FBI's Cyber Division. "The FBI and our partners are working hard to stop these threats at the source, but everyone has to play a role. Use common sense; for example, don't click on a link from an unsolicited e-mail, and remember that if an online deal seems too good to be true, it probably is. And overall, remain vigilant to keep yourself and your family safe in the online world, just as you do in the physical world."

How can you protect yourself?

- **Learn about the IC3—and use it if you're ever a victim.** The Internet Crime Complaint Center (IC3) is a reliable and convenient reporting mechanism for the public to submit complaints about Internet crime and scams to the FBI. The IC3 uses the information from public complaints to refer cases to the appropriate law enforcement agencies and identify trends. The IC3 has received nearly 4 million complaints since it was created in 2000. Anyone who is a victim of an Internet enabled crime, such as an online scam, should file a complaint with IC3 at www.ic3.gov to help the FBI stop hackers and other cyber criminals.

- **Practice good cyber hygiene at work.** When you're at work, you're a target. From personal data to financial information to company secrets, company networks are a gold mine for hackers and fraudsters. One common scam that victimizes companies is business e-mail compromise, in which a hacker will gain access to a company official's e-mail to defraud the company or access employees' private information. Additionally, ransomware, in which hackers will place malware in digital files that demands a ransom, is a serious threat to companies and other large organizations.

- **Know the risks of the Internet of Things (IOT).** Cyber security goes beyond your computer and phone. Many homes are now filled with Internet-connected devices, such as home security systems, baby monitors, smart appliances, and medical devices. All of these devices present opportunities for hackers to spy on you and get your personal information. Using strong passwords and purchasing IOT devices from companies with a good security track record are just a few of the things you can do to protect your family and home.

- **Cyber savvy? Uncle Sam wants you.** As the cyber threat continues to grow, the FBI is similarly ramping up its efforts to recruit cyber experts to work as special agents, intelligence analysts, computer scientists, and more. The FBI partners with universities and other educational institutions with a science, technology, engineering, and math (STEM) focus to encourage students to pursue an FBI career, whether as an agent investigating hackers, an analyst looking strategically at threats, or a scientist evaluating evidence. The FBI offers a rewarding career in thwarting cyber attacks and bringing hackers and other criminals to justice. Visit FBIjobs.gov to apply.

- **Learn how the FBI and partner agencies are protecting critical infrastructure.** Terrorist groups and other adversaries view the U.S. critical infrastructure—ranging from the financial sector to hospitals to electricity grids—as high-value targets that would disrupt American life if attacked. The FBI plays a key role in thwarting these attacks by stopping plots against critical infrastructure and investigating cyber attacks. Protecting these targets is a team effort among federal, state, local, and private sector partners. Three of the key partnership organizations the FBI is a member of are InfraGard, the Domestic Security Alliance Council, and the National Cyber-Forensics and Training Alliance. These strategic relationships promote timely information sharing between the FBI and the private sector, which helps to keep critical infrastructure networks safe from hackers and terrorists.

Scan this QR code with your smartphone to access related information, or visit www.fbi.gov/ncsam2017.

Crimes Against Children

Help Us Identify a Child Predator

The FBI is asking for help to identify Jane Doe 39, a woman who may have information about a child victim in an ongoing investigation.

The FBI is seeking the public's help to stop a child predator.

The unidentified woman being sought—known only as Jane Doe 39—can be seen in a video with a child who is being sexually exploited.

The video was obtained during an FBI investigation and forwarded to the National Center for Missing & Exploited Children (NCMEC), an organization that works closely with the Bureau to stop child predators. Further investigation revealed that the images have surfaced elsewhere online, said Special Agent Susan Romash, who investigates child exploitation cases as part of the FBI's Violent Crimes Against Children program. "We know the video has been traded on the Internet," Romash said, "and we know this child is a victim who needs our help."

In the video, an adult woman is heard speaking Vietnamese, and at one point her face is shown. "Our hope," Romash said, "is that someone will recognize this individual's face—or her voice—and come forward with information."

The publicity efforts to identify and apprehend Jane Doe 39 are part of the FBI's Operation Rescue Me and Endangered Child Alert Program (ECAP) initiatives.

Operation Rescue Me identifies child victims of sexual exploitation by using sophisticated image analysis to obtain evidence. ECAP seeks public and media assistance to help identify the John and Jane Does who display their faces—and other distinguishing characteristics such as tattoos—in pornographic images and videos of children.

The FBI has a longstanding partnership with NCMEC, which maintains a database of pornographic images traded online to help law enforcement coordinate and solve investigations. Working closely with NCMEC, FBI investigators look for metadata embedded within images that might contain GPS or other details that can reveal critical information.

"We also search for clues within the images," Romash said. "Those clues often help us determine where the image was produced or who created it. If those approaches don't work," she explained, "but there is an adult in the image whose face is shown, we publicize it through ECAP and ask for the public's help."

The video depicting Jane Doe 39 and a child victim was first noted by NCMEC in April 2016. The woman is described as an Asian female, likely between the ages of 25 and 35, with long black hair. She is wearing a white, yellow, blue, and red floral dress. In addition, she could be heard speaking Vietnamese.

Anyone with information can submit a tip online or call the FBI's toll-free tip line at 1-800-CALL-FBI (1-800-225-5324).

Since its inception in 2004, ECAP has resulted in the identification of 26 of the 39 John/Jane Does, and in the recovery of more than 40 child victims. Operation Rescue Me, established in 2008, has resulted in the recovery of more than 200 child victims. "These programs work," Romash said, "and we are again asking for the public's help to save an innocent child from being victimized."

Note: This case may have been resolved since this information was posted on our website. Please check www.fbi.gov/wanted/seeking-info for up-to-date information.

Scan this QR code with your smartphone to access related information, or visit www.fbi.gov/janedoe39.

Coup Attempt in The Gambia

Military Action Violated Federal Neutrality Act

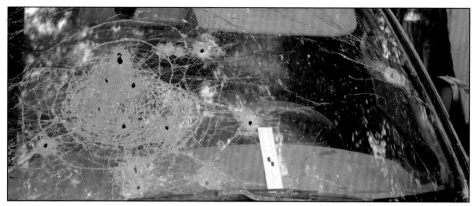

One of two cars used in a 2014 attack on the Gambian State House during a coup attempt in The Gambia. Several naturalized Americans from the West African nation helped plan and carry out the failed coup, violating U.S. federal law.

When a group of naturalized Americans from The Gambia tried to help overthrow the government of their West African homeland in 2014, they thought they would be hailed as heroes. Not only did they fail, they were charged in the United States under the Neutrality Act—a little-known federal law that prohibits Americans from waging war against friendly nations.

Two Americans were killed in the failed coup on December 30, 2014. The next day, distraught Gambian-American Papa Faal entered the U.S. Embassy in neighboring Senegal.

"He said, 'I need to get back to the United States. The Gambians are looking for me,'" said Special Agent Jeffrey Van Nest from the FBI's Minneapolis Field Office. "When embassy staff asked why, Faal said he was part of the attempted coup. That's when we got involved."

Embassy staff immediately notified the legal attaché—the FBI special agent assigned to the U.S. Embassy. The legal attaché interviewed Faal, quickly determined there was a possible violation of the Neutrality Act, and notified the Department of Justice and the FBI office in Faal's hometown of Minneapolis; Van Nest was the squad supervisor over the investigation.

Faal's cooperation led to conspirators in other U.S. states, requiring involvement from FBI field offices in Atlanta, Baltimore, Charlotte, Louisville, Memphis, San Antonio, and Seattle. Agents also traveled to The Gambia, Senegal, and Germany. The FBI coordinated with other federal agencies, including the Department of State; the Bureau of Alcohol, Tobacco, Firearms and Explosives; and the U.S. Army Criminal Investigation Command.

FBI agents interviewed subjects, searched their computers, and reviewed financial, travel, and phone records. The evidence helped agents piece together the conspiracy.

Members of the Gambian diaspora who had formed the Gambia Freedom League hatched the plan in 2012 to overthrow then-President Yahya Jammeh.

The group included Gambians living in America, Europe, and Africa. Cherno Njie, a naturalized American who lived in Texas, planned to serve as the interim leader in The Gambia.

Njie also financed much of the operation and arranged for another conspirator to buy weapons for the coup. Njie kept meticulous financial records showing how much he paid for ammunition and weapons, as well as their serial numbers. The weapons were smuggled into The Gambia hidden by clothes inside 55-gallon barrels.

The attack plan, developed by a co-conspirator with U.S. military experience, had coup members meet at safe houses in The Gambia. Two teams—one of six men and one of four—armed with the smuggled weapons and wearing military gear, attacked the Gambian State House.

Gambian soldiers killed several of the attackers, including two Americans; others escaped or were captured. Security forces also collected numerous weapons and military equipment.

Soldiers in The Gambia seized military gear and weapons provided for the participants in the attempted coup in 2014. The equipment was paid for by a naturalized American and shipped to the country; some of it was stored in safe houses.

As part of the investigation, FBI agents from Minneapolis received permission to travel to The Gambia to look at the evidence—and the bodies of the two Americans killed in the attack.

The trip into The Gambia was tense because President Jammeh initially believed the U.S. military was behind the attack. Gambian military and intelligence officials escorted FBI agents during the visit.

Agents identified more than 20 weapons purchased by Americans using money Njie provided. They also examined the cars used in the attack as well as the safe houses, and they took DNA samples from the two dead Americans.

The FBI has investigated only a handful of violations of the Neutrality Act. Despite the investigative complications—with numerous conspirators acting in several states and overseas—agents knew just how to proceed.

"The steps in these investigations are the same as for most cases," said Special Agent Margaret Thill, who also worked the case from the FBI's Minneapolis office. "You have a potential violation, you gather evidence, you build rapport with witnesses to elicit cooperation and information, and you work closely with the assistant U.S. attorney who is prosecuting the case."

Five men ended up pleading guilty in the case: four were sentenced

in 2016 on counts relating to the Neutrality Act, and a fifth was sentenced in March 2017 for buying weapons. None was sentenced to more than a year and a day in prison.

Short sentences notwithstanding, the successful investigation delivered several important messages, Van Nest said. "Rapid identification, arrest, and guilty pleas of those responsible ensured continued safety and security of American diplomatic personnel posted to the region," he explained. "More importantly, the U.S. government capably reinforced accountability to the rule of law in a part of the world which has been cursed by cyclical violence between warring factions for generations."

Coup Attempt in The Gambia
December 30, 2014

Five Americans were convicted for their roles in participating in the plot; two others were killed in the attempt.

Convicted of Conspiracy to Violate the Neutrality Act
(ages as of 5/12/17)

- Papa Faal, 48, Brooklyn Center, Minnesota. Also convicted of a firearms violation. Sentenced to time served.

- Cherno Njie, 59, of Lakeway, Texas. Also convicted of a firearms violation. Sentenced to one year and one day.

- Alagie Barrow, 44, of Lavergne, Tennessee. Also convicted of a firearms violation. Sentenced to six months.

- Banke Manneh, 44, of Jonesboro, Georgia. Also convicted of a firearms violation. Sentenced to six months.

Convicted of Conspiracy to Export Defense Articles

- Alhaji Boye, 46, (as of 3/27/17) of Raleigh, North Carolina. Sentenced to nine months.

Soldiers in The Gambia seized these weapons and ammunition from vehicles and safe houses used during a coup attempt in 2014. American participants were prosecuted under the Neutrality Act, a little-known federal law.

Law Enforcement Officers Killed and Assaulted

66 Officers Feloniously Killed in 2016

A total of 118 law enforcement officers were killed in the line of duty in 2016, according to the FBI's annual *Law Enforcement Officers Killed and Assaulted* (LEOKA) report released today. Of those deaths, 52 were accidental and 66 were felonious.

Additionally, 57,180 officers were assaulted in the line of duty, with nearly 30 percent of those officers being injured in the incidents.

All of these numbers increased from figures reported in 2015, when 45 officers died accidentally and 41 were feloniously killed in the line of duty. There were 50,212 assaults against law enforcement listed in the 2015 LEOKA report.

Through its Uniform Crime Reporting Program, the FBI collects data about the circumstances surrounding assaults against law enforcement and officer deaths. The data is collected from campus, local, state, tribal, and federal law enforcement agencies, as well as FBI field offices and non-profit organizations that track line-of-duty deaths. The LEOKA Program uses the data it collects to provide data-driven officer safety training to law enforcement officers around the country.

Of the 66 officers who were killed in criminal incidents:

- The average age was 40 years old, with an average of 13 years of law enforcement experience.

- Sixty-four of the officers feloniously killed were men, and two were women.

- Nearly all of the officers were killed by firearms—62 out of 66. Of the 62 officers killed by firearms, 51 were wearing body armor at the time they were killed.

- Four officers were killed intentionally with vehicles.

- The most common categories of circumstance surrounding officers' line-of-duty deaths were ambushes (17), followed by answering disturbance calls (13), and investigating suspicious people or circumstances (nine). (For more information on these incidents, see the summaries section of the report.)

Of the 52 officers who were killed in accidents:

- The average age was 38 years old, with an average of 11 years of law enforcement experience.

- Fifty of the officers accidentally killed were men, and two were women.

- Half of the law enforcement officers killed accidentally in 2016 were killed in auto accidents—26 of the 52. Additionally, 12 were struck by vehicles, and seven were killed in motorcycle accidents.

The annual LEOKA report also contains a separate section on federal law enforcement officers who were killed or assaulted in the line of duty last year. According to the 2016 federal data, one federal law enforcement officer was killed and 324 were injured.

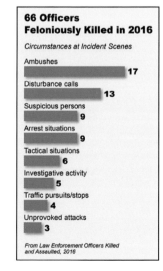

66 Officers Feloniously Killed in 2016

Circumstances at Incident Scenes

Ambushes **17**

Disturbance calls **13**

Suspicious persons **9**

Arrest situations **9**

Tactical situations **6**

Investigative activity **5**

Traffic pursuits/stops **4**

Unprovoked attacks **3**

From Law Enforcement Officers Killed and Assaulted, 2016

New Top Ten Fugitive

Help Us Catch a Killer

A North Carolina teen charged with murdering his former girlfriend has been named to the FBI's Ten Most Wanted Fugitives list, and a reward of up to $100,000 is being offered for information leading to his capture.

Alejandro Castillo—17 years old at the time of the killing—is wanted in connection with the 2016 murder of a 23-year-old woman, Truc Quan "Sandy" Ly Le, whom he had previously dated. The two became acquainted while working together in a Charlotte restaurant.

A joint investigation by the FBI and the Charlotte-Mecklenburg Police Department (CMPD) revealed that Castillo owed the victim money—approximately $1,000. Text messages between Castillo and the victim showed they agreed to meet in Charlotte on August 9, 2016, so he could repay the loan.

When the victim arrived at the meeting place that evening, Castillo apparently had no intention of returning the money. Instead, according to CMPD Det. Brent Koeck, Castillo had the victim withdraw a large sum of money from an ATM. Investigators believe Castillo drove the woman to a remote, heavily wooded area outside Charlotte, where she was shot in the head and her body dumped in a ravine. Castillo and his new girlfriend then fled the state in the victim's car.

The families of the victim, Castillo, and his accomplice all filed missing persons reports with the police when their children did not return home, and it took a week before the victim's body was found and identified. The victim's vehicle was located after the murder by the

FBI TEN MOST WANTED FUGITIVE

UNLAWFUL FLIGHT TO AVOID PROSECUTION - MURDER

ALEJANDRO CASTILLO

Photograph taken in 2015 — Photograph taken in 2016

FBI's Phoenix Division at a bus station in Arizona.

> *"The FBI has a long reach, and no matter where he is, we will not rest until Castillo is captured and brought to justice."*

Castillo and his accomplice had driven to Arizona and then crossed the border in Nogales into Mexico. Two months after the homicide, the woman who was with Castillo turned herself in to Mexican authorities and is now back in North Carolina facing charges related to the homicide. Castillo remains at large, and investigators believe he may be in the cities of Pabellón de Arteaga or San Francisco de los Romo, in the Mexican state of Aguascalientes. He may have also traveled to the Mexican states of Guanajuato or Veracruz. He is a fluent Spanish speaker.

Castillo has been charged with murder in North Carolina, and in February 2017 he was charged federally with unlawful flight to avoid prosecution.

"This crime was horrific," said Special Agent Marc Weingrad of the FBI's Charlotte Division. "Sandy was an innocent woman who was shot in the head." Weingrad believes the significant reward in the case—tipsters can remain anonymous and still be eligible for the reward—will motivate someone to come forward.

"The FBI has a long reach, and no matter where he is, we will not rest until Castillo is captured and brought to justice," Weingrad added.

Castillo is considered armed and dangerous. If you have information regarding Castillo, contact your local FBI office or the nearest U.S. Embassy or Consulate, or submit a tip online at https://tips.fbi.gov.

Note: This case may have been resolved since this information was posted on our website. Please check www.fbi.gov/wanted for up-to-date information.

Virtual Kidnapping

A New Twist on a Frightening Scam

Law enforcement agencies have been aware of virtual kidnapping fraud for at least two decades, but a recent FBI case illustrates how this frightening scam—once limited to Mexico and Southwest border states—has evolved so that U.S. residents anywhere could be potential victims.

Although virtual kidnapping takes on many forms, it is always an extortion scheme—one that tricks victims into paying a ransom to free a loved one they believe is being threatened with violence or death. Unlike traditional abductions, virtual kidnappers have not actually kidnapped anyone. Instead, through deceptions and threats, they coerce victims to pay a quick ransom before the scheme falls apart.

Between 2013 and 2015, investigators in the FBI's Los Angeles Division were tracking virtual kidnapping calls from Mexico—almost all of these schemes originate from within Mexican prisons. The calls targeted specific individuals who were Spanish speakers. A majority of the victims were from the Los Angeles and Houston areas.

"In 2015, the calls started coming in English," said FBI Los Angeles Special Agent Erik Arbuthnot, "and something else happened: The criminals were no longer targeting specific individuals, such as doctors or just Spanish speakers. Now they were choosing various cities and cold-calling hundreds of numbers until innocent people fell for the scheme."

This was significant, Arbuthnot said, because the new tactic vastly increased the potential number of victims. In the case he was

investigating, which became known as Operation Hotel Tango, more than 80 victims were identified in California, Minnesota, Idaho, and Texas. Collective losses were more than $87,000.

The incarcerated fraudsters—who typically bribe guards to acquire cell phones—would choose an affluent area such as Beverly Hills, California. They would search the Internet to learn the correct area code and telephone dialing prefix. Then, with nothing but time on their hands, they would start dialing numbers in sequence, trolling for victims.

When an unsuspecting person answered the phone, they would hear a female screaming, "Help me!" The screamer's voice was likely a recording. Instinctively, the victim might blurt out his or her child's name: "Mary, are you okay?"

And then a man's voice would say something like, "We have Mary. She's in a truck. We are holding her hostage. You need to pay a ransom and you need to do it now or we are going to cut off her fingers."

Most of the time, Arbuthnot said, "the intended victims quickly learned that 'Mary' was at home or at school, or they sensed the scam and hung up. This fraud only worked when people picked up the phone, they had a daughter, and she was not home," he explained. "But if you are making hundreds of calls, the crime will eventually work."

The scammers attempt to keep victims on the phone so they can't verify their loved ones' whereabouts or contact law enforcement. The callers are always in a hurry, and the ransom demand is usually a wire payment to Mexico of $2,000 or less, because there are legal restrictions for wiring larger amounts across the border.

Although victims were typically instructed to wire ransom payments, two individuals in Houston were coerced into paying larger amounts—totaling approximately $28,000—that could not be wired. The victims were directed to make money drops, and they believed they were being watched as they were directed to the assigned location. When the drops were made—in specified trash cans—a Houston woman, 34-year-old Yanette Rodriguez Acosta, was waiting to pick up the ransom money. After taking her portion of the payment, Acosta wired the rest in small amounts to several individuals in Mexico to transfer to the Mexican prisoner believed to be running the virtual kidnapping scheme.

Acosta was taken into custody for her involvement in the scam, and in July 2017, a federal grand jury in Houston returned a 10-count indictment against her. Among the charges were wire fraud and money laundering.

Arbuthnot noted that the Mexican prisoners who carry out virtual kidnappings use the ransom money to pay bribes and to make their lives behind bars easier. "And sometimes they use the money to buy their way out of jail. That's the ultimate goal."

He added that virtual kidnapping cases are difficult to investigate and prosecute because almost all of the subjects are in Mexico, and the money is wired out of the country and can be difficult to trace. The charges against Acosta represent the first federal indictment in a virtual kidnapping case. In addition, many victims do not report the crime, either because they are embarrassed, afraid, or because they don't consider the financial loss to be significant.

Regardless, Arbuthnot said, "victims of virtual kidnapping scams are traumatized by these events, because at the time, they believe that a loved one has been kidnapped and is in real danger."

Don't Become a Victim

The success of any type of virtual kidnapping scheme depends on speed and fear. Criminals know they only have a short time to exact a ransom before the victims unravel the scam or authorities become involved. To avoid becoming a victim, look for these possible indicators:

- Callers go to great lengths to keep you on the phone, insisting you remain on the line.
- Calls do not come from the supposed victim's phone.
- Callers try to prevent you from contacting the "kidnapped" victim.
- Calls include demands for ransom money to be paid via wire transfer to Mexico; ransom amount demands may drop quickly.

If you receive a phone call from someone demanding a ransom for an alleged kidnap victim, the following should be considered:

- In most cases, the best course of action is to hang up the phone.
- If you do engage the caller, don't call out your loved one's name.
- Try to slow the situation down. Request to speak to your family member directly. Ask, "How do I know my loved one is okay?"
- Ask questions only the alleged kidnap victim would know, such as the name of a pet. Avoid sharing information about yourself or your family.
- Listen carefully to the voice of the alleged victim if they speak.
- Attempt to contact the alleged victim via phone, text, or social media, and request that they call back from their cell phone.
- To buy time, repeat the caller's request and tell them you are writing down the demand, or tell the caller you need time to get things moving.
- Don't agree to pay a ransom, by wire or in person. Delivering money in person can be dangerous.

If you suspect a real kidnapping is taking place or you believe a ransom demand is a scheme, contact your nearest FBI office or local law enforcement immediately. Tips to the FBI can also be submitted online at tips.fbi.gov. All tipsters may remain anonymous.

Operation Cross Country XI
Recovering Underage Victims of Sex Trafficking and Prostitution

An FBI agent in Denver interviews a young woman during Operation Cross Country, a multi-agency effort to recover underage victims of prostitution and hold sex traffickers accountable.

Operation Cross Country, the FBI's annual law enforcement action focused on recovering underage victims of prostitution and drawing the public's attention to the problem of sex trafficking at home and abroad, has concluded with the recovery of 84 sexually exploited juveniles and the arrests of 120 traffickers.

Now in its 11th iteration, Operation Cross Country has expanded beyond the United States, with Canada, the United Kingdom, Cambodia, the Philippines, and Thailand undertaking similar operations. Their efforts were coordinated with the FBI and its local, state, and federal law enforcement partners—along with the National Center for Missing & Exploited Children (NCMEC)—during the four-day law enforcement action that ended October 15.

"We at the FBI have no greater mission than to protect our nation's children from harm," said FBI Director Christopher Wray.

"Unfortunately, the number of traffickers arrested—and the number of children recovered—reinforces why we need to continue to do this important work."

This year's Operation Cross Country involved 55 FBI field offices and 78 FBI-led Child Exploitation Task Forces composed of more than 500 law enforcement agencies. Hundreds of law enforcement personnel took part in sting operations in hotels, casinos, truck stops, and through social media sites frequented by pimps, prostitutes, and their customers.

All of the recovered minors were offered services by specialists who are either part of the FBI's Victim Services Division or members of other local and state law enforcement agencies. More than 100 victim specialists provided on-scene services that included crisis intervention as well as resources for basic needs such as food, clothing, shelter, and medical attention.

During operations by FBI Denver's Rocky Mountain Innocence Lost Task Force, for example, a 3-month-old girl and her 5-year-old sister were recovered after a friend who was staying with the family made a deal with an undercover task force officer to sell both children for sex in exchange for $600.

"The threat of child sex trafficking is something the FBI works on every single day," said Calvin Shivers, special agent in charge of the Denver Division. "Operation Cross Country gives us the opportunity to shine a light on this threat and to educate the public." He added that while the focused law enforcement action has "an immediate impact" of recovering a significant number of juvenile victims, "we recognize that there is a lot more work to be done to identify and recover even more victims."

Operation Cross Country is part of the FBI's Innocence Lost National Initiative, which began in 2003.

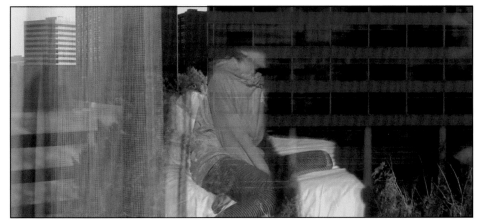

A young trafficking victim is seen in the reflection of a hotel window as she speaks to investigators and victim specialists during Operation Cross Country.

Since its creation, the program has resulted in the identification and recovery of more than 6,500 children from child sex trafficking and the prosecution of countless traffickers, more than 30 of whom have received life sentences for their crimes.

"Child sex trafficking is happening in every community across America," said John Clark, the CEO of NCMEC. "We are working to combat this problem every day," he explained, adding that NCMEC is "proud to work with the FBI on Operation Cross Country to help find and recover child victims."

"This operation isn't just about taking traffickers off the street," FBI Director Wray said. "It's about making sure we offer help and a way out to these young victims who find themselves caught in a vicious cycle of abuse."

 Scan this QR code with your smartphone to access related information, or visit www.fbi.gov/occxi.

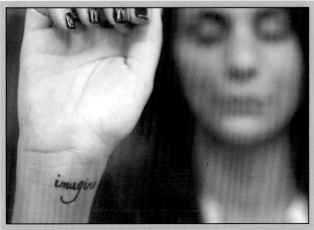

Ali's Story

Ali grew up in a middle-class suburb outside Philadelphia with parents who loved her and a wide circle of friends. She played sports and was a good student. In high school and in college—where she received an undergraduate and master's degree in criminal justice—she drank alcohol and experimented with marijuana and other drugs, like many of her friends. Then she tried heroin.

William Johnson is a deputy sheriff with the Philadelphia Sheriff's Office and a member of the FBI's Violent Crimes Against Children Task Force in Philadelphia. One of the task force's priorities is to combat human trafficking.

Although Johnson says he was just doing his job, Ali credits him with saving her from a life of addiction, prostitution, and being on the streets—a life, she believes, that would not have lasted much longer. Watch her story online.

THE FBI STORY

Commodities Fraud Sentencing
Word of Warning to Investors: Do Your Due Diligence

Self-professed investment professional Pedro Jaramillo was a pro at promoting himself and his financial prowess. Through a slickly produced online video, phony office space on Wall Street, and promises of unrealistic financial returns, this Peruvian national living in New York managed to convince more than two dozen investors to trust him with more than $1.2 million of their hard-earned money.

Jaramillo, however, never invested a dime of their money—instead, he used it to line his own pockets and keep his Ponzi scheme going. Even his claim to be an investment professional was false—he wasn't licensed to do anything remotely connected to financial advising and/or investing.

"He was stealing other people's money just to fund his own lifestyle."

But, as with most Ponzi scheme operators, Jaramillo eventually ran out of funds to keep his fraud scheme afloat, and two unhappy investors reported their concerns to the FBI. After an intensive investigation by the FBI's New York Field Office—in close coordination with the U.S. Attorney's Office for the Southern District of New York—Jaramillo was arrested and charged with commodities fraud in December 2016, pleaded guilty in April 2017, and was sentenced last month to 12 years in federal prison.

Investigators determined that, beginning at least in January 2014 until his arrest, Jaramillo—using his Latin American heritage as a common bond—had been soliciting potential victims mostly from Latin American immigrant communities in the U.S. to invest in commodity futures contracts. He told would-be investors that their money would be invested in short-term commodities contracts with a guaranteed (and unrealistically high) rate of return.

And he established his financial bona fides with potential clients using various methods.

His online video, done in Spanish, opened with flashy depictions of Wall Street and the New York Stock Exchange. Then, Jaramillo himself made his pitch to potential investors, telling them, "Money is being earned on every transaction. All you have to do is work with a proven winner." He delivered all sorts of promises about how client investments would be handled—including being set up in individually managed and federally protected accounts. Unfortunately for his investors, none of what Jaramillo said in the video was true.

To further impress potential investors, Jaramillo met with many of them in rented office space on Wall Street, where he touted his prior financial successes and his relationship with a well-known global investment bank. Again, this "relationship" with the bank proved to be non-existent, and he had no prior Wall Street investment successes.

Jaramillo also created and handed out documents with simple charts and graphs that purported to illustrate past successes and his high rates of return, more false facts he fed to his victims.

The FBI investigation included numerous interviews with the victims of Jaramillo's scheme. Many of these people—including retirees, working professionals, and manual laborers—lost their life savings, retirement money, or homes.

For example, a married couple in their 50s with $110,000—which included retirement funds—gave Jaramillo a total of $100,000 to invest but eventually stopped

hearing from him after they made repeated redemption requests. And a 75-year-old woman, hoping to earn enough money to move back to her native Colombia and purchase a small apartment, first gave Jaramillo $25,000 and then another $88,000, which included the $50,000 her children had given her to purchase an apartment after she got nothing back on her initial investment. Again, the woman lost everything.

Their individual background stories differed a bit, but the con Jaramillo perpetrated against his victims generally followed the same pattern. By misrepresenting who he was and what he did, he convinced investors to give him money to invest on their behalf. But instead of investing the money, he used the bulk of it to fund his lavish lifestyle (e.g., flying family and friends to vacation resorts). And the remaining funds went toward paying some of his early investors a small portion of what he owed them—figuring that by doing that, he could buy more time and continue soliciting new investors to keep the scheme going.

According to Alex Kurgansky, the FBI New York case agent who worked the investigation, getting Jaramillo off the streets before he could victimize even more investors was his primary motivation. "He was stealing other people's money just to fund his own lifestyle," said Kurgansky, "and had two of his victims not come forward, he would have continued the cycle for who knows how long and victimized even more people."

Kurgansky, noting that Jaramillo's scheme ran for nearly three years, said he hopes that cases like this one will serve as "a warning to potential investors to do their due

diligence before investing, and to recognize the warning signs of fraud early enough to get out of a bad situation." He also thinks cases like this serve as a deterrent to would-be fraudsters, putting them on notice that they will serve some serious prison time if they get caught.

"And ultimately," he added, "cases like this help ensure the integrity of our financial markets so the public will continue to trust in them."

Avoid Becoming a Victim: Do Your Homework Before You Invest

According to the U.S. Commodity Futures Trading Commission (CFTC), commodity futures and option markets are high-risk investments. Before you invest, do your homework.

- Check out the individual or company you're contemplating doing business with. Ask what state or federal agencies they are regulated by and then verify.

- Ask for written materials detailing the investment opportunity, the risk, and the fees and commissions charged.

- Beware of limited time offers or high-pressure sales tactics. Be suspicious if they demand an immediate commitment or ask you to expedite payment, regardless of the method (cash, money transfer, credit card, etc.).

- Beware of testimonials about an investment professional's performance that can't be verified.

- Beware of get-rich quick schemes. If it sounds too good to be true (i.e., higher-than-average rate of return or a guaranteed return), it probably is.

- Ask what recourse you have if you're not satisfied, and get any warranty or refund provision in writing.

Crash Cows

Connecticut Group Staged Car Accidents for Insurance Money

These vehicles were among those involved in more than 50 car crashes staged by a group of Connecticut residents to collect insurance money.

After an autumn evening of drinking and using drugs in 2013, a group of friends got into an Audi A6 and drove to the remote Wilderness Road in Norwich, Connecticut. The car slid off the road, hitting a tree.

Everyone in the car survived, but this seemingly typical crash was no accident.

Despite their impairment, the driver and passengers had purposely planned the crash to collect the insurance money. It was one of many crashes that a group of Connecticut residents were connected to over several years—contributing to higher car insurance premiums for all drivers and wasting public resources like ambulance responses.

In the October crash, driver Mackenzy Noze got out of the

Audi and drove away in a getaway car, while his friend, Jacques Fleurijeune, climbed into the driver's seat of the damaged Audi and called 911. Fleurijeune told police he had hit the tree while swerving to avoid a deer—though no witnesses or police ever saw the alleged deer.

The four passengers were all taken to the hospital and eventually received insurance settlements for their injuries, which were fake. Fleurijeune also received payment for the value of the car, and others in the car gave some or all of their injury payouts to Noze and Fleurijeune.

This scenario played out numerous times with various combinations of co-conspirators from 2011 through 2014, with insurance companies paying out $10,000 to $30,000

per crash in about 50 crashes. Many of them happened under similar circumstances—late-night, single-car crashes on remote roads without witnesses. In the fall, the drivers would claim to have swerved hitting a deer. In the winter, they said they lost control on a snowy street. To up their payout, they used older, European cars, which tend to hold their value over time.

"When insurance companies pay fraudulent claims, everyone's premiums go up."

For the insurance companies, these repeat crashes raised red flags. So the National Insurance Crime Bureau (NICB), a non-profit organization that serves as a liaison between law enforcement and insurance companies, shared crash data with the FBI and the U.S. Attorney's Office for the District of Connecticut. The NICB's suspicious accident data helped investigators hone in on the worst offenders.

"It was just a good, old-fashioned case, conducting interviews and reviewing documents—such as police reports and insurance company records—looking for patterns," said Special Agent Daniel Curtin, who investigated the case out of the FBI's New Haven Division. "With a lot of these staged crashes, the fraudsters made interstate telephone calls to file the insurance claims, and the calls were recorded, forming the foundation for many of the wire fraud counts."

Noze, 33, the group's ringleader, was convicted of conspiracy to commit mail and wire fraud and sentenced last month to four years in prison. Six others, including Fleurijeune, have been charged and convicted.

While insurance fraud may seem to be a victimless crime, that's far from the case.

Estimates show car insurance fraud costs the average policyholder about $300 per year in higher

The group often used rural sites—such as this one on Green Hollow Road in Killingly, Connecticut—to stage the car accidents.

premiums, according to NICB Supervisory Special Agent John Gasiorek, who assisted the FBI with the investigation.

Additionally, staged accidents are a safety hazard, both to those involved and other drivers. While in this ring, the conspirators generally did not involve other motorists, criminals sometimes

do stage accidents involving unsuspecting drivers.

"You never know who's going to come around the corner. You could hit an innocent person. It's really a public safety issue," Gasiorek said, noting that even willing participants in the staged accidents are unexpectedly injured.

"When insurance companies pay fraudulent claims, everyone's premiums go up," Curtin said. "More importantly, the staged crashes pose risks to first responders. You had police officers and EMTs rushing to crash scenes. The wasted time of medical professionals was also a concern with ER doctors and nurses treating these fraudsters for non-existent injuries. It took time away from other patients who really needed medical attention."

At least in the local region, Curtin said word has gotten out that law enforcement is working these cases and bringing perpetrators to justice.

"The insurance companies have said that suspicious claims, especially those involving single-car accidents on remote roads, are down in southeastern Connecticut," Curtin said. "They're not seeing these types of suspicious accidents because this case has sent a message."

Could Your Fender Bender Have Been Staged? Tips from the NICB

Staged accident fraudsters sometimes target innocent drivers in their dangerous schemes. If you think your car accident has been staged, the NICB suggests:

- If you are not injured and can safely do so, take pictures of the accident scene.
- Observe the details of what happened, such as how many people were in the other car. Fraudsters will often lie about how many people were in the vehicle.
- If you suspect car insurance fraud, visit the NICB's Speak Up page to file a report. Tips can be shared anonymously.

Father/Son Tutoring Company Executives Sentenced for Fraud

More Than 100 School Districts Victimized

Although financial fraudsters target all sort of victims, perhaps the worst type of financial criminals are the ones who go after the most vulnerable. A prime example of those types of criminals? A father/son pair, the subjects of a recent FBI Chicago-led investigation, who perpetrated a multi-million-dollar fraud against the Department of Education that ended up victimizing low-income students from more than 100 public school districts in Illinois and other states.

Jowhar Soultanali, 62, and his son, Kabir Kassam, 38, ran tutoring companies in the Chicago area—Brilliance Academy, Inc., offered on-site school tutoring, while its wholly owned subsidiary Babbage Net School, Inc., provided online training. The two advertised their services mostly to schools with large numbers of low-income students. These schools were recipients of federal funding from the Department of Education earmarked for "supplemental educational services," or tutoring.

But Soultanali and Kassam brazenly misrepresented the nature and quality of the tutoring services their companies actually provided, both in their marketing materials and in their state provider applications. The two promised to create customized tutoring programs to address students' academic needs, pre-test and post-test students to determine where students needed help and how effective the tutoring was in providing that help, and create useful student progress reports for parents and schools.

Instead, what schools—and their students—got were mostly generic tutoring programs configured at or below students' grade levels, partial or missing pre-test and post-test

assessments that did little to help students, and fraudulent progress reports that, in some cases, were automatically generated by a computer program.

As part of the fraud scheme, Soultanali and Kassam also engaged in fraudulent billing, including creating invoices based on false attendance records and spreadsheets that contained inflated tutoring time summaries.

But the two didn't undertake this scheme by themselves. They also bribed school officials and others to ensure that the fraud remained hidden. Bribes included a Caribbean cruise for an assistant principal in Texas and a trip to a gentlemen's club for a state education official in New Mexico.

All told, the two companies received about $33 million from school districts around the U.S. Investigative activity revealed that Soultanali and Kassam fraudulently obtained at least $11 million of that for themselves during the 2009-2010 school year, using it to buy lavish properties, luxury vehicles, and expensive jewelry.

In the summer of 2010, an employee of one of Soultanali and Kassam's companies—suspicious of company activities—reported concerns to the FBI's Chicago Field Office. The Bureau opened an investigation, working closely with the Department of Education's Office of Inspector General and with valuable assistance from the Chicago Public Schools' Office of Inspector General.

Investigators worked methodically to build a case—forensically analyzing financial records from more than 100 school districts and 60 bank accounts; reviewing company records and e-mails; and

interviewing numerous individuals, including employees of the two tutoring companies and school officials in Illinois and a number of other states. By April 2014, there was enough evidence to indict Soultanali, his son, their two companies, and four other co-conspirators. Shortly after that, Soultanali and Kassam—in order to stay out jail—paid their $500,000 bond with diamond and ruby rings, plus several luxury vehicles.

But that attempt at keeping their freedom was for naught. Both men eventually pled guilty to fraud charges, and, last month, were sentenced to federal prison. Both were also ordered to pay $11,393,762 in restitution to the Department of Education.

And fortunately, both Brilliance Academy and Babbage Net School went out of business, and the victim schools are now able to contract with legitimate and highly qualified tutoring services to enhance the academic skills of their students.

According to Mark Prejsnar, the Chicago case agent who headed up the investigation, the scheme perpetrated by Soultanali and Kassam "demonstrated how the greed of a few individuals can have such a negative impact on our most vulnerable citizens and communities." And he's hopeful that the results of this investigation will serve as a deterrent to others who might be contemplating similar frauds.

THE FBI STORY

STEM and the FBI

Recruiting the Best and the Brightest

The acronym STEM—science, technology, engineering, and mathematics—describes a range of academic disciplines that have become more important than ever to the FBI's mission of protecting the American public.

"The country's enemies, be they terrorists, computer hackers, spies, or financial fraudsters, are exploiting the newest technologies at every turn," said Special Agent Avatar Lefevre. "If the FBI doesn't recruit and train the best qualified people in the STEM fields, our adversaries will undoubtedly gain an advantage."

Lefevre heads a unit in the FBI's Human Resources Division created two years ago to specifically recruit individuals with cyber skills. But he pointed out that "employees with STEM backgrounds are required across the entire gamut of FBI programs." And that applies not just for special agents, but also analysts, engineers, and a variety of scientists and other professionals who help solve crimes through the analysis of DNA, fingerprints, trace evidence, and other cutting-edge methods.

"With regard to the cyber realm," Lefevre said, "the FBI has computer scientists, computer engineers, IT specialists, digital forensic examiners, electronics engineers, electronics technicians, and computer analysis and response teams." He added, "We are also moving heavily into data analytics. We have needs for data analysts and data scientists. Those are just a few of the positions specific to the cyber field."

Industry is also competing for highly skilled STEM employees, Lefevre noted, and private companies often pay more than

SCIENCE | TECHNOLOGY | ENGINEERING | MATHEMATICS

FEDERAL BUREAU OF INVESTIGATION | #ServewithSTEM

one can make as a public servant. But salary is not the only thing to consider when contemplating a career.

"We sell the mission, and our employees interact with the communities they serve," Lefevre said. "At the FBI, if you have a computer science or engineering degree or some other technical background, you are going to do things you would not likely do anywhere else. Using your technical skills," he explained, "you are going to see the direct effect of your work. You are going to see people's lives saved. You are going to see money being returned to victims of fraud. You are going to see the mitigation of terror attacks. And you are going to know that you played a vital part in all of that because of the skills you brought to the table."

Recruiting individuals with STEM training is a top priority for the FBI, and Bureau personnel regularly visit colleges across the country to talk with prospective job candidates. "We are now also working at the high school level doing the same thing," Lefevre said, "to let kids know at an earlier age that the FBI is here and we

are doing a lot of cool things they might not know about. We want to put the FBI on their radar."

Reaching out to a younger audience is important. "If you think the FBI is something you might like to do in the future, now is the time to start planning," Lefevre said. Because of the Bureau's exacting security clearance process, "young people have to be aware that their actions now will have a bearing on their ability to gain government employment later," he explained.

"We are the FBI. We are the ones expected to stop the next potential terror attack," he said. "We have high standards, and we are going to make sure that you are the best person for this organization before we give you that job offer."

On the other hand, he added, some would-be job candidates rule themselves out before ever applying. "My experience is that some folks think they are not competitive enough," Lefevre said. "My recommendation to them would be to apply—you have no idea until you apply."

2016 Hate Crime Statistics Released
Report Details Offenses, Victims, Offenders, and Locations of Crimes

Today, the FBI's Uniform Crime Reporting (UCR) Program released *Hate Crime Statistics, 2016*, its latest annual compilation of bias-motivated incidents reported throughout the U.S.

The newest report—which provides information about the offenses, victims, offenders, and locations of hate crimes—reveals that for 2016, law enforcement agencies reported 6,121 criminal incidents that were motivated by bias toward race, ethnicity, ancestry, religion, sexual orientation, disability, gender, or gender identity.

As part of the 2016 report, participants in UCR's Hate Crime Statistics Program included 15,254 law enforcement agencies. These agencies provided from one to 12 months' worth of data about bias-motivated crime, and of those agencies, 1,776 reported one or more incidents. The remaining agencies reported no hate crimes occurred within their jurisdictions.

Of the 6,121 criminal incidents reported, 6,063 were single-bias incidents (there were also 58 multiple-bias incidents). Of the single-bias incidents:

- 57.5 percent were motivated by a race, ethnicity or ancestry bias;

- 21.0 percent were motivated by a religious bias;

- 17.7 percent were motivated by a sexual orientation bias;

- The remaining incidents were motivated by a gender identity, disability, or gender bias.

Where were these crimes committed? The two largest percentages of hate crime incidents took place in or near residences (27.3 percent) and on or near some type of roadway (18.4 percent). The remaining incidents were perpetrated at a variety of other locations, including schools and houses of worship, commercial and government buildings, restaurants and nightclubs, parking lots and garages, playgrounds and parks, and even medical facilities.

In short, hate crimes can and do happen just about anywhere.

What about the victims of these crimes? Hate crime victims can be individuals, businesses, government entities, religious organizations, or society as a whole, and they can be committed against persons, property, or society. In 2016, law enforcement reported a total of 7,615 victims of hate crimes.

Of the 7,615 overall victims, 4,720 were victims of crimes against

persons (both adults and juveniles), 2,813 were victims of crimes against property, and 82 were victims of hate crimes categorized as crimes against society (e.g., weapons violations, drug offenses, gambling).

Going forward. The FBI, through its UCR Program, will continue to collect and disseminate information on hate crime—as a means to educate and increase awareness of these types of crimes for the public as well as for law enforcement, government, community leaders, civic organizations, and researchers around the country.

The Bureau will also continue to combat hate crimes that fall under federal jurisdiction—the number one investigative priority under our civil rights program—and offer operational assistance to our local and state law enforcement partners during their hate crime investigations.

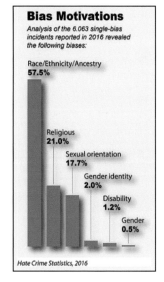

Bias Motivations
Analysis of the 6,063 single-bias incidents reported in 2016 revealed the following biases:

Race/Ethnicity/Ancestry
57.5%

Religious
21.0%

Sexual orientation
17.7%

Gender identity
2.0%

Disability
1.2%

Gender
0.5%

Hate Crime Statistics, 2016

New Top Ten Fugitive

Help Us Catch a Killer

A convicted felon wanted for the brutal murder of his wife is the newest addition to the FBI's Ten Most Wanted Fugitives list, and a reward of up to $100,000 is being offered for information leading to his capture.

Jesus Roberto Munguia, a known gang member with a violent criminal history, is charged with the July 2, 2008 kidnapping and murder of his wife in Las Vegas, Nevada.

"This was a vicious killing," said Special Agent Andrew Attridge, who is investigating the case from the FBI's Las Vegas Division. Munguia and his wife were estranged—each having accused the other of infidelity. When Munguia threatened to kill his wife and their four children, ages 6 through 12, she left their Las Vegas home with the children.

"A few nights later he convinced her to come home," Attridge said. When she did, Munguia locked the kids in the bedroom and forced his wife into her car. He drove her to an unknown location, where he bound her hands with seatbelts and used jumper cables to tie her neck to the car seat's headrest. "At some point," Attridge said, "he beat her to death with a blunt object, possibly the handle of a tire jack."

After the murder, Munguia drove back to his house, parked the car in the driveway, and fled. The victim's sister found the body in the car, bound and beaten.

Munguia was charged in Nevada with kidnap and murder with a deadly weapon on July 3, 2008. Soon after, he was charged federally with unlawful flight to avoid prosecution.

At the time of the murder,

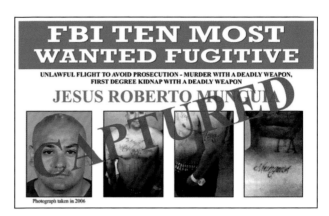

FBI TEN MOST WANTED FUGITIVE

UNLAWFUL FLIGHT TO AVOID PROSECUTION - MURDER WITH A DEADLY WEAPON, FIRST DEGREE KIDNAP WITH A DEADLY WEAPON

JESUS ROBERTO MUNGUIA

CAPTURED

Photograph taken in 2006

Munguia was 31 years old. Born and raised in Los Angeles, he is a known member of the Southern California gang TEPA 13 and has an extensive criminal record, Attridge said, including several counts of car theft, and assault with a deadly weapon on a police officer when he was 18 years old. Prior to the murder, there were several outstanding warrants for his arrest.

"We believe Munguia continues to have extensive family ties and gang ties to Southern California," Attridge said, especially in Los Angeles and Bakersfield. He may have also fled to Tijuana, Mexico, or deeper into Mexico.

Being named to the Ten Most Wanted Fugitives list means the reward for information leading to Munguia's capture has increased to as much as $100,000. "We are hoping that will be a motivator for somebody to come forward," Attridge said, adding that tipsters can remain anonymous.

Munguia has several distinguishing features that may help someone recognize him. He has a tattoo of a teardrop near his left eye, and a tattoo of the letters "PA" on the

back of his neck. He is also missing his right index finger.

"We know he is a violent individual," Attridge said, "and he also appears to be smart in terms of evading capture." Munguia has been known to use his deceased brother's identity to get jobs—using his real name could lead authorities to him because of the outstanding warrants for his arrest.

"We believe that Munguia will do anything to evade capture," Attridge said. "He should be considered armed and extremely dangerous." If you have information regarding Munguia, contact your local FBI office or the nearest U.S. Embassy or Consulate, or submit a tip online at https://tips.fbi.gov.

Note: Jesus Roberto Munguia was arrested without incident in Mexico on February 15, 2018.

Indian Country Cold Case in Montana

Seeking Answers to a Young Man's Disappearance

Special Agent Steve Lowe hangs a sign on the Crow Reservation in Montana seeking information in the case of Robert Garrett Stewart, Jr.—known to family and friends as "Baby Garret"—who went missing in October 2013.

With his wife beside him at the kitchen table in their home on the Crow Reservation in Montana—and many of his children, grandchildren, and extended family members nearby—Robert Garrett Stewart, Sr., talks about his son, who disappeared four years ago.

"I miss him every day," Stewart said. "Every morning I give him a little prayer in my bedroom. Every day I think about him and wonder where he's at. Is he hungry? Does he need money? Every day is a question mark."

Named after his father, Robert Garrett Stewart, Jr.—affectionately known to family and friends as "Baby Garrett"—went missing in October 2013. Since then, the FBI has been working to provide answers for the Stewart family.

"We don't know exactly what happened to him or if he came into some kind of harm," said Special Agent Steve Lowe, who has been

investigating the disappearance from the FBI's office in Billings, Montana. "But we have not forgotten Baby Garrett. This case is still active; it's still open. We are pursuing all available leads."

Baby Garrett, 25 years old when he went missing, was last seen in Billings with acquaintances. He never returned to his family's home on the reservation and hasn't been heard from since.

The FBI became involved with the case because Stewart, an enrolled member of the Crow Tribe, had been living on the reservation. On many reservations throughout the United States, the FBI is responsible for investigating major crimes that occur on federal lands, such as murder, violent assaults, and the sexual exploitation of children. Agents work closely with local and tribal law enforcement personnel as well as with the federal Bureau of Indian Affairs.

"Knowing that we had a missing person, which sometimes turns into a death investigation," Lowe said, the FBI began assisting local law enforcement after the disappearance and became the primary investigative agency on the case in late 2013.

> *"We feel that there are people in the area who know something about what happened to Baby Garrett. We want them to come forward, even if they remain anonymous."*

Since then, despite promising leads, the case has gone cold. "We still do not know exactly what happened to Baby Garrett," Lowe said. More than a year ago, seeking additional help from the community, the FBI launched a publicity campaign about the case and offered a $10,000 reward for

information. "We feel that there are people in the area who know something about what happened to Baby Garrett," Lowe said. "We want them to come forward, even if they remain anonymous."

"I want somebody to step up and let us know, help us at least to understand what happened to him," said Baby Garrett's father. "Where is he? That's always my question every day. What happened?"

In addition to Lowe's efforts, an FBI victim specialist has kept in contact with the family to let them know of any developments in the case and to ease their concerns when rumors or news accounts surface about unidentified bodies being found in the region.

"I have been on this case for several years," Lowe said. "Agents before me have worked it as well with our local partners, our victim specialist, and other support people. To meet the family, to see how much they miss their son, their brother, their uncle, it just tears at your heart."

And although the case is several years old, Lowe explained, it remains "extremely important to the FBI and to me, because we're talking about a person's life. We're talking about a person's family who loves him, who misses him dearly, whose lives are not the same since he disappeared."

Sitting with his family in the home that he and his son built together from the foundation up, Baby Garrett's father said he is not sure what the future will bring. "My hope is to see him back," he said. "In my dreams, he always comes up, and I'm the only one that's talking to him, trying to get him caught up, you know. This happened to

this one, this happened to her. This happened to one of the kids. I'm always talking to him about getting him caught up, and all the things that happened in the last four years. That always happens in my dream, and I want it to be real."

Submit a Tip:

If you have any information concerning the disappearance of Robert Garrett Stewart, Jr., please contact the FBI Salt Lake City Division's resident agency in Billings, Montana, at (406) 248-8487 or toll free at (877) 569-7449. You can also contact your local FBI office or the nearest American Embassy or Consulate. Tipsters can remain anonymous, and there is a $10,000 reward for information leading to the resolution of the case.

Note: This case may have been resolved since this information was posted on our website. Please check www.fbi.gov/wanted/kidnap for up-to-date information.

Internet Crime
IC3 a Virtual Complaint Desk for Online Fraud

That holiday card in your inbox? Think twice before clicking. That deep discount in your newsfeed on the season's hot gadget? Does it seem too good to be true?

The FBI's authority on Internet scams suggests keeping your guard up as holiday shopping season kicks in. The Internet Crime Complaint Center, or   , is the Bureau's virtual complaint desk for people who believe they have been victimized or defrauded online. The unit, established in 2000 in the FBI's Cyber Division, receives about 800 complaints every day through its website, www.ic3.gov.

"The scams that we get all year long are the same scams that happen around the holiday season," said Donna Gregory, head of the IC3 unit, which is based in West Virginia. "It's just that people are more apt to maybe fall for them during the holidays—especially for non-delivery scams or clicking on links for greeting cards that are actually malware."

Non-delivery scams—ordering and paying for goods or services online that are not delivered—were by far the most prolific complaint in 2016, accounting for 81,029 victims and $138 million in losses, according to the IC3's most recent annual report. Business e-mail compromise (BEC) scams—which dupe company representatives into wiring money to fraudsters—and romance scams accounted for the biggest financial losses last year: more than $579 million.

> *"The scams that we get all year long are the same scams that happen around the holiday season. It's just that people are more apt to maybe fall for them during the holidays."*

The IC3 consists of special agents, technical experts, and analysts who look for patterns and trends in the complaints. Some, but not all, complaints are referred to law enforcement agencies for investigation.

"We're looking at the complaint for other potential victims," said Gregory, "We might find that the same e-mail address is being used in 15 other complaints. And then we can start seeing a pattern and put information together."

Gregory said social media platforms are being used more often to advance online schemes, given their access to networks and freely shared personal information. Social media played a role in more than $66 million in losses last year.

While victims reported more than $1.3 billion in losses last year to IC3, the problem is believed to be much larger, since only about 15 percent of fraud victims report the crimes to law enforcement, according to FBI estimates.

If you think you might be the victim of Internet fraud, go to www.ic3.gov to file a complaint. If you think that letter from the Nigerian prince is going to make your holiday dreams come true, think again.

Theft from the Most Vulnerable

Group Stole Millions Designated to Feed Hungry Children

Gladys and Anthony Waits seemed to be living successful lives. He was a business owner; she worked for the state of Arkansas. They lived in a large, renovated home and drove high-end cars.

But the Waits' lifestyle was a fraudulent one of the worst kind: They lined their pockets with money earmarked for feeding needy children through Gladys Waits' job at the Arkansas Department of Human Services (DHS), the agency that administers U.S. Department of Agriculture (USDA) grants to feed children in low-income communities. Along with their co-conspirators, they stole $11 million that was meant to feed children from low-income families.

"These investigations are so important because they hit at the heart of what these programs stand for—taking care of children," said Special Agent Jacob Stokes, who helped investigate the case out of the FBI's Little Rock Division. "These people are taking advantage of that, and people that are truly hurt by it are the children. Money was taken away from a program that could have helped children in need."

The premise of the state program was relatively simple. Organizations or individuals applied to the state to host a program and find a feeding site, such as a school or daycare center. Applicants went through an initial site visit and were approved by Gladys Waits' agency, the Arkansas DHS. The sites reported back to the state how many children were fed, and Arkansas paid the site sponsors per child who participated.

In the case of the fraudulent sites, the numbers of children fed were grossly inflated, and the excess funds the site sponsors received became kickback money—both for a group of the site sponsors who were in on the fraud, as well as for Gladys and Anthony Waits and a few state employees.

The fraud went on for more than two years, ending in 2014, with additional site sponsors being recruited with the promise of kickbacks. As the conspiracy went on, Gladys Waits was promoted to a management role in her agency, giving her more power to keep the fraud going undetected. For example, she would give site sponsors a heads-up before the state conducted an "unannounced" site visit to ensure children were being fed properly.

"Some of these sites were simply fronts; they didn't feed any children. Others would feed a few and claim they fed many more," said Special Agent Richard McLain, who also worked the case out of the FBI's Little Rock office.

The group went to great lengths to cover their tracks.

Investigators pored through numerous pages of falsified documentation, such as fake invoices and spreadsheets. The investigation, worked jointly with the USDA, Internal Revenue Service, and U.S. Marshals Service, showed about 10 percent of the state program's budget was fraudulent.

The investigation was truly a team effort, with each agency bringing their own capabilities and resources.

"Our agency has the knowledge and expertise in USDA-funded programs, but you can never have enough help," said Special Agent David Rucker of the USDA Office of Inspector General, who worked on the investigative team. "In addition to having an FBI agent on the team, the FBI's financial analyst analyzed bank records, and team members from all the agencies, including the FBI, made simultaneous arrests of several of the subjects."

While much of the money may never be recovered, thanks to the asset forfeiture process, the government seized more than $850,000 of the group's ill-gotten gains, much of it from one of the site sponsors.

Gladys Waits pleaded guilty to conspiracy to commit wire fraud, and in July, she was sentenced to nine years in prison and ordered to pay $9.7 million in restitution. Anthony Waits was convicted of conspiracy to commit wire fraud and was sentenced to more than 14 years. Twelve others involved have either been convicted or pleaded guilty.

Officials from the Arkansas DHS were also key partners in helping to facilitate the investigation. For the FBI personnel who worked this case, the years-long effort was worth stopping those who would take from such vulnerable victims.

"By falsely inflating those numbers, you remove money from a program that only has so much funding. The government's stance was they were taking food from the mouths of children," McLain said.

Heroism in Hostile Territory

The Argentine Operations of the FBI's Special Intelligence Service

Although the FBI effectively shut down Nazi intelligence operations within the United States during World War II, our southern neighbors remained targets of Nazi spies, saboteurs, and smugglers throughout the war. Most of our southern neighbors were politically neutral as the war was not at their doors, but their policies tended to be anti-Nazi, providing the U.S. with various degrees of assistance against German threats to the Allied war effort.

One of the exceptions was Argentina, which—as a result of its policies—distanced itself from the U.S. and drew itself closer, diplomatically, to Germany. This meant that Argentina was a hotbed of intrigue, and it proved to be a tougher environment for members of the FBI's Special Intelligence Service (SIS), the U.S. intelligence component whose mission was to identify and counter Nazi operatives in South America.

Although it obtained little official cooperation from Buenos Aires, the SIS was able to work with local officials, funneling them evidence that would result in the arrest of German operatives. To do this, the Bureau had assigned its first non-official cover agent to Buenos Aires in September 1940, and by mid-1942, agents had been assigned in an official liaison capacity to the U.S. Embassy and two consulates. By late 1943, at the height of SIS operations, the FBI had several agents operating as official liaisons as well as 37 agents working against the Nazis in undercover positions.

These agents had their work cut out for them. Although Buenos Aires was ostensibly neutral, U.S. Undersecretary of State Summer Welles had identified it—in 1942—as being a base for Axis espionage operations. The Nazis were using Argentina's ambivalence to funnel their own intelligence agents into the Western Hemisphere, to enhance radio communications across South,and Central America for its agents, and to smuggle strategic minerals back to Germany. The FBI needed to put a stop to all of these actions.

Through one investigation, our agents discovered that an official in one of the American firms that provided cover jobs in Argentina for SIS members was strongly pro-Nazi and used the company to the detriment of the U.S. The FBI was successful in bringing this derogatory information to the attention of the firm's New York headquarters, which fired the employee before he "succeeded in doing either the SIS program or his company any particular harm."

Smugglers were an even bigger concern. The Bureau wanted to ensure that the Nazi war machine did not have access to valuable commodities that would allow them to build higher-tech weapons. In one of our biggest successes, SIS

agents learned that the German naval attaché in Argentina, Dietrich Niebuhr, was orchestrating the smuggling of strategic war materials through the British naval blockade. He and his operatives would buy mica, platinum, and industrial diamonds on the black market and use seamen aboard Portuguese and Spanish freighters to courier it back to German industries.

SIS personnel faced many dangers as they were surveilled, harassed, and—in one instance—arrested.

FBI SIS agents surveilled these operations and collected a wealth of intelligence against Niebuhr's smugglers that could be shared with local law enforcement willing to work with us. The intelligence also helped the U.S. to develop an extensive "List of Certain Blocked Nationals" (a predecessor to today's U.S. Department of Commerce's Entity List) that U.S. and British customs officials could use to disrupt Niebuhr's smugglers in the Caribbean. And Niebuhr was eventually expelled from Argentina.

SIS personnel faced many dangers as they were surveilled, harassed, and—in one instance—arrested. The arrested agent, though, maintained his discipline and did not divulge his true affiliation. He

was eventually released and quickly sent out of the country, but his cover was compromised and he could not return to SIS service.

The work of the SIS in Argentina came to an abrupt halt in 1944. As a result of the indiscretion of several hard-drinking SIS informants whose roles were uncovered, FBI Director J. Edgar Hoover—fearing that his agents could be compromised—quickly ordered all SIS personnel out of the country.

Implementing a plan already in place, the agents left Argentina using a motor launch that the Bureau maintained on the Río de la Plata River, which borders Argentina and Uruguay. This escape path was known as "Crosby's Navy"—after Francis Crosby, the FBI's legal attaché at the U.S. Embassy in Buenos Aires and the head of the SIS contingent in Argentina. The potentially compromised agents were whisked down the river in the dark of night to Montevideo, Uruguay.

Considering the dangers they had faced, the SIS did a remarkable job maintaining an Argentine presence, and its work hampered many Nazi plots over the war years. And as a result of its efforts, the Bureau—and the United States—gained significant experience operating in potentially hostile territory.

Health Care Fraud
Texas Doctor, Nurses Exploited Trust-Based Systems

When a federal judge in Texas sentenced a 52-year-old Dallas woman to 10 years in prison recently—and ordered her to pay more than $23 million in restitution to Medicare and Medicaid—it marked the end of a massive health care fraud case in which the government was systematically defrauded and the care of vulnerable patients was placed at risk.

Cynthia Stiger was the last of seven defendants to be sentenced in the long-running scheme. The ringleader, Dr. Jacques Roy, received a 35-year sentence in August 2017 and was ordered to repay the government more than $268 million. Roy and his co-conspirators—some of them nurses—perpetrated a home health care fraud that involved thousands of patients over a period of eight years.

"It's sad when people in the medical community who enjoy a level of trust and responsibility choose to callously take advantage of sick and elderly patients," said Special Agent Chelsie Drews, who investigated the case from the FBI's Dallas Division. "But that is exactly what happened here."

Dr. Roy, Stiger, and others improperly recruited individuals with Medicare coverage to sign up for home health care services. One co-conspirator, nurse Charity

Eleda, sought out patients from a homeless shelter, sometimes paying recruiters $50 for each eligible patient they found. Among their many crimes, the fraudsters falsified medical documents to make it appear as though Medicare patients qualified for home health care services that were not medically necessary

> *"It's sad when people in the medical community who enjoy a level of trust and responsibility choose to callously take advantage of sick and elderly patients."*

In 2004, when Dr. Roy began to exploit the system, home health care was a relatively new concept. Medicare would pay for doctors to visit patients in their home—usually the elderly or infirm—who might not otherwise be able to receive treatment. "The practice quickly became popular," Drews said, "and Dr. Roy was intent on capitalizing on that."

Evidence showed that Dr. Roy approved plans of care for 11,000 unique Medicare beneficiaries. "The more patients he had, the more services he could bill for," Drews said. "When the case went to trial," she added, "it was the largest single-physician home health care fraud in the country."

Dr. Roy was certifying patients for Medicare home health services from more than 500 home health companies. "Those kinds of numbers were unheard of in the industry," Drews said.

After an individual was certified for services, the fraudsters falsified home visit notes to make it appear as though skilled nursing services were being provided and continued to be necessary. Dr. Roy performed unnecessary home visits and then ordered unnecessary medical services for patients. At his instruction, hundreds of millions of dollars in fraudulent claims were submitted to Medicare. And in many cases, patients were deprived of care or received inferior care.

It took time for the fraud to be discovered, Drews explained, because Medicare and Medicaid are trust-based systems. "There are so many eligible beneficiaries. In order for patients to get the care they need and then to get their claims processed in a timely manner, the system trusts that providers are submitting a true and accurate billing for their services," she said. Dr. Roy exploited that process.

The case was investigated jointly by the FBI, the U.S. Department of Health and Human Services Office of Inspector General, and the Texas Attorney General's Medicaid Fraud Control Unit as part of the Department of Justice's Medicare Fraud Strike Force. Dr. Roy and his co-conspirators were arrested in 2012 on a variety of health care fraud charges.

"We are pleased with the outcome of this case," Drews said. "The lengthy sentences handed down send a strong message of deterrence to that industry."

10 Years of Digital Billboards
Partnership Brings Safety Messages Directly to the Public

When alleged Florida gang member Demeko Wells was wanted for credit card fraud and identify theft earlier this year, he noticed his own photo on a digital billboard alert in the Tampa area, and he knew his days of freedom were numbered.

The next day, Wells turned himself into police and pleaded guilty to several charges. In October, he was sentenced to nearly five years in prison.

This is just one of many examples of the FBI working with the outdoor advertising industry to place timely, critical information directly in the public's view on electronic roadside billboards. These messages can be produced and posted quickly after a crime occurs or a person goes missing, and they can be targeted to specific geographic areas.

While some billboard alerts focus on wanted criminals, including the FBI's Ten Most Wanted Fugitives, many also cover important safety reminders, often tailored to the local area. Public safety messages on billboards remind the public to call the FBI with information on issues such as Internet crime, laser strikes, border corruption, human trafficking, and identity theft.

"Our digital billboard program gets results and helps us keep the public safe."

Electronic billboards are also a key tool in getting information from the public in a crisis when investigative speed is critical. In the immediate aftermath of the Route 91 Harvest Festival shooting on October 1, the FBI posted a seeking information message on billboards around Las Vegas and received more than 4,000 tips from the public.

Created in December 2007, the National Digital Billboard Initiative has directly led to 57 fugitive captures and has assisted with numerous other investigations. The FBI can place information on up to 7,300 billboards in 46 states. Additionally, in some cities, the messages can be broadcast via digital message boards in bus shelters or digital newsstands.

"Our digital billboard program gets results and helps us keep the public

safe," said FBI Office of Public Affairs Unit Chief Christopher Allen, whose office manages the program. "Our private sector partners in the outdoor advertising industry help us target critical messages to the public in a timely fashion. These billboards have helped us solve complex crimes, arrest dangerous fugitives, and raise awareness on threats ranging from sex trafficking to border corruption."

Outdoor advertising companies donate available space, as a public service, and the FBI's messages rotate in and out along with paid advertising. The FBI messages are visible for approximately 10 seconds.

"Posters empowering the public to help law enforcement pre-date Jesse James," said Nancy Fletcher, president and CEO of the Outdoor Advertising Association of America (OAAA). "As media changed, the FBI has kept pace by using digital billboards and other modern media to communicate with a mobile public on behalf of safety."

2016 NIBRS Crime Data Released

Report Contains New Data, Including Animal Cruelty

Today, the FBI released information on more than 6 million criminal offenses that were submitted to the Uniform Crime Reporting (UCR) Program's National Incident-Based Reporting System (NIBRS) in 2016—and for the first time last year, the annual NIBRS report included data on animal cruelty. Additionally, hacking and identity theft were added to the overall fraud offense category.

While NIBRS data is not yet nationally representative, 6,849 law enforcement agencies (about 37 percent of the country's law enforcement agencies that participate in the UCR Program) contributed their data to the *NIBRS, 2016* report, a 201-agency increase from 2015. By 2021, NIBRS is scheduled to become the national standard for crime reporting, replacing the Summary Reporting System. NIBRS provides additional information and context for criminal offenses, and when fully implemented, it will assist law enforcement in using their resources efficiently and effectively.

"Information that is accurate, accessible, and complete enhances and informs conversations about policing," FBI Director Christopher Wray said in his message in the report. "It helps us learn how and why crimes occur and what we can do to prevent them from happening in the first place. It helps law

enforcement to be more proactive, helps communities use resources more strategically, and it improves the safety of our nation's citizens and law enforcement officers."

In the new categories, there were 1,126 animal cruelty cases reported to NIBRS. In recent years, law enforcement and other groups have advocated for adding animal cruelty to FBI crime statistics as a way to better understand it as a crime against society and also because animal cruelty is sometimes linked to domestic violence and other violent crimes.

Of the more than 250,000 fraud offenses reported by law enforcement to NIBRS in 2016, 22,894 were identity theft offenses and 581 were hacking/computer invasion offenses.

Some additional highlights from *NIBRS, 2016:*

- Based on aggregate data, NIBRS agencies reported 5,237,106 incidents involving 6,101,034 offenses with 6,437,018 victims.

- There were 4,963,644 offenses with known offenders (in which at least one characteristic of the offender was known.) Of those offenders whose age was known, 43.5 percent were between the ages of 16 and 30. Sixty-three percent of known offenders were men, and 25.6 percent were

women. In other cases, sex of the offender was unknown.

- Of the reported offenses, 62.5 percent were crimes against property, 22.7 were crimes against persons, and 14.8 percent were crimes against society (such as gambling or animal cruelty).

- More than half of the victims (52.4 percent) knew their offenders (or at least one of the offenders if the incident included more than one offender). Additionally, 24.3 percent of the victims were related to their offender (or at least one offender if more than one was present.)

- The NIBRS report contains data on 3,261,521 arrestees. Of those who were arrested, 34.1 percent were 21 to 30 years old. More than 71 percent of arrestees were men, and 28.3 percent were women.

More NIBRS data can be found online in the NIBRS interactive map or the Crime Data Explorer tool.

FBI Launches Crime Data Explorer Tool

The FBI recently released its Crime Data Explorer (CDE), an interactive tool that enables law enforcement and the public to more easily use and understand the massive amount of published UCR data. CDE users can easily search, sort, and compare crime statistics; create charts and graphs; download tailored reports; and use application programming interface (API) to build their own web applications. For mobile users, CDE offers a streamlined, mobile-responsive web design that works on cell phones and tablets as well as computers. CDE currently includes data on hate crime, assaults on law enforcement, police employees, agency participation, cargo theft, and human trafficking. Additional datasets and tools will continue to be added to the tool.

National Academy's 270th Class
Graduates Receive Presidential Congratulations

The FBI's National Academy—a prestigious 11-week educational program for law enforcement officers from around the world—graduated its 270th class today, and on hand to congratulate the graduates were Director Christopher Wray, Attorney General Jeff Sessions, and President Donald Trump.

"I'd like to extend a special welcome to President Trump and Attorney General Sessions," Wray said, addressing the 222 students in this session's class, who represent 49 U.S. states, 20 countries, four federal agencies, and three branches of the U.S. military.

"For more than 80 years," Wray said, "this program has served as a bridge between state and local law enforcement to international law enforcement. Today, you join the ranks of more than 50,000 graduates from more than 170 countries."

Founded in 1935, the National Academy program offers mid-career law enforcement leaders an advanced training program at Quantico, Virginia, the same location where the FBI trains its agents. National Academy students take courses in subjects ranging from behavioral science to counterterrorism to intelligence theory and engage in intense physical training. Just as importantly, they network with their peers.

Forging friendships and partnerships, Wray said, "is what the National Academy does best. As the world becomes smaller and perils loom larger, we've learned that a threat to one of us can be a threat to all of us. We've learned that working together isn't just the best option, it's really the only option."

Class spokesperson Craig Wiles of the Drug Enforcement Administration addresses the graduates of the 270th session of the FBI National Academy as President Donald Trump, Attorney General Jeff Sessions, FBI Director Christopher Wray, and other officials look on.

In welcoming Trump, Wray noted that it has been 46 years since a U.S. commander in chief participated in a National Academy graduation. "Mr. President, there is no better place to talk about the importance of partnerships than here at the National Academy, surrounded by some of the finest law enforcement leaders from here at home and around the world."

"It is an honor to join you today and to stand with the incredible men and women of law enforcement," Trump said during his remarks. "I am here not only to congratulate you, but to honor you for your courage and devotion."

In addition to thanking the many family members in the audience, the president said, "Now, more than ever, we must support the men and women in blue." Trump addressed a number of issues related to policing and national security and said the Department of Justice has announced more than $98 million in grant funding to help local police departments hire new officers. "If we want to bring down violent crime," he said, "then we must stand up for our police."

Wray noted that last February, the president addressed the Major County Sheriffs Association, calling for a national partnership and a new beginning between law enforcement and the citizens they serve. "By joining us today," he said, the president is "renewing that call."

Trump also recognized the National Academy's class president and spokesman, Drug Enforcement Administration officer Craig Wiles, whose father graduated from the National Academy 40 years ago and was in the audience today for his son. Wiles reminded the graduates and their families that "evil lives around the world," noting that during his session's nearly 11 weeks at Quantico, 24 law enforcement officers lost their lives, several terror attacks occurred in the U.S., and 10,000 individuals died of drug overdoses.

But Wiles remained hopeful. Based on his experience at the National Academy, he said, "I have never been more enthusiastic and optimistic about the future of the law enforcement community." He added, "There is no greater calling than this honorable profession."

Affinity Fraud

White-Collar Criminals Use Bonds of Trust to Prey on Investors

Financial fraudsters are known to be an unscrupulous lot, but it is particularly loathsome when these white-collar criminals exploit trusting members of their own church or social circle to line their pockets.

Financial crimes based on bonds of trust—known as affinity fraud—occur throughout the United States but are especially prevalent in Utah, where members of The Church of Jesus Christ of Latter-day Saints too often are victimized by savvy fraudsters who claim to be just like them.

"These are greedy individuals who will stop at nothing," said John Huber, the U.S. Attorney for the District of Utah, a lifelong resident of the state and member of the Mormon Church. "What's so disconcerting is that these criminals approach us at church or through associations at our work or referrals from friends. They are silver-tongued devils—wolves in sheep's clothing who will take our money and we'll never see it again."

So serious is the problem of affinity fraud in Utah that in 2015 the state legislature passed a law establishing an online white-collar crime registry—similar to sex-offender registries—which publishes the names, photographs, and criminal

details of individuals convicted of financial fraud crimes in the state going back a decade. Currently, there are 231 individuals listed on the registry.

In addition, a collaboration between federal, state, and local law enforcement partners has resulted in the Stop Fraud Utah campaign, which aims to educate the public about affinity fraud—what people can do to avoid it and how best to report it if they have been victimized.

"Within the Mormon population, there is a well-known sense of trust," said Special Agent Michael Pickett, a veteran white-collar crime investigator in the FBI's Salt Lake City Division. "Unfortunately, that trust can sometimes take the place of due diligence, and that's when individuals are more susceptible to being victimized."

Affinity fraudsters are expert manipulators. "They are great salesmen," Pickett explained. They will approach members of their social or religious circle with a promising investment opportunity—one that pays a high rate of return—and then use a variety of high-pressure tactics to get their victims' money.

Pickett described some of the fraudsters' ploys: "This is a once in

a lifetime opportunity. You don't want to be the one who passed up buying Amazon when it was first offered. You don't want to be the one that blows that opportunity, but you have to do it now. If you wait, the opportunity is gone. And by the way, you are one of the few people I am making this offer to, so let's just keep it between ourselves."

"This type of fraud is significant," Pickett said. "Within the Utah area, we are investigating more than $2 billion worth of fraud. In the last four months, we've opened 10 new cases." He added that Utah consistently ranks among the top five states for the FBI's most significant white-collar crime cases.

Too often, individuals dreaming about getting the great deal promised to them by a trusted friend or associate fail to see the red flags. "A key to this is communication," Pickett said. "You have to do your due diligence. Talk to a neighbor or a family member. Add a little common sense to the equation, and try to separate truth from fiction."

That's where the Stop Fraud Utah campaign comes in. "The strategy for law enforcement is not to deal with fraud as a reaction, but to deal with it on the front end," said Richard Best, regional director of the Salt Lake City office of the U.S. Securities and Exchange Commission (SEC), a partner in the campaign. "The best way to stop fraud is to avoid fraud, and the best way to do that is to educate the community so that when they are confronted with situations—opportunities, as fraudsters would say—they know to ask the right questions."

Established earlier this year, the Stop Fraud Utah campaign has

A Utah woman who believed she had done her homework on retirement investments later discovered she was part of an elaborate scam that cost her thousands.

John Huber, U.S. Attorney for the District of Utah, illustrates how affinity fraud takes advantage of established "relationships of trust."

Michael Pickett, supervisor of the white-collar crime squad in the FBI's Salt Lake City office, shares tactics fraudsters use to prey on potential affinity fraud victims.

Richard Best, regional director of the Securities and Exchange Commission's Salt Lake office, describes taking precautions against affinity fraud.

sponsored several fraud seminars around the state, which are free and open to the public. And because victims of affinity fraud typically call their local police departments to report these crimes, there is also an effort to train local law enforcement personnel on how to identify white-collar fraud, what evidence to collect, and the proper state and federal agencies to report it to for further investigation.

The high level of collaboration among Stop Fraud Utah campaign partners is "crucial to our success here," Best said. "I cannot stress that enough. The SEC's relationship with the FBI and the U.S. Attorney's Office is one of the best I have ever seen." Other members of the campaign include the Utah Attorney General's Office, the Internal Revenue Service, and the state's Consumer Protection Division.

"In Utah, we have to do something to stop fraudsters from exploiting people who trust them," said U.S. Attorney Huber. That's why the state's top law enforcement official has personally attended fraud seminars to caution the public about affinity fraud. "I know Utah very well," he said. "It troubles me to see good people who have worked very hard to set aside retirement funds and nest eggs lose that to people who seemingly have no conscience."

Unlike a drug addict who might rob a bank out of desperation, Huber added, financial fraudsters' crimes are ruthlessly premeditated. "These perpetrators, with a smile on their face and a twinkle in their eye, approach with a handshake and a hug, with intent and with persistence, to violate the trust of their victims and to take their life's earnings."

Scan this QR code with your smartphone to access related information, or visit www.fbi.gov/utahaffinityfraud.

Wolves in Sheep's Clothing

The white-collar criminals who commit affinity fraud are often charismatic salesmen capable of deceiving even sophisticated investors.

Special Agent Michael Pickett, a veteran financial fraud investigator in the FBI's Salt Lake City Division, offers a case in point:

His team was investigating a scam artist who had fraudulently collected approximately $5 million from investors—and who would later go to jail for his crimes.

"We talked with one of his victims, an elderly lady, who knew this gentleman very well," Pickett said. "She had been associated with him for years. Her husband, who had recently passed away, had been good friends with him as well."

The woman had invested and lost more than $100,000 with the individual. Investigators spoke to her and made her understand that she had been the victim of a fraud. "Ultimately, she agreed to wear a wire for us and talk with the individual to get his sales pitch so we could use that in court against him," Pickett explained. "She knew it was fraud and agreed to help us." Wearing the wire, the victim spoke with the man who had taken her money. "She came back about two hours later," Pickett said, "ready to invest more money with this individual."

FBI agents were able to talk her out of investing more funds, Pickett said, "but that's how good a salesman he was—and it was all based on that relationship of trust."

Civil Forfeiture

Sale of Child Abusers' Home Benefits Organization That Serves Victims

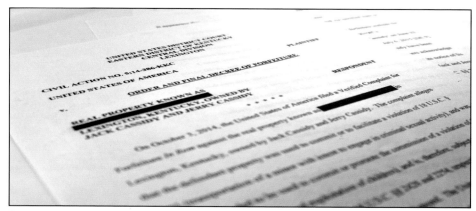

The home of Jack and Jerry Cassidy, who were convicted of sexually abusing children, was subject to civil forfeiture because their home was "used to commit or to facilitate" their crimes.

A Kentucky home where two brothers abused dozens of children over more than two decades has been sold following its civil forfeiture, and the proceeds will benefit a local advocacy group that serves young abuse victims.

The unique arrangement emerged following the investigation of twins Jack and Jerry Cassidy, of Lexington, who pleaded guilty in 2015 to state charges of child pornography and sexual abuse of minors. The brothers were longtime Boy Scout leaders and trusted members of the community, and many of their criminal acts were committed in the house where they held their meetings. Because the property played a central role in the crimes—including facilitating the movement of minors across state lines—local investigators and prosecutors worked with the U.S. Attorney's Office to seize the property under federal asset forfeiture laws. The effort set in motion a novel approach to supporting a program for young victims like those the Cassidy brothers abused from 1963 to 1986.

"It's a good example of what can be done for the good of the community," said Wade Napier, an assistant U.S. attorney who helped implement the civil forfeiture.

The "good" in the case was how officials used a powerful federal law enforcement tool to punish criminals and benefit the community where so many—at least 30 victims—were affected.

"This is a great example of how we can work together as one for the community."

Here's how it worked: Proceeds from the auction of the Cassidy brothers' house went to the FBI, which shared the funds with its partners in the case—the Lexington Police Department, which led the criminal investigation, and the Fayette Commonwealth Attorney's office, which prosecuted the state criminal case. The sharing framework is outlined under the federal government's asset forfeiture equitable sharing program, which says the FBI can transfer up to

80 percent of forfeiture proceeds to local law enforcement who assist in a case, and partners can then share up to $25,000 a year with community-based organizations that serve a law enforcement purpose. In this case, the beneficiary was the Lexington-based Children's Advocacy Center of the Bluegrass, a non-profit serving abuse victims across 17 counties in Central Kentucky.

"The civil asset forfeiture was directly applicable to the terrible conduct we saw from the defendants in this case," said Napier, who serves in the Eastern District of Kentucky.

The Cassidy brothers' crimes were uncovered on August 11, 2014, when police responding to a 911 call by a concerned friend found Jack Cassidy at the front door of the rambler, refusing their entry, and his brother on the floor bound and motionless—apparently the result of a consensual game. When they finally got inside, police saw framed photographs of young, semi-naked boys in suggestive poses, many with taped-on labels of "sweet," "pretty," and "wow." Police also discovered the brothers' hand-written journals documenting their victims and the abuse that occurred in the house and on Scout trips.

Special Agent Kimberly Kidd, who investigated the case out of the FBI's Louisville Field Office, said "there was no question" of whether the brothers' home should be seized. "It's not like the abuse happened just one time in this house," she said. "For decades, they were molesting children in this home."

As the investigation progressed, Lexington Police Department officers focused on the criminal case while Kidd traced the brothers' travels to determine if federal crimes occurred. The brothers, who were in their 70s at the time of their arrest, ultimately pleaded guilty to nine state charges, assuring they would spend the rest of their lives in jail.

Meanwhile, the federal focus turned to seizing the home, since Kentucky state law doesn't have a pathway for real property seizures and forfeitures in child exploitation cases. For Kidd, who has had numerous cases that relied on the use of the Children's Advocacy Center, it seemed like a natural fit to help fund the center with proceeds from the brothers' assets.

"They are always available to support law enforcement, and I would love to see law enforcement give back," Kidd recalled thinking. "This is a great example of how we can work together as one for the community. We're in this together and we recognize that."

The brothers were each sentenced to 20 years in jail; Jerry Cassidy died in September at age 79.

Proceeds from the sale of the Cassidy brothers' home is benefiting the Lexington-based Children's Advocacy Center of the Bluegrass, a non-profit serving abuse victims across 17 counties in Central Kentucky.

Investigators documented more than 30 victims, but the case was cemented on the testimony of three individuals who told the court how they were exploited decades ago. Kidd described the case as unnerving because the Cassidy brothers were in positions of authority and trust in their own community. "They completely took advantage of that for three decades," Kidd said.

The auction of the Cassidy brothers' home netted proceeds of about $84,000, which was distributed through the equitable sharing program with the Lexington Police Department and commonwealth's attorney's office. Under the arrangement, the agencies are giving the money to

the Children's Advocacy Center, which has already put the funds to work in the form of a new roof, upgraded technologies and new recording equipment in the center's forensic interview suites.

Winn Stephens, executive director of the center, said the funding and support from the FBI and the local agencies affirmed his organization's role with law enforcement.

"They have the option of expending those funds themselves or passing them through to an organization like ours," he said. "I think it really made us feel validated in the work that we do and the type of partners we are that they were so willing to share those funds with us."

Snake Oil Salesman
Man Cheated Would-Be Investors in Oil Boom Housing

Convicted fraudster Ronald Johnson showed this photo to investors in his Bakken housing project to convince them that their money was being used as intended—but this construction site was not the property the investors had visited. This was an initial clue that the investment was a scam.

Like many who are looking for economic opportunity, Ronald Johnson saw the oil-booming Bakken region in North Dakota and Montana as a chance to make money.

Yet unlike oil workers putting in an honest day on the job, Johnson was a con artist who simply separated innocent investors from their money while enriching himself.

The Bakken Formation, a vast, oil-rich territory that runs from North Dakota to eastern Montana and north into Canada, has experienced an influx of workers in recent years who need housing while they work in the oil industry. When Johnson visited Watford City, North Dakota, he noticed oil workers were parking their RVs in indoor RV parks to get out of the cold and take advantage of shared

services, like laundry. He decided to pitch investors on the idea of building indoor RV parks for Bakken workers.

His sales pitch offered investors "memberships" that would entitle them to a percentage of rental and other income generated by the parks based on how much they invested. Johnson also sold his scheme as a good deed to help oil workers who needed warm, indoor housing in the harsh North Dakota winters.

"Some of the victims were completely taken in by the concept of a financial investment with the opportunity to help people," said Special Agent Christopher Lester of the FBI's Minneapolis Division, who investigated this case along with Special Agent Julie Barrows of the Internal Revenue Service-

Criminal Investigation. "He preyed on their values to get them excited about investing in something that had the potential for profit and also to help these workers in the Bakken."

Johnson told his investors he would buy property in North Dakota and begin the building process. Instead, he stole their money and spent it on himself or repaid previous investors clamoring for their money back. He also funded his own cattle farm, bought land (including a Minnesota island), and purchased more than a dozen vintage cars.

Johnson's investors soon started questioning him about the park and what he had done with their money. He went to great lengths to cover his tracks, including sending one investor a picture of a construction site that wasn't actually of the property the investors had visited. Once they found each other and began comparing the stories Johnson had told them, Johnson's scheme began to unravel. Through search warrants, interviews, and other investigative tactics, the FBI and IRS-CI discovered Johnson was not simply a bad businessman—his intent was to defraud his victims all along.

"Johnson is a smooth talker, just a career con man who would basically say anything to separate a person from their money."

"His sales pitches were very targeted to what the person was looking for," Lester said. "If they wanted a solid investment, he'd point to existing RV parks and their success. If another person was more interested in the philanthropic aspect, he would highlight how these poor workers were freezing outside, and it was God's work to help them."

Some of Johnson's victims were close to him—such as his former girlfriend and his pastor—making them more susceptible to the pitch. Other victims were a couple in the RV business Johnson recruited by offering a business partnership, as well as a Minnesota businessman looking to help the Bakken workers. The victims lost anywhere between $200,000 and $800,000 each.

Thanks to the asset forfeiture process, some victims will recoup a fraction of their money through the sale of Johnson's ill-gotten gains, but it will be a minimal amount compared to what they lost. Losing such a significant amount of money has had life-altering effects on the victims. At Johnson's sentencing hearing, one victim said she will have to change her retirement plans and will struggle to take care of her aging mother.

"Johnson is a smooth talker, just a career con man who would basically say anything to separate a person from their money," Lester said. "We understood it was important Johnson had his day in court. If he didn't, he was just going to continue to defraud people."

Johnson was convicted of wire fraud and money laundering in June. In November, Johnson was sentenced to more than 10 years in prison.

"Mr. Johnson took advantage of every opportunity—and dollar—provided to him," said Acting Special Agent in Charge Hubbard Burgess of the IRS-CI St. Paul Field Office. "Investment decisions are difficult enough without individuals like Mr. Johnson trying to steal hard-earned dollars. Fortunately, the IRS-CI and FBI work side by side in a united front against financial crime and to help keep the public safe."

These vintage cars and private island in Minnesota were just some of the ill-gotten gains obtained by Ronald Johnson as a result of his scheme.

THE FBI STORY

THE FBI STORY

Index

Index

Index

THE FBI STORY

Index

FBI OFFICE OF PUBLIC AFFAIRS
935 Pennsylvania Avenue NW
Washington, D.C. 20535

The FBI Honolulu Division's Adopt-a-Scho
program brings together students from
two different high schools to solve a mock
kidnapping case that culminates in a dig a
fictional crime scene.